"A riveting read! Over 50 years, critics an
Oliver Ford Davies' distinguished actin
plays. Perceptively and modestly he now
the ups and downs, the many hits and fe   ....
stage and screen. Long may it continue!"
Sir Ian McKellen

"Oliver Ford Davies is one of our best writers about theatre. I was
educated and entertained in equal measure."
Sir David Hare

"This is a first-rate book. Oliver Ford Davies is both a fine actor and
an excellent historian. The result is a book that doesn't just chart the
growth of a career but that also records seismic changes in theatre
and society and that deals with the practical economics of an actor's
life. I learned something on every page."
Michael Billington OBE

"Oliver Ford Davies manages to knit together all the overlapping
social, political and artistic strands of the past sixty years with a
genuine curiosity about how his own life has been reflected in these.
All this with a lightness of touch which makes it a swift and always
engaging read."
Dame Harriet Walter

"As a playwright there are great actors you want to work with and
write for again and again – Oliver Ford Davies is one of them.' No
one who reads it will look at acting – or indeed the theatre – quite in
the same way again."
David Edgar

AN ACTOR'S LIFE IN 12 PRODUCTIONS

Oliver Ford Davies

The Book Guild Ltd

First published in Great Britain in 2022 by
The Book Guild Ltd
Unit E2 Airfield Business Park,
Harrison Road, Market Harborough,
Leicestershire. LE16 7UL
Tel: 0116 2792299
www.bookguild.co.uk
Email: info@bookguild.co.uk
Twitter: @bookguild

Typeset in 12pt Sabon MT

Printed and bound in the UK by TJ Books LTD, Padstow, Cornwall

ISBN 978 1915352 033

British Library Cataloguing in Publication Data.
A catalogue record for this book is available from the British Library.

MIX
Paper from
responsible sources
FSC® C013056

For Jenny and Miranda

CONTENTS

LIST OF PHOTOGRAPHS

INTRODUCTION

This is an account of my acting life, mainly in the British theatre. It is not intended to be an autobiography, but in order to understand my development as an actor from an uncertain start to limited success I have included certain personal details. I have highlighted twelve productions, because they seem to me representative of my fifty-odd years in the theatre, but I have included a brief summary of other important stage and screen appearances, leaving out dozens of unremarkable performances.

I hope the seven decades it covers may both entertain and illustrate the changes in the performing arts scene through one person's ups and downs. Although I have done many new plays, worked with many fringe companies, my acting life has mainly been in classical theatre, Shakespeare, Shaw, Chekhov and Pirandello. I doubt that such a life is available to an actor starting out today. Acclaimed actors in their thirties nowadays disappear into movies and television or decamp to America, occasionally emerging to play Medea or Hamlet. The sort of stage life that Judi Dench or Ian McKellen enjoyed for so many decades is a thing of the past. In that sense this book details a career that has become almost historic, but I hope it illuminates the history of British theatre in the last sixty years.

Production One

THE SEAGULL (1956)

In December 1956 I directed and acted in Chekhov's *The Seagull* in my last year at school. This may now seem unremarkable, but I see it as a symptom of a cultural sea-change. Today we may lament that over half the West End theatres are occupied by often mediocre musicals (16), while plays (8) and comedies (5) bring up the rear. In the 1950s we lamented that over half were occupied by often mediocre comedies (10), revues (5) and thrillers (5). At my school, King's Canterbury, each of the eight houses presented a play to the school on a stage in the medieval chapter house, and in this incongruous setting comedies and thrillers represented theatre to teenage boys. I performed in an Agatha Christie, a 1930s thriller *The Amazing Dr Clitterhouse*, and *The Happiest Days of Your Life* (something of a hostage to fortune). When it was my turn to choose the house play I decided the school was ready for, or at least might endure, Chekhov.

My awakening to the power of acting came in 1950, when at the age of eleven I played Richard II at school in a scene from Gordon Daviot's *Richard of Bordeaux* (the play that made John Gielgud a star in 1933). For casting me I owe a debt of gratitude to my English teacher, Athelstan Newall, the first person to believe that I had real acting talent. My approach to the script was, I now realise, instinctive: if you don't have that instinct don't bother setting out in such a

1

difficult profession. I understood how much I loved my wife Anne and how much I regretted the exile of my best friend Robert de Vere, but above all I relished being someone else, which has I think been the bedrock of my acting – I've always been intent on promoting the character rather than myself. It may well stem from teenage angst of not knowing who I was and taking refuge in another persona, or rather expanding my own personality beyond my teenage limitations. Fifty years later I worked with several eleven-year-olds on two productions of the children's classic *Goodnight Mister Tom*, and I observed how well children understand and relate to emotions, whether love, anger, fear or jealousy. They don't stop to work out how to express these, as an adult actor might; they just play them. There is a purity of intention and delivery. From the age of eleven I wanted, deep down, to become an actor.

When my voice broke at the age of thirteen I found that I had developed a powerful, resonant baritone register, which I produced quite naturally. This was pure luck, presumably to do with the configuration of my head, chest and diaphragm, and it has proved a mainstay of my professional life – 'Old Brass Lungs', as I was called at one point at the RSC. When fourteen I was already the barn-storming Pistol in *Henry V*, who was played of course by the captain of rugby. In the night scene with Williams and Bates he was urged by the director to put more conviction into his pro-battle arguments. "But I don't think they're very good arguments," said Henry. My fourteen-year-old-self recoiled: how dare anyone suggest Shakespeare had given the king poor arguments? But the more I thought about it the more I agreed. The analogy between a master sending a servant on a journey and a king sending soldiers into battle, 'purposing not their death', was a poor one. Had Shakespeare slipped up, I wondered? No, I decided, he knew perfectly well the soldiers were right. A more complex way of reading Shakespeare opened up. In my teens I was also inspired by over a dozen productions I saw at Michael Benthall's seasons at the Old Vic in the early fifties, including Richard Burton's Hamlet and Iago. I would cycle up from Ealing and sit in the back rows of the stalls for 2/3d (11p), half price at matinees for under 16s – a huge concession unthinkable today.

In 1955 Ronald Harris, my history tutor, was to direct an outdoor production of *Romeo and Juliet*. He asked me what part I wanted to play, and I cautiously suggested Capulet, but to my surprise he suggested Mercutio: he must have thought that if you recognise someone of talent you should trust him with one of the best parts. I reveled in the freedom the part gave me and the verse seemed second nature to me. The only downside was the duel, since the Tybalt fought with his eyes closed and therefore had no idea where his sword was aimed. Each night I was so relieved to be dead but unscathed. The cast were made up by a professional father and son, the Berts – 'Wigs

Romeo and Juliet, King's Canterbury, 1955.
L to R: OFD (Mercutio), Anthony Austin (Romeo),
Jeremy Paul (Benvolio), Nick Freeman (Tybalt).

by Bert' are listed in many of the West End programmes of the mid-century. Bert senior was putting some sort of foundation on me when he stopped and said, "You have one of the most rubbery faces I have ever come across."

"Good for comedy," I suggested.

"Very good for clowning," he said. So I have a clown's face, I pondered. A seed was sown.

The play was seen one night by Clifford Williams, then running the local Marlowe Theatre (and from 1962 a director with the RSC), and he singled me out to a staff member as 'an actor'. When this was passed on to me I knew my ambition had been given some kind of confirmation, but I didn't allow myself to think that I might actually become a professional actor. The idea seemed too remote, too hazardous, perhaps too improper. Twenty-five years later I was being directed by Clifford in an RSC production of Solzhenitsyn's *The Love Girl and the Innocent* and I reminded him of this happy coincidence. After some thought he replied, "I have absolutely no memory of your Mercutio, and I apologise if I'm in any way responsible for your becoming an actor." Thus are golden moments destroyed. We remained friends.

I had been introduced to Chekhov quite by chance. I was sitting in the school library by the drama section, trapped by the rain, when I noticed the title *The Cherry Orchard* and thought it might be a cheering light read about nature. It proved like no other play I had ever read, and I was captivated for life. Early in 1956 I saw *The Seagull* in the John Clements season at the Saville Theatre, and I was so swept away by the experience that I knew I had to work on it. I think I was particularly attracted to the play because the central quartet comprise two writers and two actors, and I identified strongly with all four. I was also much influenced by David Magarshack's *Chekhov the Dramatist* (1952), in which he argues that Chekhov's full-length plays are in one sense a number of short stories skillfully woven together, and that the leitmotif of *The Seagull* is that 'people who have nothing to live for are doomed to a life of constant disappointment and unhappiness', a thread that runs right through Chekhov's plays and stories – indeed seemingly through Russian life at the end of the century. I realised that while plays chronicle an important period in certain people's lives, they set out the problems without making any claim to solve them.

Arkadina's acting may not be to the taste of Moscow and St Petersburg, but she is very popular in the regions and is determined to carry on touring in leading parts. Trigorin is a much read and admired novelist, always busy, though conscious he is no Turgenev: 'I have a feeling for nature, it arouses a sort of passion in me, an irresistible desire to write…[yet] in the end I feel that all I can do is to paint landscapes, and that everything else I write is a sham – false to the very core'. Both reluctantly admit they are not in the front rank, an example I was to accept in the early part of my own career. Konstantin and Nina are more problematic because we see them at the outset of their artistic lives. Nina can see she acted 'abominably' when she started – Konstantin talks of 'false intonations and violent gestures' – but now 'I am a real actress, I act with intense enjoyment, with enthusiasm… What really matters in our work is not fame or glamour but knowing how to endure things… and when I think of my vocation I'm not afraid of life'. Konstantin on the other hand feels he's 'still floating about in a chaotic world of dreams and images, without knowing what use it all is'. Dorn thinks his stories are 'vivid, full of colour', but 'he doesn't set himself any definite goal'. Trigorin has a more brutal summing-up: 'and not a single living character!'. You can imagine how powerfully these contrasts worked on a seventeen-year-old with ambitions to act and write. 'Knowing how to endure' was to be central to my life in the theatre.

I could only undertake such a difficult play because I thought I could cast it. John Underwood, our Juliet in 1955, adept at female roles, played Arkadina, and Ian Thompson (later a very good professional actor) played Konstantin. Jeremy Paul Roche, my first choice as Trigorin, was forbidden to take part as he was coming up to university entrance, so I decided to play the part myself. Nina was played by a first-year student, David Stedall. Fourteen-year-old boys can play girls very effectively, as Elizabethan theatre knew only too well. His final scene with Konstantin was probably beyond him, but then it has defeated many talented young actresses (though not Vanessa Redgrave). Our Dorn was Robert Horton, always an outspoken and ambitious member of the house. He regarded Jeremy and myself as 'arty-farty', went into engineering and oil, eventually became chairman of British Petroleum and then Railtrack, both of which companies he drastically reorganised. He played a crucial part in John Major's privatisation of the railways, and was duly knighted in 1997. He has always seemed to me a character out of Anthony Powell's *A Dance to the Music of Time*. If only I had given him Trigorin, which he craved, perhaps the railways might have remained nationalised.

These productions had the habit of bringing the whole house together in one concerted effort. Team games are often invoked for creating a community among schoolchildren, but drama and the other arts can be even more inspirational. I was fortunate in going to a school where being good academically, musically or dramatically was considered just as important by students and staff as prowess at football or cricket. Everyone wanted to contribute; two of the least cooperative house members told me they understood I needed a fir tree for the outdoor set. I tentatively agreed. "Leave it to us," they said, and the next day they appeared dragging a ten-foot fir tree behind their bicycles, which they had clearly cut down in some neighbouring private wood. I asked no questions, grateful that at least they hadn't gone out and shot a seagull. I realised that putting on a play can create a family, short-lived perhaps, but for a period extremely intense. I have been grateful for many such families throughout my career.

We rehearsed for most of the winter term with no clear idea of how it would come together. What encouraged me was the way the cast responded to the text and to the situations their characters found themselves in. I remembered my father saying to an amateur cast rebelling at doing Bernard Shaw, "Surely if you are going to the trouble of learning all those lines it's worth learning something that's well written." It was my first intimation that the script lies at the basis of everything. I suspect my production was a pale copy of the

John Clements I had seen, but it gave me a great deal of confidence as a director, and more particularly as an actor. I had put on a play, directed it and acted in it. I also found I liked being in charge, if only of my own performance in front of an audience. This is probably why I came to relish the stage rather than film, where you are so much in the hands of the director and editor, who often reshape to such a degree that both you and the original concept are lost. Acting is so much about communication: on stage with fellow actors and the audience; on film with a fellow actor only, who when it gets to your close-up may have already gone home. The part also introduced me to the variety a great writer threads into a character. Trigorin is intelligent, successful, likeable and highly respected, but he is also weak, impetuous, disloyal and hypocritical. It is an aspect of Chekhov's genius that he suggests that Trigorin knows he is all these things. I feel sure the play puzzled and bored at least half the school audience, used to a play with a recognisable plot, sure laughs and suitable climaxes: the first night audience in 1896 St Petersburg are witness to this bewilderment – and in many cases derision.

Many people, however, were challenged and impressed. Ronald Harris wrote to me: "Congratulations – I admire the audacity which prompted you to choose it, and I greatly enjoyed the production. You had an exceptionally talented cast and you must have enormously enjoyed producing so worth-while a play." As to the 'talented cast' I was later to learn that 80% of your decisions may have been made once you have assembled a cast. Frank Hauser, who ran Meadow Players at the Oxford Playhouse for seventeen years, once said to me: "There's no such word as 'better' in the theatre. You cast someone and on day one of rehearsals you realise your mistake, but you work hard and he improves and improves. And then on the first preview your best friend comes and says, 'Why did you cast him, he's terrible?' And you reply, 'But he's so much better...' and as you say the word it freezes on your lips."

I also made a discovery that has impacted on me throughout my career. Neither Ian Thompson nor myself were conventionally good-looking, but how important is this in playing Konstantin and Trigorin? In the case of Konstantin, not at all. Nina is his girlfriend because he's the only suitable young male around, he writes plays for her to act in, and she likes visiting Arkadina's household. The best Konstantin I have ever seen was Simon Russell Beale for the RSC in 1990, and Simon was never one of nature's juvenile romantic leads. Trigorin's allure for women is that he is a famous writer, and this is what attracts both Arkadina and Nina. In fact Chekhov displayed little interest in male good looks, as neither did Shakespeare. Vanya and Astrov, Andrey and Tusenbach, Trofimov and Lopakhin are never identified as handsome. In *Three Sisters* Olga says of Tusenbach, 'It's true he's not good-looking... when he came to see us in his civilian clothes I thought he looked so plain that I started to cry'. Yet Tusenbach is routinely cast with a good-looking actor, who then tries to disguise his looks with glasses and an ugly hairstyle. Jonathan Miller is the only director in my experience with the intelligence to cast someone unusual – Roger Hammond, a plump, good-natured actor who probably, like me, never got to play a young lover in his life. Producers and directors will always advance the same arguments: firstly, that audiences want to see good-looking actors, and secondly, that 'plain' actors have never acquired the experience to play major parts – it's a Catch-22. Female actors suffer such discrimination in a more extreme form. There are rules: beautiful people are only attracted to beautiful people; a non-beautiful couple is of no public interest (except on the rare occasions when that is the point of the story); a beautiful person attracted to a non-beautiful person is an impossibility.

I left school in 1957. The years 1956/7 were a turning point in Britain in so many ways. The death of Stalin and the end of the Korean War in 1953 had given hope that the Cold War and the threat of nuclear annihilation might recede. In February 1956 Khrushchev made his famous speech denouncing Stalin for 'the cult of personality', and he and Bulganin made a state visit to Britain which included a much-criticised tour of Canterbury Cathedral at the invitation of the communist 'Red Dean' of Canterbury, Dr Hewlett Johnson. As we were rehearsing *The Seagull* we witnessed the humiliation of Eden's Suez invasion and the crushing of the Hungarian uprising by Soviet tanks. Egged on by my headmaster Canon 'Fred' Shirley (who loathed his Dean), I wrote an editorial in the school magazine attacking Hewlett Johnson for failing to denounce the invasion of Hungary. To general surprise this made headlines in the national press (I was later interviewed on television by Jeremy Thorpe), and I had to go into hiding while reporters roamed the school trying to establish the writer of the editorial. It gave me a taste for political journalism which has never entirely left me.

1956 was a radical year in theatre and music. Today we are fixated on the myth of 'The Sixties', but things were clearly on the move by the late fifties. In 1955 I had seen the first English production of *Waiting for Godot*, though I failed to see it as a turning point in drama. In August 1956 the Berliner Ensemble came to Britain for the first time. Brecht had just died, and I saw his widow Helene Weigel in *Mother Courage* in all of all places the Palace Theatre, later home to *The Sound of Music*. The Moscow Arts Theatre also made a first visit with *Three Sisters* – Olga Knipper, Chekhov's widow now in her nineties and the original Masha, was thrilled at this initiative. In September I saw the first revival of Osborne's *Look Back in Anger* at the Royal Court and immediately organised a reading back at school, Jeremy Paul as Jimmy, Ian Thompson as Cliff and myself as Alison – I have always fancied female parts. The language was so anarchic, free-wheeling and liberating, the class war and the sex war were laid bare and I felt validated and inspired by this apparent socialist cry for freedom. I transferred my groupie instincts from the Old Vic to the Royal Court and the plays of John Arden, Arnold Wesker and Ann Jellicoe: Shakespeare and new writing were to dominate much of my career. That autumn I also saw Paul Scofield in an adaptation of Graham Greene's *The Power and the Glory* directed by Peter Brook – the best male performance I have ever seen (more later). At the same time American cinema, from *On the Waterfront* to *Rebel Without a Cause* with Brando and James Dean, proclaimed a new approach to acting, as did Albert Finney and Tom Courtenay in *Saturday Night and Sunday Morning* and *The Loneliness of the Long-Distance Runner*, but we were just as enthralled by Ingmar Bergman's *The Seventh Seal* and *Wild Strawberries* (my all-time favourite). A university friend claimed to have seen *The Seventh Seal* fourteen times and, though he knew no Swedish, learnt the entire dialogue by heart. Many years later when filming with Max von Sidow I told him this and he burst into happy, if incredulous, laughter.

In music pop had been through a barren crooning time but Elvis released *Heartbreak Hotel* in 1956, and when the film *Rock Around the Clock* arrived in Britain my school put the local cinema out of bounds for fear we might tear up the seats and jive in the aisles (alas, highly unlikely). What I most remember listening to were soundtracks of musicals, *Oklahoma*, *High Society* and *Guys and Dolls*, until *West Side Story* blew everything out of the water. Today in the same way my granddaughters Alice and Rosalind know many of the numbers in *Hamilton* by heart. My school teemed with classical music: Bach, Mozart, Beethoven and Schubert have influenced much of my life. A great awakening came with Simone de Beauvoir's *The Second Sex*, which set me on the path to becoming some form of feminist. It was also the year of my first visit to Stratford-on-Avon with my father, when we queued for hours to see Alan Badel's Hamlet, Harry Andrews' Othello and Peter Hall's first production there, his Watteauesque *Love's Labour's Lost*. I was smitten. However unlikely it seemed, I wanted to be part of that.

My parents were great theatre lovers. My father, Robert Davies, taught English at the Latymer Upper School in Hammersmith for forty years, played the violin, founded the dramatic society and was a devoted director in the amateur theatre. My mother, Cicely Ford, came from Ledbury in Herefordshire and was a theatre-lover and voracious reader, particularly of Anglo-Saxon history. She was twenty-six when she met and married my forty-two-year-old father. They moved to Ealing in West London, my brother Simon (later a solicitor and district judge) was born in 1936 and I followed in August 1939. I owe so much of my love of literature, history, music and drama to my parents, and I also suspect that having a father in his sixties when I was in my teens may even account for my ability – predilection, maybe? – to play so many middle-aged parts in my twenties.

1957–67: Oxford student, Edinburgh lecturer, Birmingham Rep actor

Passing history exams is essentially memory plus journalistic flair. You have forty-five minutes to set down the causes of the 1914–18 War, and I proved good at that ridiculous compression. My school pushed scholarship boys hard, so I did my 'O' levels at thirteen, my 'A' levels at fifteen, and I got an open scholarship to Oxford at sixteen. It was not without personal cost. The stress of attempting ten 'O' levels in a class mostly a year older than myself caused me to develop a stammer. I dreaded being put on to translate French or Latin in class because I knew I couldn't manage certain consonants. I found myself clutching a handkerchief in my lap, sodden with sweat. My release came in acting: there I was stammer-free, yet another incentive, it seemed, to pursue drama. Within a couple of years the stammer had more or less receded, though the 'D' of Davies remained a stumbling block long after.

I seemed set on an academic path, but my practical interest in theatre had been stimulated by the outstanding amateur theatre in Ealing, The Questors. I got to do little acting there in 1956/7, but a good deal of bricklaying on their new studio theatre. I am now a vice-president (Judi Dench is president and the main theatre bears her name) and every time I attend I inspect my brickwork to check that it doesn't need repointing. I had a gap year before university could take me, but Voluntary Service Overseas had their full quota; travelling abroad, from the 1980s the great student solution, was too problematic and expensive in the 1950s, so I fell back on the last resort followed by W. H. Auden and so many others, prep school teaching. Without any training I was let loose on seven- to twelve-year-olds. My vague plan was to become a teacher, so this might prove an illuminating, or possibly disheartening, experience.

Betteshanger School, near Deal in Kent, had a relaxed and artistic environment based on partial Montessori lines. As no punishments were allowed one had to rely on personality and the ability to create interest in the subject, no bad test of one's professional suitability. I did send one extremely disruptive boy to the eighty-three-year-old headmaster, and as he came back grinning broadly I was so curious I asked him at the end of the lesson what had happened. The head had apparently said to him, "Mr Davies is a scholar and a gentleman, and you, sir, are a cad and a bounder." I felt we were back in the 1920s, possibly the 1880s: clearly no point in sending anyone else to the head. As a would-be historian one fact that came to light interested me greatly. An old boy had recently reminded the school to their surprise that in 1940–41 Robert and Edward Kennedy had been pupils when their father Joseph Kennedy had been the American ambassador in London. He also recalled that Jack Kennedy, on leave from the navy, had visited his brothers and had volunteered to umpire in a cricket match, a sport about which he knew nothing. Many a president and prime minister has seized the chance to take on a job they are quite unqualified for. A search in the school records did reveal R. and E. Kennedy, and what fascinated me was that in less than twenty years these facts had been buried and forgotten. As Dr William Urry, the Canterbury Cathedral librarian, had drummed into me: "Somewhere in some archive or attic is a piece of paper saying, 'I, William Shagspeare of Stratforde-upon-Avon, writ these 42 plays.' You just have to keep looking."

In 1958 I arrived at Merton College Oxford – I had missed National Service by six weeks. Our immediate political preoccupations, apart from hoping for an end to seven years of 'You've never had it so good' Tory government, were twofold: reducing the threat of nuclear war and working for the abolition of the death penalty. We marched and held rallies accordingly. A contemporary caused a stir by leaving the university after a year to live in Cornwall, which he reckoned the safest place in England from nuclear fall-out. I also plunged into the university theatre world, and one of the first productions I saw bowled me over. Earlier that year Patrick Garland, President of the Dramatic Society (OUDS), had asked the television director Peter Dews, a very down-to-earth Bradfordian, to find a play for him and the Oxford Theatre Group to do on the Edinburgh Festival fringe. Dews came up with an idea submitted to him by Willis Hall, based on his own experience, about a small squad of British soldiers trapped in the Malayan jungle by the advancing Japanese army. Willis Hall agreed to write the play, then called *The Disciplines of War*, and tailor it for the available university cast, with Patrick Garland as Bamforth, the leading part. It went to Edinburgh, was a great success and was snapped up by Lindsay Anderson and the Royal Court. Renamed *The Long and the Short and the Tall*, with a cast that included as Bamforth the then-unknown Peter O'Toole (replacing Albert Finney, who had appendicitis), Robert Shaw, Alfred Lynch, and as O'Toole's understudy Michael Caine, it was again a success, won awards, and a film version followed in 1961, with hardly any of the original cast – the 'stars' Laurence Harvey and Richard Todd being no substitute for O'Toole and Shaw. As you can imagine, Peter Dews was not pleased at being sidelined from his commission. The version that I saw took place in a lecture room without set, costumes and only a few props, and a small audience on three sides. What it showed me was that what counts in theatre is the script and the acting. If they are sufficiently enthralling you can imagine the rest – set, costumes, lighting, music, sound (the work of the so-called 'creative team').

In my first year I had the good luck to work with three very inspirational directors. Colette King, a postgraduate, was auditioning for *Oedipus at Colonus*, and asked me to improvise a scene where I lost my temper. I did so: I relish becoming angry on stage because I find it so difficult in life. "You've obviously done impro before," she said. "No, that was my first." Colette, a very early advocate of improvisation, was not prepared to make the compromises needed in professional theatre and perhaps thought as a woman director she was unlikely to find work she relished, and later taught acting and writing at Dartington College of Arts. She seemed to me to direct without directing, like certain great orchestral conductors, and yet achieve extraordinary results. The distinguished director Ronald Eyre once told me he thought she was the best director in England – never condescend to non-professionals. In my second term I had one line in *Coriolanus*, 'Let's see him out at gates', it's engraved on my soul. I may have played Mercutio and Toby Belch at school, but then so had a dozen others: I was starting again from the bottom. The play was directed by a guest, Anthony Page, with Patrick Garland as Coriolanus, Susan Engel as Volumnia, and as an assistant the young Ariane Mnouchkine, who went on to found the Parisian avant-garde stage ensemble *Theatre du Soleil* in 1964. Anthony Page, who later part-ran the Royal Court, clearly liked working with actors, had a great eye for detail and a strong visual sense. I had entered an Oxford one-act play competition with a piece about the Black Death called *Knock Death Knock*, which won and was performed. Anthony liked the play and for the next twenty years whenever we met, and I was hoping/desperate for acting work, would ask how the writing was going. He had a point: we need writers far more than actors.

My third, and most important, influence was Vladek Sheybal. He had been a member of the Polish National Theatre in Warsaw, where he directed *Three Sisters*, and had been forced to leave Poland after the 1956 uprising. He knew no one in Western Europe and had gone from menial job to menial job, until Vernon Dobtcheff noticed him washing up in an Oxford tea rooms and, typical of Vernon's almost cosmic knowledge, had asked him if he was indeed Wladyslaw Sheybal who had starred in Andrzej Wajda's film *Kanal*. He agreed, and Vernon suggested he could earn more money teaching acting and directing to students. As a result eight of us, including Caryl Churchill and Michael Kustow, each paid him five shillings for a two-hour group session. All summer term we worked on the second act of *Three Sisters* in such depth that we never in fact reached its end. Vladek was of course teaching us pure Stanislavski, and to this day I cannot help but judge all productions of the play by how they handle the strange little tragicomic scene between Andrey and Ferrapont, two characters who have nothing in common apart from their loneliness, which we had worked on for so many hours. As an exercise I directed a little one-act play, and Vladek said, "It is light and funny, but please, Oliver, do not mistake it for theatre." I often think of a 'mistake' being committed when I sit miserably watching a mediocre play or production. Vladek was soon snapped up by the profession, moved to London and later Paris, and appeared in many films, often as Eastern European villains, most notably in the second Bond film *From Russia with Love* and Ken Russell's *Women in Love, The Debussy File* and *The Boy Friend*, and was filming right up to his death in 1992. The tragedy is that Vladek could have been a great stage actor in London had British theatre not been so intolerant of English with a foreign accent.

There were few outstanding Oxford actors at the time, but playwrights and would-be playwrights abounded: Denis Potter, Caryl Churchill, John McGrath, Julian Mitchell, Alan Bennett, John Wells, Don Taylor, Roger Smith, David Wood, Michael Palin and Terry Jones. When I was drama critic of the student magazine *Isis* the film critic was David Rudkin, about to write *Afore Night Come*. Despite this plethora of writers it is noticeable that we performed very few new plays. In both student and professional theatre revivals, translations and classics dominated: no wonder that in their frustration George Devine and others set up the Royal Court as a beacon of new writing. Frank Hauser's time at the Oxford Playhouse was, however, a vast resource of contemporary European drama, particularly from France, then very much in the theatrical ascendant: Anouilh, Sartre, Giraudoux, Montherlant, Genet, Ionesco, and also Moliere and Racine. Hauser was also a great devotee of Shaw, Brecht, Pirandello and the Greek classics – the complete *Oresteia, Lysistrata*, and the *Bacchae* (with Sean Connery and Yvonne Mitchell). I feasted on them, confirmation that good writing lies at the root of theatre. He also enticed so many good actors to the Playhouse, including Judi Dench,

Prunella Scales, Joan Greenwood, Diane Cilento, Barbara Jefford, Leo McKern, Dirk Bogarde, Roger Livesey, Jeremy Brett and John Hurt. These were seasons that put our current national and West End theatres to shame with their very Anglo-centric repertoire. Since the demise of the World Theatre Seasons at the Aldwych (1964–75) we have turned our backs on Continental European theatre. Such parochialism, such philistinism.

At the end of my first year Ken Loach (a very good comic actor) and I played the two villains, Knockem and Whit, in Ben Jonson's *Bartholomew Fair*, an Oxford production by Ken and David Webster which went to the Stratford Festival of University Theatre in the garden by Holy Trinity Church. Ken and I had one entrance by boat, with me rowing, Ken steering. One night the rudder got stuck in the reeds, and I can still see Ken tearing at the foliage and crying, White Rabbit-like, "We shall be too late, too late!" We were. It was the 1959 Centenary Year (the hundredth season) at Stratford with the starriest of casts – Olivier as Coriolanus, Paul Robeson and Sam Wanamaker (an improbable pairing) as Othello and Iago, Charles Laughton as Lear and Bottom, and a young company including Vanessa Redgrave, Albert Finney, Ian Holm, Zoe Caldwell, Robert Hardy and Julian Glover. It was one of the hottest summers of the century and I saw all the productions, an unforgettable few weeks. Our play went well, though to our annoyance Dudley Moore, with one line as an apple seller, got far too many notices. He did, however, outshine us all at a party we gave, attended by Vanessa, Albert and many of the professional company, with an hour-length improvised stand-up with a harmonium and a collapsing chair: Dudley was set to be an inspired clown and a great jazz pianist. My second year I directed and acted in play after play, including both parts of *Tamburlaine*. My third year I foreswore acting and just worked. With finals over I was free to go to the Edinburgh Festival fringe with the Oxford Theatre Group, who had a tradition of presenting a newly written play and revue on the Royal Mile.

The venue was the Cranston Street Hall, belonging to the Edinburgh Parks and Burials Department, who liked to surround our thrust stage with flowers and foliage, which we had politely to remove. The play we chose to premiere was *Songs for an Autumn Rifle* by the historian and novelist David Caute (*At Fever Pitch*, *Comrade Jacob*, *The Fellow Travellers*). The intricate plot charted the reactions of the communist *Daily Worker* to the 1956 Hungarian uprising contrasted with their opposition to the Suez invasion. I played the *Daily Worker* editor, while my son on his National Service stint languished in an army prison for refusing to go to Suez, and was interrogated by an officer played to the manner born by Peter Snow. The plot centred on our Budapest correspondent, played by Gavin Millar, who was sending back reports on the Russian invasion which the *Worker* was unwilling to print until it had the official party line from Moscow. Copies of the *Worker*, as a communist paper, were allowed back into Budapest, whereupon local freedom fighters were turning on our correspondent for failing to report the truth. In the course of the run we were startled by a visit from the real correspondent, Peter Fryer, who endorsed David Caute's account (and in 2006 was awarded the Hungarian Order of Merit for 'his continuous support of the Hungarian revolution'). This was August 1961 when to our surprise a striking parallel emerged. We were taking the *Daily Worker* as part of our research when on August 13th the Berlin Wall started to be erected. Once again the paper was at a loss how to explain it – history does occasionally repeat itself – until word eventually came from Moscow that the wall was essential not to keep East Germans in but to keep Western fascists out.

In 1961 we were still in the era of the Lord Chamberlain, who not only vetoed certain passages but sometimes made 'helpful' suggestions. In the play we sent our imprisoned son various provisions including a box of chocolates, which the guard removed as 'we don't want you shitting bricks all over the place'. The Chamberlain objected to 'shitting bricks', but suggested 'spreading marzipan' would be permissible. We declined the offer. The play was a great critical success. Harold Hobson in *The Sunday Times* went overboard and wrote that together with the exhibition of Epstein sculptures and the great Castle itself it was one of the glories of the festival. The play, as far as I know, has never been revived or printed. As a footnote to the Oxford Theatre Group at the Edinburgh Fringe, in 1966 they presented the premiere of a play many professional companies had passed on, Tom Stoppard's *Rosencrantz and Guildenstern Are Dead*. The local notices were not very enthusiastic, dismissing it as some whimsical sub-Beckettian joke, but it seemed to me a fascinating hour-length idea overstretched. Then Ronald Bryden in the *Observer* wrote that it was 'the most brilliant debut by a young playwright since John Arden's seven years ago', the National Theatre seized upon it and faced with a cancelled production allowed it twenty-five performances on a minimum budget. It was so well reviewed that it stayed in the National repertoire for three years, played for a year on Broadway, won a Tony for best play, launched Tom's career, and has been frequently revived. Such is the nature of chance in the theatre.

During the run of the play I received some surprising news. My plan had been to do a Diploma of Education, enabling me to teach in state schools, and then go to drama school – still hedging my bets, you notice. But I found I had been awarded a State Studentship (£450 p.a. for three years) to do a DPhil in seventeenth- and eighteenth-century history. Such interventions can determine the course of one's life. I was, however, now free to go on acting at Oxford, much to the annoyance of my departmental head Professor Hugh Trevor-Roper. Peter Dews, who having directed all Shakespeare's history plays entitled *An Age of Kings* for BBC television (black and white hour-length episodes that went out live, Robert Hardy as Henry V, Sean Connery as Hotspur), returned to Oxford in 1962 to direct the two parts of *Henry IV* for OUDS and cast me as Falstaff on the grounds that 'you have the twinkle, lad'. He concentrated ferociously on the meaning of the lines, and was a brilliant and witty paraphraser (he called it his version of subtext). Many an actor struggling with Shakespeare has cried out in despair, "Oh, if only we could say your version, Peter!" His guidance also taught me so much about Shakespeare's acute sense of prose rhythm – 'If I be not ashamed of my soldiers, I am a soused gurnet: I have misused the King's press damnably.' The production and my performance were judged a success, my vocal control was pronounced 'stunning', and as a result the RSC showed great interest in taking me on, as did a very good London agent. Suddenly I seemed to have made a great leap forward. A crucial choice was now before me – should I chuck in my doctorate and go to Stratford, following the example of Alan Bennett, who had recently left his postgraduate thesis to be engulfed by *Beyond the Fringe*? But it is always a gamble. The RSC could have used me for a season, not re-engaged me, and my boats would have been burnt. I decided I was set on the path to be a history teacher, either at school or university, and theatre would remain a hobby. I hoped in forty years to have another crack at Falstaff.

Meanwhile I became president of OUDS and probably ill-advisedly played Othello, directed by my friend Adrian Brine. It was early 1963, the coldest English winter some claim since 1814, with a frozen River Cherwell and ice-cold rehearsal rooms. It featured a number of students who later turned professional, Michael York, Giles Block, Sheridan Morley, Annabel Leventon, Braham Murray, Michael Elwyn and Neil Stacy. Such a flood was unusual; most Oxbridge actors reject the siren call. Nancy Lane, our Bianca, remained a cell biologist, and later advised the government on education and became world-renowned for her work on invertebrate cell junctions. We toured French universities, where in Lyon I got one of my most unexpected notices, 'féroce comme Orson Welles'. The photos suggest I was indeed a ferocious Othello, probably because ferocity escaped me in real life. Forty years later I was a very ferocious Lear – the same reason might apply. Adrian Brine soon afterwards settled in Amsterdam and for fifty years became a sought-after director in Holland and Belgium. Despite the probable limitations of my performance, playing Falstaff and Othello gave me a great deal of confidence. I could at least hold my own playing two great Shakespearean heavies at the Oxford Playhouse, a fully professional theatre. It also confirmed to me that I was, in a phrase I came across much later, an 'ambivert', an extrovert when performing and an introvert when studying and writing in isolation. I have found it a trait common to many actors.

I started work on 'The wealth and political Influence of the greater aristocracy 1688–1714', a subject not close to my heart but which I was assured urgently needed tackling. It involved many visits to archives in stately homes, which proved not without interest. At the Duke of Devonshire's Chatsworth House I picked up by pure chance a bound copy on an open shelf of Thomas Hobbes' *Leviathan* (one of my Oxford set books) in his own handwriting – worth perhaps half a million. In August 1963 I watched President Kennedy visiting his sister's grave in nearby Edensor churchyard – three months before his own death. A welcome diversion came via Ned Sherrin, who got me a job with Bert Shevelove and Larry Gelbart (authors of *A Funny Thing Happened on the Way to the Forum*). I first 'Englished' their script for a film *The Wrong Box,* substituting biscuit for cookie, etc. Despite a stellar British cast, Peter Sellers, Michael Caine, Ralph Richardson, Peter Cook and Dudley Moore, the film flopped – though at least no one accused the script of sounding American. I then started research for an idea Bert and Larry had for a theatre revue on the theme of 'Human Folly'. It was the vaguest of briefs but it kept me occupied in my spare time for many months, the bonus being occasional tutorials from Larry Gelbart on scriptwriting – he was later to part-write one of my favourite films, *Tootsie.* Despite my reams of material, perhaps because of, they decided quite rightly it wasn't going to work and went back to America.

In my third year of ducal archives I was advised to try for some academic posts. Leeds turned me down, and I expected Edinburgh to do the same as, to my dismay, they had been forewarned by someone of my dramatic interests. The panel asked me my views on devising a language for plays set in a historical period, and by chance the night before the interview I had travelled across to Glasgow to see the first production of John Arden's *Armstrong's Last Goodnight* at the Citizens Theatre, and was able to hold forth on Arden's pastiche of language of the period. I think it was on the strength of my evident interest in Scottish history and language that they offered me an assistant lectureship at the unprincely salary of £1,000 p.a. (perhaps

£20,000 in 2022 terms). I was launched: wonderful city, great university, very good history department. Could this be me for life?

Three weeks into the job I had what I describe as my Damascene moment. I was entering the staff club in Chambers Street for lunch when I suddenly thought, "This isn't what I want to do with my life." I seemed to see the next forty years ahead of me, perhaps in Edinburgh, and I knew that if I had two lives I would teach and write history in one and act in the other, but one life would have to be the theatre. I talked it over with my sympathetic professor, Denys Hay, and he advised me, "Go soon. If you leave it till you have a mortgage and perhaps a family you won't go." Academia is full of lecturers regretting they didn't become a politician, an editor, a scientist, a barrister. He even promised me that if things didn't work out he would try to find me a post back in the department. I hazard that he did this not because he thought me likely to be an important historian, but because he had attended and enthused about one of my seventeenth-century European lectures (acting and vocal dexterity are great helps). Indeed, the student newspaper had voted me the best lecturer in the department, much to the amusement, and in some cases annoyance, of my twenty senior colleagues. Needless to say, the student paper was rapidly forbidden to review any more lectures.

I stayed two years in all, taught Robin Cook among others, and just missed Gordon Brown and Ian Charleson, who both arrived as students in 1967. I enjoyed the teaching and the staff/student camaraderie, but not the exam preparation. I felt students were over-examined, a situation that has continued to worsen. In the vacations I worked with a very good amateur society the Edinburgh Graduate Theatre Group (still going strong), for whom I directed *The Relapse* and *The Cherry Orchard*. This, my second Chekhov production, I was particularly proud of, the venerable *Scotsman* critic calling it the second-best production of the play he'd ever seen (I never discovered the first). But it also taught me that the theatre could never be a hobby for me. Apart from members being periodically unavailable for rehearsal, ten performances are the most an amateur group can usually manage, and you close just as things are beginning to come together and you can make progress. I had also been working for four years as a regional drama critic for *The Guardian*, at three guineas a review (£60 today?), first at Oxford and then in Edinburgh, covering mainly the recently opened Traverse Theatre in the Lawnmarket. I found it a largely frustrating experience, partly through the cuts sub-editors made to suit their layout and partly because I had to phone through three or four hundred words by 11pm (often from a phone box), which gave little time for considered thought. Faced by such a deadline many reviewers were therefore content to sketch in the background of the play, outline the plot, and say simply what they liked and didn't like. I wanted to be more thorough and analyse what the writer, director and actors were trying to do, consider how far they had succeeded, and decide whether it was worth attempting. I found that near impossible to do in perhaps thirty minutes, and in recognition these days very few notices are what the trade calls 'over-nighters'. I envied classical music critics who are allowed to write that it will take several more performances of a new work to be sure what the composer is saying. Theatre critics have to give instant judgement at first hearing, and are sometimes driven to write things which the playwright, director and cast know to be naïve and ill-considered. Such critics usually come from a literary background and have no practical knowledge of theatre (and it shows), unlike classical music critics who have at least gone to music college and could once play an instrument. I bowed out with relief, though it taught me to respect the few critics who can achieve instant analysis.

I felt it was too late to go to drama school, I was twenty-seven, had done a great deal of acting and directing, had taught students myself, and had no hope of getting a grant. But was I any good and how could I tell, acting being such a subjective craft? There are no eight grades, no opportunity to demonstrate you can play a Chopin nocturne note-perfect. Actors emerge from such different channels. Some are hooked from youthful experiences and never deviate, even if it means sweeping the floor or playing a ninja turtle. Some, like myself, are similarly hooked but chary of committing until other more secure channels are explored. You lose out on the juvenile leads but, I believe, benefit from the very different experiences other professions have given you. Some actors drift into it because they don't seem good at anything else: it's often the classroom clown syndrome. Some have been going to theatres and acting classes since they were five; conversely, one actor told me he got into drama school without ever having seen a play in the professional theatre. Some have parents who act and direct and just follow the family business as it's the only thing they feel familiar with, as plumbers, policemen and priests do. Some are plucked, usually because of their looks or potential charisma, from school, university or random venues, and thrust into film or television, without having given the matter much thought. Some just hope to be famous and/or make money. It's a great melting pot: sometimes talent rises to the top, sometimes not. Sometimes mediocrity prospers, sometimes not. There is nothing fair about acting as a career. Chekhov had warned me of difficulties ahead when he wrote to Olga Knipper: 'There are in store for you many unsuccessful days and whole unsuccessful seasons. You must he prepared for all this, accept it, and nevertheless stubbornly, fanatically, follow your own way'.

Following my own way was not without cost. A five-year relationship which seemed to be nearing marriage collapsed as I felt I could not commit to settling down, perhaps starting a family, at the same time as taking on the uncertainties of an entirely different profession. The theatre is not kind to personal relationships. My father was very supportive of my change of direction, my mother less so. She worried about the insecurity I would face, and for the next ten years would regularly say, "You've given it a good go, why not go back to lecturing?" I think too it was a matter of status: she would rather her son was a university lecturer than an out-of-work actor. Among my friends and relations some were incredulous at my turning my back on a university career; some thought acting had always been going to win. I have never thought of myself as a courageous person, but looking back I think it was the most daring action of my life. At the time it just seemed inevitable.

I started looking for work by writing letters to the few people I knew in theatre, the shameless Oxford network. Peter Dews, who had recently taken over the Birmingham Rep, was the only one who replied, and I have kept his letter:

'O.K. You can, if you wish, join the company in January to rehearse *Richard II* and *As You Like It*, playing Salisbury and the Groom in *Richard* and Duke Senior in *As You*. The salary for beginners is ten guineas [the Equity minimum, perhaps £200 in 2022 money]. Which is all I dare, in conscience, offer you weekly. You would also play in the third play, *The Holy Terror*, based on Fr. Rolfe's *Hadrian VII*.'

I accepted like a shot, full of romantic notions of Olivier, Richardson, Scofield and Finney starting their careers at Barry Jackson's theatre in Station Street. It was also monthly rep, a luxury compared with the many theatres still operating on a weekly basis. Ten guineas was a blow (though I got very good digs for £2 17s 6d), but Peter immediately upped it to £12 – "I took thirty bob off someone else's salary," he unblushingly told me. I felt daunted as an untrained amateur joining the company of a premier rep, but fortunately many of the company were new to Birmingham and may not have initially realised my lack of professional experience. My familiarity with Shakespeare also disguised many faults, and Salisbury and the Groom were hardly taxing parts. I thought if I kept my head down I might survive.

One hurdle was overcome when Peter kindly granted me the essential Equity card: in those closed-shop days major reps were allowed to give out two cards a year. My name Oliver Davies was a bigger stumbling block. Equity insist on a unique name (there are instances of the 'wrong' actor turning up on the first day of rehearsal), and they claimed they already had an Oliver Davies. I suggested Oliver Ford (my mother's surname and my third forename) and this was accepted. Two months later they wrote that they already had one of those (though neither was in *Spotlight*). I was in a quandary: I was twenty-seven and many people were familiar with my name. My friend from university Michael Johnson had happily chosen to become Michael York, taking the surname from a brand of cigarettes, but I was strangely reluctant to become Oliver Dunhill, Olly Capstan or Ford Camel. Peter Dews suggested Oliver Ford Davies. This was only a minor change and had a good rhythm to it, but I feared (rightly, as it turned out) that it would condemn me to classy parts. Equity accepted the name but insisted on a hyphen (alas, even classier). Twelve years later I checked and Equity said they had neither an O. Davies or an O. Ford any longer, but it seemed too confusing to change. I dropped the hyphen, though forty years later journalists still put it back. Today, of course, double-barrelled names are frequent, particularly among the African and Caribbean communities. Fashion has caught up with me.

I started on January 2nd 1967, and two days later was drafted into the Christmas show 1066 and All That, taking over Oliver Cromwell (a prescient piece of casting), which luckily made me feel part of the company. The first time I saw Brian Cox walk on stage as some Roman captain I thought how can a squat twenty-year-old actor have such weight and presence? First impressions are so vital in theatre. Peter Dews was not only directing Richard II but also playing Gaunt, and he asked me to understudy him in case there was a crisis. I immediately learnt it, and after ten days we had a run-through of the first half of the play, and as things weren't shaping well Peter told me he had to sit out front and I was to play Gaunt ("You better bloody know it, lad"). At notes he opened with, "Olly is a total bastard and he's playing Gaunt. I'm not competing with that. But you've still got to play Salisbury and the Groom." I think I can claim that as a unique treble, Gaunt is usually in the pub by 8.30. I felt I could cope vocally with Gaunt but was brought up short when Henry Knowles, playing Richard, said, "If you're going to play the part you bloody well need to look me in the eye." First useful note of my career – I realised in my nervous state I was acting in a bubble of my own making. One of the reasons Peter gave me a job was that he had deliberately assembled a very young ensemble company, and he needed someone who could play older parts, setting me on a path that dogged me for years.

He was a great spotter of talent, he had directed Brian Cox as Andrea Sarti in Brecht's *Galileo* at the Lyceum Edinburgh and brought him to Birmingham along with Alison Key and Paul Chapman. Michael Gambon he saw at the Belgrade Coventry and knew he was ready for a first stab at Othello, with Brian as Iago. Timothy Dalton, Anna Calder-Marshall and Anthony Higgins he took straight from drama school. At twenty-seven I was the oldest company member. In the *As You Like It* Rosalind my daughter, played by the guest Andrée Melly, was actually older than I was and had taught Brian Cox, her Orlando, at drama school, which made for a very probing relationship. Once the Shakespeares were on we turned to the Rolfe play, now renamed *Hadrian VII*.

Production Two

HADRIAN VII (1967–69)

Since the play and the novel on which it is based may be unfamiliar a little background detail might help. Frederick William Rolfe (1860–1913) wrote his fourth novel and masterpiece *Hadrian the Seventh* (under the pseudonym Baron Corvo) in 1903 in attic lodgings in Hampstead. Rolfe became a Roman Catholic convert at the age of twenty-six, and was twice refused ordination as a priest on the grounds of 'devoid of vocation'. Into his novel he poured all his bitterness and frustration against both life and Roman Catholics by making his hero, a thinly disguised Rolfe, unexpectedly become pope, whereupon he sets about purging and reconstructing the church. Although the novel had good reviews and was later praised by D. H. Lawrence, Graham Greene and others, the first imprint of 600 copies failed to sell out and Rolfe never received a penny from it in his lifetime. He worked ceaselessly, but his libellous letters to erstwhile friends and his vituperative attacks on them in the press made him many enemies. He died in Venice in 1913, destitute and undernourished.

Peter Luke (1919–95), a BBC producer, writer and director adapted the book and made Rolfe himself the central figure and his ascent to the papacy a day-dream while waiting for the bailiffs to arrive. I was cast as one of the bailiffs who in Rolfe's dream turns into a bishop and later a cardinal, Rolfe's right-hand man and 'good friend' (I was

Hadrian VII, Birmingham Rep, 1967.
OFD (Talacryn, seated), Alec McCowen (Hadrian).

to play a lot of those). Peter Dews evidently still had faith in my 'twinkle', though some company members I realised were put out by the promotion of this untrained, inexperienced 'intellectual'. To the company's excitement Alec McCowen was joining us to play Rolfe. I had seen him as a dazzling Mercutio in Franco Zeffirelli's production of *Romeo and Juliet* at the Old Vic in 1959, and in 1962 the Fool to Paul Scofield's Lear at Stratford. I was so nervous at the first read-through I felt sure that when it came to my first line to Alec no sound would emerge. In fact Alec proved a delight to work with, though his darting eyes missed nothing. I learnt a great deal from watching the decisions he made; he was one of the best explorers of language I was ever to encounter. Rolfe had given Hadrian a wonderfully literate invective, full of biting sarcasm, bumptious conceit, passionate self-loathing and arrogant self-satisfaction, and Alec inhabited every twist and turn as if it were second nature. He also had great wit, relishing every chance to see the comic side of word and deed. This was all allied to a fastidious, burnished technique, a word often undervalued, sometimes derided, though as Olivier wrote, 'Talent is very plentiful, skill is rather rare'. Ben Kingsley once said that he'd always managed to keep very good company: I too have been very lucky with the company I've kept. Alec could be very down-to-earth about the basics of acting. I once asked him if he knew when he was acting well. "That's when I clear my mind, listen to what's being said to me, and find myself replying with the words the author has given me." And how often does that happen? "On a good night perhaps 70% of the time." And on the press night? "Oh, never on the press night." Poor critics, I thought, never to witness actors listening to one another.

Peter's production was simple and direct; pace and clarity were always his passion, and he placed great emphasis, and most of the budget, on ceremonial with cardinal red to the fore. Audibility was ever his watchword: at company notes he was apt to say to an actor: "The audience have come to hear a play; your final line only a passing bat would have picked up." Our company were mostly too young for the parts they were playing, myself included, but rose to the challenge, Paul Chapman, Brian Cox and Gabrielle Laye in particular. Alec received universal praise, but the play did mediocre business. The reviews were curiously contradictory. Irving Wardle in *The Times* thought the decision to put Rolfe himself at the centre of the play was 'an unworkable scheme... a trick which always strikes one as a cheat'. Gareth Lloyd-Evans in *The Guardian* went further: 'It is in effect a no-play... in all conscience I could find little of the real stuff of drama'. And yet Wardle went on to say: 'Relieved of its shaky superstructure and with some tightening up the play would be well worth a London transfer', and Lloyd-Evans concluded: 'Alec McCowen miraculously succeeds by force of technique in holding the piece together'.

The play's weakness lay inevitably in the second half. Once Rolfe was installed as pope the energy of the plot dwindled, as it does with

Marlowe's *Dr Faustus*. It's a Cinderella story, and who's interested in how the princess's plans for model housing work out? The novel describes in arcane detail Rolfe's reconstruction of the Church in the context of European politics, but this is hardly audience-friendly and Luke had to limit himself to clashes with outraged cardinals and visits from old friends and malignant enemies, culminating in his assassination. The initial critical reception therefore would seem to be 'faulty play, good production, great central performance'. On that basis the play could well have disappeared, a coterie offering for the few hundred admirers of Frederick Rolfe. Why then did it survive? Because there were two managements who believed in both the play and Alec, and were determined to give it a London run. Bernard Miles wanted it for his Mermaid Theatre which was not in a flourishing state, and Bill Freedman and Charles Kasher were prepared to back it. It taught me that a producer and a management are crucial to a playwright and a production's chance of a future: think of Max Stafford-Clark and Caryl Churchill; Peter Hall, Richard Eyre and David Hare; Michael Codron and Tom Stoppard. I have written about *Hadrian*'s gestation at some length because it is an issue that has concerned me throughout my career: how many worth-while plays given a try-out in a regional theatre have folded, never to be heard of again? Getting a first production is difficult enough; getting a second or a transfer can assume mammoth proportions. The British theatre is extremely wasteful of writing talent.

As if to illustrate the importance of a management's whim Peter Saunders, owner of the Vaudeville Theatre, took a surprising fancy to The Birmingham *As You Like It* and transferred it to his theatre for the summer months, by which time I was playing both the dukes as Peter Brookes, the bad duke, had wanted to stay with his young family in Birmingham. It also saved them money: two dukes would have cost £35; I was promoted to £25. Peter Dews wanted to keep the company together, something almost impossible in regional theatre today, and I returned to Birmingham to do a season of six classic plays, which included Somerset Maugham's *The Circle*, Shaw's *The Doctor's*

Dilemma and Iris Murdoch's *A Severed Head*. The most ambitious of the season was *Peer Gynt*, with Brian Cox as Peer, Anna Calder-Marshall as Solveig, Michael Gambon as the Button Moulder and myself as Troll King and Madhouse Keeper (fifty-two years later at the National Theatre I graduated to the Button Moulder, the theatre can be a long game). In nearly every play I was, like Mike Gambon, either a middle-aged or an elderly character. This ability was to bring me a great deal of work in the regions and even at the RSC, but it also proved limiting. Not only could I not fully express my own age and personality, but film, television and commercial London theatre weren't interested in a young actor aping middle-age. Gambon, with his extraordinary physicality and maverick talent, managed to escape these limitations.

Peter Dews looked at me shrewdly one day and said, "You seem able to play anything I put in front of you." I think this was the moment I realised that one of my main strengths was an ability to see things from other people's point of view. My training as a historian was an aid to this: I had never tried to judge Napoleon or even Hitler; I tried to understand where they were coming from. I have never been an actor who closely observes people's behaviour, I have always been more interested in their minds – 'I may not be sympathetic to what you say and do, but fascinated by how you have come to believe it'. Peter's analysis of my looks then concluded, "You'll be alright when you're forty, and even better when you're fifty." This is not what you want to hear when you're twenty-eight. He was to prove right, almost to the month.

In the meantime the various managements must have liked my performance in *Hadrian* because for some months I was pencilled in to play Talacryn again, the 'good friend', when it opened at the Mermaid. Alan MacNaughtan, a fine actor, had accepted to play the archbishop, but on rereading the script understandably decided Talacryn was the better part and my name was removed. I left the Rep in March 1968 and went back to my parents' home in Dorset to finish my thesis since my seven years, the maximum period allowed, were almost up. I had managed to keep my research going at Birmingham by working in the university library (entirely without permission) whenever I had a few hours off. I did finally get my DPhil, but when my external examiner Sir Jack Plumb suggested, "If you did another three families you'd have an interesting book," I knew wild horses wouldn't drag me back into an aristocratic archive.

When the play opened in London in April 1968 the daily critics were still divided. And it was therefore left to the posh Sundays to have the conclusive word. Harold Hobson in *The Sunday Times* called it 'this splendid, colourful, recklessly melodramatic and vituperatively brilliant drama', while Ronald Bryden in *The Observer* concentrated on Alec's performance:

> 'The ovation at the end was the most rousing I've heard since the opening of *The Prime of Miss Jean Brodie*. Like the cheers that night for Vanessa Redgrave, it had little to do with drama but with the perishable, precarious excitement of a special theatrical occasion: a performance in which an actor of long promise comes into his own... We have a new star of the order of Alec Guinness.'

I felt so happy for Alec. He had been stuck well into his thirties playing juveniles. Now at last he had a leading part that showed off his strength, intelligence and charisma. As a result the play was deemed a hit, and this was further enhanced when the Lambeth Conference of Anglican bishops paid a group visit and proved to be a uniquely receptive audience for ecclesiastical jokes. During the summer I heard that Alec and Alan MacNaughtan would be leaving the production in October, and that I was offered my old part which Peter Dews urged me to accept. In less than two years as a professional I would be playing a major part in a London success. So far luck was on my side.

Alec was to be replaced by the Canadian actor Douglas Rain. Douglas was largely unknown to British theatre, though in the early fifties he had trained at the Bristol Old Vic school, which had left him "depressed by the stagnant atmosphere which pervaded the school and all of the English theatre". In 1953 he understudied Alec Guinness as Richard III in the inaugural season of the Stratford Ontario Festival Theatre, and had played in all fifteen seasons since, his wide range of parts including Henry V, Malvolio and Iago. Taking over from Alec was never going to be easy, especially as many of the initial cast stayed on, and Douglas' rather withdrawn personality meant that he remained on somewhat formal, even uneasy, terms with some of the old hands. His performance was extremely intelligent and ferociously committed, but without some of Alec's wit and speed of thought. As a result he put time on the production. On Fridays and Saturdays we played 6 and 8.40, standard at the Mermaid, and at the first performance we came down at 8.30, due to start again in ten minutes. We did get a little faster, though we never had time for anything more than a quick mug of soup.

I got on well with Douglas, perhaps because I was also new to the Mermaid, perhaps because I was playing the 'good friend'. I met his wife Martha Henry, another hugely talented actor from the Ontario theatre, who later became known as 'the first lady of Canadian theatre' and in 2018 played Prospero there at the age of eighty. As the run continued Douglas confided in me more and more his exasperation at the tired performances many of the cast after 500 performances were giving. 'Anticipation' was his great bugbear. I finally plucked up courage to ask him if I was anticipating him at any point.

"Yes, you are."

"But how, I'm not cutting off your sentences?"

"No, but I see in your eyes that you are preparing your reply before I have given you sufficient information to warrant it."

For the next nine months I tried to follow Alec and now Douglas' advice, empty my mind and listen to what was being said to me. The dangers of anticipation, far too little talked about in the theatre probably because from out front it is hard to detect even for the director, has now become a bugbear of mine. I also learnt that playing the good friend/wise counsellor it pays to keep still on stage and allow the leading player their freedom. Stillness has turned out to be one of my strengths, upheld by a Lindsay Anderson note to Brian Cox, "Don't just do something, stand there." Patrick Stewart once said when accepting a best supporting actor award in the early seventies that there are two grooves either side of the RSC stage where support operates while the star occupies the middle. I was to experience this for many years.

One evening Douglas told me he had been spending several days with the director Stanley Kubrick, who was looking for a 'bland mid-Atlantic accent' for a voice-over narration of a film. When the first narration was abandoned Douglas recorded hours of computer dialogue, including numerous different versions of the Daisy Bell singing sequence. Douglas later found that he was the voice of HAL 9000, the computer who governs the space-ship in the film *2001 – A Space Odyssey*. Ironic that for all the great parts Douglas has played a computer voice remains his abiding claim to international fame – and I believe he has never seen the film.

In March 1969 we left the Mermaid for the Theatre Royal Haymarket, a signal commendation and a great help in refreshing the production. I continued to share a dressing room, the beautiful wood-panelled room on the stage level of the Haymarket, with an elderly actor Donald Eccles (the archbishop), and we had the most absorbing conversations about theatre as Donald delved back before the war. I remember we discussed an actor in the company who seemed of little talent, and I suggested with all the effrontery of youth that perhaps it would be a kindness to advise him to look for another profession. Donald said, "Be careful. I've only done that once, at Stratford in the 1930s. A good-looking, well-built young man, good cricketer, but very wooden. His name was Trevor Howard." I have taken Donald's warning: it is so difficult to know how actors will develop, as any drama-school teacher will confirm. Also what can appear wooden on a stage can turn out to be very helpful for film, where stillness of feature can be a bonus – think Spencer Tracy, Bill Murray, and indeed Trevor Howard in *Brief Encounter*. At the end of my year they asked me to stay on when Paul Daneman took over Hadrian, but I felt it would be a mistake, not to say soul-destroying, and left. I have been careful never to do a year's run again.

Michael Bryant once told me he regarded the first thirty performances as his "experimental period, and then I more or less do the same thing every night". If you are fortunate enough to be playing one of the big beasts with a multiplicity of facets and a story with continual twists and turns (Lear, Cleopatra, Gynt) then exploration can be never-ending, but in good supporting parts, with what I term 2½ dimensions, the chances of experiment are limited: Horatio can't start despising Hamlet, Miss Prism can't fall in love with Cecily, without wrenching the play off course. I also learnt that being part of a take-over cast is no route to further work, as directors, producers and casting directors have all seen the original. I had, however, risen to the giddy heights of £50 per week – perhaps £850 in 2022 terms, a handsome amount but not the goldmine some people imagine. It did, however, enable me to rent a five-room flat in Paddington for £12 per week, which I shared with one and sometimes two people. At £4 or £6 p. week. I could afford to keep on my London base when I went out later into £30 rep, something that young actors today can rarely manage with grossly inflated rentals.

Meanwhile Alec had opened on Broadway to great acclaim and a Tony nomination; Peter Dews actually won the director's Tony. Columbia announced a film version with Alec as lead, and took a full-page ad in the *New York Times* showing the now-iconic photo of Alec in papal white smoking a fag before the throne. It was an almost unprecedented demonstration of faith in a relatively unknown movie actor – and this was a 'coterie' script which threatened to have no life after Birmingham. Then *The Shoes of the Fisherman* with Anthony Quinn opened, and bombed. Papal films were out, so no *Hadrian VII*: timing is everything in Hollywood. As a postscript, in 1995 I went to see a Chichester production of the play with a fine cast headed by Derek Jacobi and realised the early critics were probably right – it isn't that good a play.

1969–74: the Rep years

In the nearly six years between leaving *Hadrian* and first joining the RSC in 1975 I acted in twenty-two plays with eight different theatre companies. My particular abilities seemed to be in demand, at any rate in regional theatres. I have thought it a period worth examining because it describes a theatre scene that barely exists today. Just as the days of weekly rep where an actor might be engaged for a long season to play often unspecified parts, so clinically described by John Osborne in *A Better Class of Person* (1985) and Michael Blakemore in *Arguments with England* (2004), had largely passed by 1970, so the '70s and '80s inhabited a different theatre landscape.

Although regional theatres were still referred to as reps, the theatres that engaged a company to perform a number of plays were fast disappearing, and so I went from theatre to theatre to act in one or occasionally two plays. Funding theatre had always been a problem, but the Arts Council decision to concentrate on 'Centres of Excellence' meant that smaller theatres went to the wall, and local councils were unwilling to bail them out. There was also the perception, not always justified, that the National Theatre and the RSC were gobbling up the available money. Reps had always operated on an administrative shoestring, but now there was a drive, partly inspired by the Arts Council, to increase the size of the administration, which in some theatres arguably became top-heavy and resulted in fewer productions and smaller casts. In the late 1960s the Bristol Old Vic and the Little Theatre were presenting twenty-seven plays on three stages: this was soon to drop to eight productions in the one main house. Television was becoming more of a threat to live regional theatre, both because it was a free alternative and in many departments, casting, sets, costumes, etc., its standards were higher. Audiences were less inclined to accept actors in their twenties 'greying up' to play older people. Actors and their agents were also increasingly keen for them to stay in London for better-paid film and television work. Fringe theatre, particularly in London, was becoming the training ground that regional rep had once been, with the crucial differences that it was ill- or un-paid and usually in very small venues.

In 1970, after a season at the Phoenix Leicester, I went back to the Birmingham Rep to direct Charles Dyer's *Staircase* and to appear in Shaw's *Pygmalion* and Coward's *Tonight at Eight*, which then went to the Ravinia Summer Festival in Chicago. American audiences, very familiar with *My Fair Lady*, were bemused by the lack of songs in Shaw's play, particularly when Higgins pronounced 'I've grown accustomed to her face'. Mary Miller, recently playing major parts at the National Theatre, came to play Eliza Doolittle. She bemoaned to me that she was on £30 p. week, which surprised me as I was on £32 10s. She took this up via her agent and the Birmingham general manager eventually confessed the outrageous fact that the top for men was £35 and for women £30. I wondered if this discrepancy was the norm throughout the theatre at the time – and perhaps still is today? Unless there is a standard company wage, theatres are still very reluctant to reveal their pay structure. In the Coward I played the doctor in *Still Life*, on which *Brief Encounter* is based, and had to cope with a line to Mary Miller, 'We're nice people, you and I, and we've got to go on being nice'. It has proved one of my very few romantic leads, and I noted how much more attractive I briefly appeared to the usherettes – ah, the perks of playing a lover. As I was not in the third play I had two free weeks, in one of which I saw with Douglas' help several plays at the Stratford theatre in Ontario, and in the other stayed on a working ranch in New Mexico – quite an eye-opening introduction to the Americas. It was to be the last time I worked with Peter Dews. He saw the Birmingham Rep into its new theatre in 1971, left a year later to direct many West End and Chichester Festival productions, and then ran Chichester 1978–80. Soon after he suffered a stroke, and though he continued occasionally to direct and teach he had lost much of his fire. He died in 1997. He had been my patron and mentor, and I owe him so much.

The 1960s hadn't fulfilled all our hopes but there had been a liberalisation of society with the movement for gay rights culminating in their 1967 legalisation for over-21s; the second wave of feminism; the abolition in 1965 of the death penalty and in 1968 the censorship of the Lord Chamberlain; the opposition to the Vietnam war and the Paris uprising. It was also a time of sexual liberation, and for five years I went through a succession of relationships veering from the improbable to the impossible. For much of society it wasn't all

Carnaby St, flower power and free love, but it seemed a start. We approached the '70s with optimism.

On my return from Chicago I went to the Oxford Playhouse to play Fenella Fielding's father in a new play about Colette (I was probably ten years younger than Fenella), and then a much too young Friar Laurence in *Romeo and Juliet* with Felicity Kendal as a particularly resourceful Juliet. In between plays in 1971 I devoted myself to helping Sam Walters and others set up a lunch-time theatre at the Orange Tree pub in Richmond. I acted there, directed Stoppard's *After Magritte*, and had a play of mine performed. In the autumn I went to Hampstead Theatre to appear in *Tonight at Eight* again – different plays apart from the perennial crowd-pleaser *Red Peppers* – directed by Gillian Lynne, her first 'straight' production. As singing was involved, and I have great difficulty singing in tune, Gillian begged me to mime during the choruses, which I accepted with alacrity (had I gone to drama school both my singing and my movement would have greatly benefited). With Millicent Martin and Gary Bond in the leads we transferred to the Fortune Theatre, where Coward himself came to see us. After the performance he talked to us on stage for half an hour, and I was much impressed. He was very direct and down-to-earth about what no longer worked and what was too dated in the plays. I think he would have been happy to talk to us till midnight had not Graham Payn reminded him that the Savoy Grill was about to close.

I then went to Manchester to appear in J. M. Barrie's *Mary Rose,* where the young woman disappears on a visit to a Scottish island, returns twenty years later totally unchanged to find her ageing parents cannot cope with her reappearance. It is a strange play, shadowed by the loss of life in the First World War and the ghosts that continued to haunt parents. It was directed by Braham Murray for Theatre 69, the precursor to the Royal Exchange Company, with Mia Farrow as Mary Rose and myself as her father, with music by John Taverner. Mia was twenty-eight and I was thirty-three, so I was at long last five years older than my daughter. Laurence Olivier had wanted to play the father at the National Theatre, with Mia as his daughter, but Tynan and others were not keen on the play and the idea was dropped. Mia of course sold the house out, but she proved to be a very good actress, very truthful to act with. When we toured the play to Brighton Mia went to have tea with the Oliviers, then living in Brighton, and cheerfully reported that Olivier had quoted the whole of the father's last speech from memory and was coming to see the play with his family at the Saturday matinee. I was introduced to him after my shell-shocked performance, and he enthused about what a wonderful play it was and what a wonderful part the father was, and then left me. I was elated for about thirty seconds until I realised he had said nothing about how wonderful my performance was – it was a stratagem Olivier had perfected over the years. Appearing with Mia, however, had numerous advantages, not least in the variety of friends she introduced me to – Katharine Hepburn, Joni Mitchell and, though I didn't recognise them till Mia prompted me, the Beach Boys.

After a short run of *Mary Rose* in London I did three weeks as a monk on my first film, John Osborne's play *Luther* with Stacy Keach in the lead surrounded by a galaxy of British theatre talent, Judi Dench, Robert Stephens, Patrick Magee, Alan Badel, Julian Glover and Hugh Griffith. In one scene Leonard Rossiter and I dressed Stacy to officiate at his first communion. The film, shot by the great Freddie Young and so full of promise, has been long buried. Christmas and New Year '72–73 found me reunited with Brian Cox in a stylish production by Colin Graham, director of so many Britten operas, of *The Three Musketeers* at the Nottingham Playhouse. Graham used William Walton's film music from *Henry V* and *Richard III* to great effect, arguing that it was quite wrong for the fifteenth century, but very suitable for the seventeenth – which I doubted. In the company playing a double of D'Artagnan's love Constance Bonacieux and Kitty, Milady's maid, was Jenifer Armitage. I had seen and admired Jenny's work, as two years previously she had played Sonya in the BBC Play of the Month production of *Uncle Vanya*, opposite Anthony Hopkins and Freddie Jones, and prior to that she had been in Peter Gill's D. H. Lawrence Trilogy at the Royal Court.

During rehearsals and the run of *Three Musketeers* Jenny and I became friends, later on partners, and have been together ever since. Our backgrounds are strikingly dissimilar. Jenny was born to communist parents, grew up on the Golders Green/Hampstead borders, and went to the progressive King Alfred School. She went on to train at both Hornsey School of Art and for drama at Webber Douglas, where she was awarded Best Actress in 1966. As Jenny says, the story of our relationship from such disparate starting points is really a story about theatre. When a group of people of differing ethnicities, classes, religions, genders, sexualities, or differently abled, come together to produce and perform a play, the shared endeavour unites us. In the process of realising the world of the play our differences fall away. It is why we love theatre.

That winter a television play I had written, *Field Work*, went out on ATV. It attracted the attention of the great BBC producer and script editor Betty Willingale, and she got me to write a specimen *Z Cars*, a treatment for a historical love story which I set in Haddon Hall in Derbyshire, and arranged for me to pitch for a Play for Today on an idea I had about a television tobacco campaign fronted by a seventeenth-century Pocahontas (judged too way out). Another moment of decision had arrived. I seemed firmly labelled a 'character actor': what were my chances of escaping into more testing parts, as 'characters' like Alec Guinness, Leo McKern and Michael Hordern had? Would I one day play Vanya, Peer Gynt, or Lear? It seemed a long shot, and perhaps I would be more fulfilled turning to full-time writing, applying to lecture in a university drama department, or turning to direction as Patrick Garland and Ken Loach had once urged me? I could still hear my mother saying, "You've given it a good go, why not..."

I knew only too well after six years the downsides to being an actor. Firstly, you are an employee, endlessly auditioning and when finally offered a part the only power you have is to say 'no'. Choice and the power to initiate hardly exists. Secondly, in the acres of unemployment there is little opportunity to hone your craft, unlike a pianist who can work at home on the Goldberg Variations or a circus artist who can at least practise juggling with five batons rather than four. Being out of work or doing near-rubbish for the money can be debilitating beyond measure, leaving you feeling that you ought to be doing something more useful with your life. But despite all this I felt, perhaps narcissistically, that I wanted to explore my potential as an actor to its limit. As a director I loved working with actors in the rehearsal room but was not drawn to the never-ending selling of myself and my concept to producers and artistic directors. Returning to lecturing seemed an admission of defeat. I knew few dramatists can make a living writing for the stage, so television would be the likely resort – with all its inherent drawbacks. My close friend Jeremy Paul had become a successful television writer (he wrote fifteen of the original *Upstairs Downstairs* scripts), and I was only too aware of the compromises he had to make in writing to a formula and being rewritten by producers, a situation that is, of course, far more extreme today. An actor makes innumerable compromises in getting work, but out there on stage you can and should be your own master.

Production Three

FEARS AND MISERIES OF THE
THIRD REICH (1973–74)

A more permanent job was thankfully offered me by Richard Cottrell with the Cambridge Theatre Company. We were contracted for nine months to appear in six plays, the first four in a form of repertoire. Inspired by the Actors Company, set up by Ian McKellen and Edward Petherbridge, the nine men were all to play a mixture of large and supporting parts. In the opening two productions, for example, I was to play Mr Hardcastle in *She Stoops to Conquer* and Valentine and various officers in *Twelfth Night*. Unfortunately the same mixture could not be applied to our three women. Both plays have three very good female parts, but no good supporting parts for women, no female equivalents of Sebastian, Antonio and Fabian in *Twelfth Night*. It is a problem not only in Shakespeare but in most plays prior to the twentieth century that there are too few medium-sized parts for actresses to learn and develop their skills: in *King Lear* women are either playing Goneril, Regan and Cordelia or nothing – that is until fifty-fifty gender casting became a reality: Lear and the Fool have already been played by women, and no doubt Gloucester, Edgar, Edmund and Oswald will follow (or have followed). Cottrell had, like Dews in 1967, deliberately chosen a young company, partly because we were cheaper and readier to work very long hours, and partly because more seasoned actors might not have agreed to playing smaller parts. Trevor Nunn later told me he had attempted a similar project at the RSC and failed to find enough experienced actors ready to play the occasional third senator. Our actresses were Diane Fletcher, Brenda Peters and Zoe Wanamaker; our actors James Aubrey, Geoffrey Bateman, Trevor Bowen, Pip Donaghy, Jack Galloway, John Green, Dennis Lawson, Roger Rees and myself. After performing in a succession of one-off productions the whole idea of an ensemble company I found immensely attractive, and I blindly plunged in.

The two initial classics yielded excellent performances from Zoe Wanamaker as Viola and Denis Lawson as Feste, and in *She Stoops* Diane Fletcher and Brenda Peters as Kate and Mrs Hardcastle and Roger Rees as Young Marlowe. I hugely enjoyed Hardcastle, and have always hoped to play him again. We then went on to modern plays, the British premiere of Ionesco's *Aunt Sally, or the Triumph of Death (Jeux de Massacre)*, loosely inspired by Camus' *The Plague*, and Brecht's *Fears and Miseries of the Third Reich* (directed by Robert Lang). Both fascinating plays, but hardly box-office draws. All the productions played initially at the Cambridge Arts Theatre for two weeks, the longest a city of 100,000 could sustain, and then went on tour, where theatres were offered a choice of the four productions, though there were few takers for the Ionesco. The scheme threw a considerable strain on actors, stage management and backstage technicians. Richard Cottrell wrote in *Plays and Players* (October 1973): 'I just find it a fucking drag, quite honestly. It's expensive; it's a tax on staff; and to have to adapt to seven theatres which have different entrances and exits is a hassle. With a lot of touring theatres you get the feeling that it's a bore for them to have you. They don't want to sell you, so we try to do our own leaflets and posters. I can't think of anyone who could say in all honesty I do touring because I love it'.

Ionesco in *The Triumph of Death* proposes that 'death is my anguish, my prison, and my freedom to be aware, because those who do not think about death cheat us out of the knowledge of our future'. In the play everyone – happy lovers, prison convicts, debutantes, doctors with universal cures – all end up dead through the plague. It was tiring and, despite the farcical humour, repetitive and predictable to perform, but I relished the anarchy it generated. This was my third absurdist outing. In 1961 at Oxford I had played the name part in Michel de Ghelderode's *Pantagleize* (1929), where a Chaplinesque figure unwittingly becomes leader of a revolution and is shot by the police, and a year later I had appeared on the Edinburgh fringe in Arthur Adamov's *Paolo Paoli* (1957), where the events leading up to the First World War are seen through the prism, both absurd and Brechtian, of a dealer in butterflies and ostrich feathers. British dramatists have never really taken to absurdism as political and social comment, though it helped to spawn the satire wave from Spike Milligan and Peter Cook to *The Thick of It*.

I enjoyed *Fears and Miseries* (*Furcht und Elend des dritten Reiches*), translated by Paul Kriwoczek, far more than the Ionesco. At Oxford I had seen university productions of *The Caucasian Chalk Circle* (with Denis Potter as Azdak and Margaret Forster as Grusha), and *The Good Woman of Setzuan* (with Annabel Leventon and David Aukin, directed by Michael Rudman). In the professional theatre I had seem Berliner Ensemble productions of *Mother Courage* and *Coriolan*, *Good Woman* again (with Peggy Ashcroft), *The Life of Galileo* (Lyceum Edinburgh with Tom Fleming), and *The Threepenny Opera* (with Vanessa Redgrave, Joe Melia and Barbara Windsor). I list these to show how frequent were Brecht productions and how devotedly actors and audiences took to them. Today, apart from occasional productions of *Galileo*, Brecht is hardly seen at all – too didactic, too heavy-going, too bad box-office. *Mother Courage*, his greatest play, has become a rarity.

I knew from our many workshops at Oxford that the Brechtian concept of 'alienation' or 'estrangement' (*verfremdung*) was partly a reaction against early twentieth-century melodrama in writing and acting, but also a rebuttal of Rheinhardt and Piscator, whom Brecht saw as trying to unite cast and audience in an emotional imagined world, which denied the reality of the world outside. Brecht wanted both actor and audience to keep the characters on stage at a distance. In workshops we were encouraged not to 'live' the characters but to 'show', to translate our speeches into the third person – 'He now argues that…' At first I thought this of limited use, but this estrangement did help me appreciate who was speaking, why, and with what intention. The object was to present the audience with a body of evidence and invite them to come to their own rational conclusions, and to this end clarity was everything. Far from being didactic, Brecht wanted both to make the audience think for themselves and to entertain them – the comic continually intrudes. The snag was, as he discovered time after time, that as the plays were not simple agitprop they had a strong emotional content that counteracted the audience's rational analysis. Audiences found themselves sympathising with Mother Courage's losses and dogged spirit rather than condemning her destructive, self-obsessed entrepreneurialism, and however much a disappointed Brecht rewrote the play they have continued to do so. Brecht's characters are subtly many-sided, but audiences tend to see only the side that attracts them.

I was so happy to be doing professional Brecht at last, but I soon realised that *Fears and Miseries* is not typical Brecht but far more naturalistic, conventional, and almost documentary in style as it describes life in Hitler's Reich, written in the mid-thirties from the safety of exile in Denmark and first performed in Paris in 1938. The twenty-three scenes vary greatly in length and subtlety; some are short revue sketches but at least half a dozen are complex and paradoxical. In *The Jewish Wife* we discover in a succession of phone calls to friends that the wife (Diane Fletcher) is not packing to have a simple break in Amsterdam but is leaving her non-Jewish husband for good to save his career. In *The Spy* Brenda Peters and I moved from mild concern to frantic agitation that our teenage son, played by a gum-chewing Zoe Wanamaker, was going to denounce us to the SS at a Hitler Youth meeting. The child returns, claiming only to have been buying chocolate and exits. All seems well for a moment, but suddenly the father's paranoia returns, 'Do you think he's telling the truth?'. In *The Sermon on the Mount* I played a dying man telling his priest (Roger Rees) that life in the next world must be better than that under the Third Reich, while my son sat silent at the foot of the bed in his SS uniform. In *The Physicists* Pip Donaghy and I were two scientists hungrily discussing Einstein's theories but pausing every time a silhouetted interloper passes by in the corridor. In *Justice* Pip as the Judge has to adjudicate between three Storm Troopers and a Jewish shopkeeper. The predictable outcome is complicated by the fact that the Jew has 'highly influential contacts' in the Ministry of Justice. The Judge's dilemma unfolds in some superb observational writing as, in a lather of sweat, he concludes to my unsympathetic fellow judge, 'I am looking out for myself. Only I don't know what advice to give myself!' It was Brecht at his best, specific, universally significant, funny, with a lethal punchline.

Fears and Miseries made me realise that what I valued most about Brecht was not his style but his content. All good plays, of course, have universal significance but are usually written on a small canvas. In *Mother Courage* and *The Caucasian Chalk Circle* Brecht's canvas is epic (favourite Brechtian word) in scale. 'Epic' theatre presents the complexity of the human condition in relation to the social and economic forces that determine the lives of millions. He was also a practical man of the theatre, famous for undermining his theoretical principles when in rehearsal. In a small book that I found by chance, *Brecht as They Knew Him* (edited by Hubert Witt), I read that an actor in his company wrote that Brecht had said to him in rehearsal:

> 'This is your moment, don't let it get away. Now it's your turn, and to hell with the play. All those taking part are interested in carrying forward the common cause of the play, yours too. But then there is also your interest, which stands in a certain contradiction to this. Everything lives from this contradiction.'

This advice chimed with my growing belief that every actor falls, however slightly, on one side or the other of this divide. We choose to do a play because we like the script and the part, but which is finally predominant? Is it the fat part or a desire to make the play work? I had always leant towards 'the common cause of the play', but I was finding from my observation of the very different actors in the Cambridge company that it was at least as important to stand up for my character as it was to serve the play. Selflessness in acting can be just as diminishing as selfishness. Three actors solely intent on pushing their own agendas without listening to one another can render a scene meaningless; three actors intent on 'making the scene work' without driving the action can render a scene flaccid and uninteresting. The problem is to keep both approaches in balance: 'everything lives from this contradiction', but it is not easy to achieve. It was a particularly hard lesson for me, after years of accommodating myself to others, a trait perhaps developed by having a dominating elder brother. Mike Gambon told me a story of Olivier directing O'Casey's *Juno and the Paycock* at the National and passionately urging the removal men in their brief but crucial appearance in the last act: "This is YOUR ninety seconds. TAKE IT!" The more he browbeat them the less inclined they were to take their moment and to hell with the play. Olivier patently couldn't understand an actor unwilling to seize his ninety seconds.

The touring and rehearsal of these four productions began to take their toll on company morale. Spending most of a Sunday travelling back from Aberystwyth to London, the circuitous rail connections being a nightmare, and being required to rehearse in Guildford 10.30 Monday morning brought a company revolt. It was therefore a relief to settle into the Cambridge Arts for five weeks to perform a pantomime *Jack and the Beanstalk*. This was written by John Moffat, who was also the expert Dame with Polly James as Jack, and was very enjoyable, though the many matinees and performances at 5 and 8pm were tiring for an exhausted company. I had a bad cold, trapped in a rubber mask and eighteen-inch-high boots as the Giant, though Roger Rees (Simple Simon) insisted for years afterwards that it was my greatest performance. I can still remember 'Fee, fo, fi, fum, Ooh I've a rumble in my tum' when I can hardly recall a line of Friar Laurence.

On January 28th 1974 we set off for another seven weeks' touring, but now there was a new and major hazard – the Three-Day Week.

On December 13th Edward Heath's Tory government announced that in order to conserve electricity and coal stocks in the face of industrial action by coal miners commercial use of electricity would be limited to three specified days and for a certain number of hours. This came into force on January 1st 1974 and meant in effect that on certain days all electricity would be turned off at, or not turned on until, 9pm, and theatres would have to cope with self-generated auxiliary lighting. At the Nuffield Theatre Southampton we were performing *Fears and Miseries* when the 9pm switch came, and we found that there were two auxiliary lights over the stage and four over the auditorium – suddenly the audience were more brilliantly lit than we were (Brecht might have approved). Our nadir was reached at the Harlow Playhouse where we were performing *Twelfth Night*. The IRA, or some allied group, had placed a bomb in Harlow town hall, and when this was discovered they announced that there was a bomb in another of Harlow's public buildings – the theatre being one such. I remember being backstage waiting for my entrance and watching security men opening hampers, turning over spare lighting, restlessly searching for a bomb while we awaited the 9pm switch which would plunge the backstage into darkness. Did the half-full house, ignorant of the danger, really need *Twelfth Night* in these circumstances? Must the show always go on? We survived, no second bomb was ever discovered, and probably never existed. The following night I drove into Harlow in total darkness, parked as best I could near the theatre, lights came back on at 9pm, and I left the theatre at 10.45 to find I had a ticket for parking on a double-yellow line. I have not been back to Harlow since.

After the pantomime we were back on tour in January rehearsing the final show, Terence Rattigan's *French Without Tears*, during the day. Since electricity was so scarce theatres were unwilling to provide us with any heating and offered only minimal lighting. Richard Cottrell, directing from the front row of the stalls, admitted at one point that

French Without Tears, Cambridge Theatre Company, 1974.
L to R: Pip Donaghy, Joanna Wake, OFD, Roger Rees.

the lighting was so dim he couldn't even see our faces. The irony of trying to rehearse a comedy set on the warm sunlit French Riviera in these conditions was not lost on us. Despite this the play went well in the final two weeks of the season. I used to watch most nights from the wings the exquisitely acted love scene between Zoe Wanamaker and Roger Rees. A play which I had unthinkingly dismissed as a trivial crowd-pleaser turned out to be very astute about the male psyche.

While the pantomime was playing in January the company, actors, stage management, wardrobe and management met several times to discuss the problems the long season had thrown up. The result was a document, drawn up by me, to be submitted to the Arts Council entitled 'The Strains of Touring in a Subsidised Company'. Certain points stand out and illuminate not only the 1970s but the perennial rigours of theatre tours. The twelve main actors were on £30 per week plus £10 touring allowance (in 2022 terms these could be multiplied perhaps thirteen times). Since it was calculated that a reasonable bed and breakfast in 1973/4 was £1.75 per night (though I found a dire room in Hull for 80p) and a notional restaurant evening meal £1.25, it can be seen that the £10 allowance was wholly inadequate and had to be supplemented out of wages. With this supplement of at least £14, £3 (10%) to the agent and an average £7 to keep on a home base, this left the actor with about £6 before tax to cover all other expenses at home and on tour. Stage management on £27 and £22 were left with little or nothing, in effect subsidising the tour. In addition the price of petrol doubled between October 1973 and March 1974.

As I noted 'a life of cheap digs, take-away Chinese meals, cadged lifts and general suitcase existence is not designed to improve an actor's health, confidence or work'. The artistic satisfaction of playing such a varied repertoire might be high but the work-load was overwhelming. We played and rehearsed six days a week for six months without any breaks, mostly doing a fifty-seven-hour week (not including meal breaks). 'These financial, physical and emotional problems would hardly be worth detailing did they not have a direct bearing on the one crucial issue – the company's ability to give a good performance each night.' The need to maintain standards was paramount because we were only too aware of the 'overwhelming response from audiences, school parties, supporters clubs etc. Far from contracting, the touring market is actually expanding. Each year new theatres are opening in towns and universities which cannot support a resident three or four weekly rep... the need for touring productions of classic and modern plays has never been greater.' We submitted our report and on February 14th 1974 Sir Hugh Willatt, Secretary-General of the Arts Council, wrote back to me that 'many of us here will find the survey very interesting and useful'. It was presumably left to moulder in some basement. It has, however, left me with an abiding interest in salary levels and the financial complexities of play production. The British, unlike the Americans, are so anxious to hide who is being paid what. I have always had a desire to blow it open.

The need for touring productions continues to this day. Fewer and fewer regional theatres can afford to be producing houses for more than half the year, and some former reps like Cheltenham and Canterbury are wholly receiving houses (apart from the panto) and are therefore increasingly reliant on tours. Straight plays have a particularly hard time since many newly built theatres – Milton Keynes, Woking, Aylesbury, the Salford Lowry, for example – seat well over as thousand and cater largely for touring musicals. Civic pride which ordered these monsters has not proved the friend of serious drama. Pay and conditions have undoubtedly improved, though the lure of television based in London has meant fewer actors are prepared to tour, particularly if they have a family. Our experiment of an ensemble company offering theatres a choice of four productions has gone, I suspect never to be repeated.

Richard Cottrell cut his next season down from six productions to three, and the tour was much shorter. Richard had let it be known that he intended to do *Hamlet*, and at one time Roger Rees and myself seemed to be in the frame, until Richard announced that he had seen a remarkable young actor, aged twenty-four, at the Young Vic – Ian Charleson. Roger and I agreed that our chance of playing Hamlet had probably disappeared for good, but such is the wheel of fortune Roger, after his success in *Nicholas Nickleby*, played the part at Stratford ten years later. I still await the call. I played Horatio (good friend again) to Ian Charleson's Hamlet, but the production never really took off. Ian had good moments and his potential was obvious but he himself admitted he wasn't happy with his performance. *The School for Scandal* fared a little better, but I never felt I found a way to play Sir Peter Teazle. It looks straightforward but isn't. When I saw Ralph Richardson on a pre-London tour in 1962 he simply recited two of the speeches, as if to say 'I haven't yet decided how to play this part so I'm just saying the words'; and John Neville at the National in 1990 gave an odd, almost caricatured rendering of old age. The part has clearly troubled the illustrious, but perhaps I was just sick, at the age of thirty-five, of playing old men. What did I really know of a sixty-year-old being married to a twenty-year-old? Pirandello's *Six Characters in Search of an Author* completed the season, and Richard made the curious decision to have the 'characters' stick to the dated translation by Frederick May, while the 'actors' were encouraged to improvise, which Heather Canning and I did with gusto. The effect was to make the actors more real than the characters, thereby reversing Pirandello's intention.

Ian and I became friends, and since at the end of the tour he had nowhere to live he became Jenny and my lodger in Paddington for a year, and I came to recognise his dispositions, part gregarious, part solitary. Six years later he became a star with the film *Chariots of Fire* and in 1989 he played Hamlet at the National Theatre, and once again I was in the cast as Player King (more later). I have many happy memories of those two tours, played violently contrasting parts while learning all the time, made many lasting friendships, and relished the sense of family, but they remain by far the most gruelling seasons I have ever undertaken. The Cambridge Company continued for another twenty-five years, finally folding in 1999. Mike Alfreds had renamed it 'Method and Madness', and the last production of his I saw was an adaptation of Hardy's *Jude the Obscure* in 1996 with a cast of four. The economics of touring had bitten deep.

Production Four

HENRY V AND CORIOLANUS
(RSC 1975–79)

O ne fortunate outcome of this second tour was that two of the plays were seen by Buzz Goodbody, the new artistic director of Stratford's The Other Place, and she offered me Horatio to Ben Kingsley's Hamlet and Sir Amorous Lafoole in Ben Jonson's *Epicene (The Silent Woman)*. I was at last to be a member of the RSC, a company I might have joined twelve years before, but Terry Hands in the main house had only small parts to offer me in *Henry IV parts 1* and *2*. The year before I was playing Sir Peter Teazle at the King's Theatre Edinburgh; now I was back to Third Traveller. It felt like my first year at university, starting at the bottom again. I accepted because I wanted to work with Buzz, but I couldn't help thinking where I might have been if I had joined the RSC in 1963. Had I made a bad decision? What use was a DPhil to me now? I had so much ground to make up. Useless speculation, I knew.

In the pre-RSC fifties Stratford had usually appointed a company for March to October headed by a well-known star – Olivier, Redgrave, Gielgud. Peter Hall in the sixties wanted an ensemble company with three-year contracts: Patrick Stewart told me when he was given another three years it was one of the happiest days of his early life. In the seventies under Trevor Nunn companies were given two-year contracts, a year at Stratford, a year at the Aldwych (later the Barbican), with a get-out for actors after sixty weeks. By the 2000s with the partial withdrawal from the Barbican this set pattern collapsed. Sometimes a company would be assembled for three or more productions; sometimes plays were cast singly. Much the same pattern had evolved at the National. Olivier's ensemble company had given way to various experiments with director-led ensembles, but increasingly separate casts were appointed to fulfil the demands of three contrasted spaces. Actors had lost the security of lengthy employment and growing together as a company, but had gained availability for better-paid work in the ever-expanding world of television. It was the same throughout society: by the '70s job security had lost its appeal; freedom to explore every avenue was the cool imperative. But at Stratford it was, I think, a loss, as actors no longer matured over a period of years to the particular demands of playing Shakespeare – Ian Holm first worked at Stratford in 1954 and continued there, and later for the RSC, for some twelve years.

A few weeks before the 1975 season opened I was told the offer had changed – the RSC has always been a law unto itself. I was to come out of *Hamlet* and play Montjoy, the French herald, in Terry Hands' opening production of *Henry V* on the Stratford main stage. I didn't feel happy about this, but Buzz had agreed, or had had her arm twisted, and I wasn't especially keen to play Horatio again so soon, even with Ben Kingsley. At least I thought I would get to work with Buzz later in the season. Then Terry informed me that I was to play not just Montjoy but 'anybody French with a message', the French Ambassador, the Governor of Harfleur, etc. I asked if I was several different characters or basically the same person. "Well, you are and you aren't," said Terry. I waited to see how this not very helpful note would turn out. It was a difficult time for me as my father had died the year before – in his sleep during a holiday in Scotland. He had been so supportive of my limited acting successes and, amid a welter of other feelings, I felt a regret that he never knew of my arrival at Stratford, almost twenty years since he had first taken me there.

Henry V, RSC, 1975.
L to R: OFD (Montjoy), Alan Howard (Henry V).

I felt a sense of relief after Birmingham and Cambridge that I was joining a secure, well-subsidised company. Not so. The RSC was likely to lose its London base, the Aldwych, through inflated costs and insufficient subsidy and the Stratford theatre itself had to appeal for funds to preserve its very fabric: it was facing a projected shortfall of £200,000. The 1974 Stratford season, which had involved two different companies, had been beset by problems. 1975, designated yet another Centenary Year, was therefore to be an economy season. For the first time there were to be only four productions in the main house (five and occasionally six being the usual number): the Falstaff plays, *Henry IV parts 1* and *2*, *Henry V* and a revival of *The Merry Wives of Windsor*, all directed by Terry Hands with Brewster Mason as the fat knight. Ignoring chronological order *Henry V* was to be the flagship opening production. If it was deemed a failure, or even mediocre, the outlook was bleak.

We started rehearsals in the dusty, creaky attic rooms in Floral Street, Covent Garden, later after vast refurbishment 'The Sanctuary', home of luxury spa and beauty treatments. The plan was to rehearse *Henry V* in the morning and *Henry IV part 1* in the afternoon, so that the second play could open as soon as possible. The Chorus starts by stating that this 'unworthy scaffold' cannot possibly evoke the 'very casques / That did affright the air at Agincourt', and the audience therefore will have to use their thoughts to 'deck our kings' and 'make imaginary puissance'. Terry Hands' radical solution was to start from scratch with the cast in rehearsal clothes and in a rehearsal situation – the audience would have to use their imagination from the very start. One company director wrote that he was 'horrified to learn from a friend that the performance is to be given with the actors dressed in boiler suits or similar garb'. The cast one day watched Trevor Nunn and Terry walking round and round the lawn at the back of the theatre while Trevor, as we later learnt, tried to persuade Terry to drop the idea. It might be an economy season, but jeans and trainers weren't going to bring in the crowds. Today, forty-seven years later, period costume is anathema to young directors; identical boiler suits might well be cutting-edge.

I proved the beneficiary of the audience's alarm because I was the first character onstage in medieval costume. As the French Ambassador who brings the tennis balls I appeared right at the back of the stage in the historically correct garb of the Bishop of Beauvais. Various audience members later told me of the intakes of breath followed by murmurs of, "Oh my god, tell me that's a costume at last."

When rehearsing this scene I learnt two valuable lessons. Before the tennis balls sent by the Dauphin are revealed the ambassador has a twelve-line speech. I delivered this and Terry told me he needed to be more arrogant. I tried again, and Terry said, "That wasn't more arrogant, that was just louder." A great note: all kinds of strong emotions aren't best served by increasing the volume. I was determined to find a way to be more arrogant, so at my third attempt I slowly walked all the way round Henry while speaking. "Now that was more arrogant," said Terry, eyes gleaming. I felt relieved.

"But he's not actually going to do that," said Alan, in clear alarm.

Terry looked at me, looked at Alan, and said, "No, no, he won't be doing that." And I thought – I see, there's a limit to how arrogant you can be in a supporting part.

Alan Howard's great strength as Henry turned out to be, in addition to his athleticism and his handling of the verse, the inner turmoil he brought to the part. The play starts in indecision and doubt. Every time Henry tries to solve a problem by action the problems and decisions compound. He eventually takes Harfleur after threatening the violation of your 'shrill-shrieking daughters' but then retreats to Calais. The story is stop-start all the way to Agincourt, a battle the English would have been relieved to avoid. Shakespeare could scarcely be more alive to the realities of warfare. Alan thought the ceremony speech, always the most difficult and searching in the play, was 'a sicking-up of everything in him, the impotence of temporal power, its inability to change or help anyone. There seems to be in Henry that constant tug between reason and passion that you will find in all Shakespeare's great tragic heroes.' We were fortunate that Alan had already played Hamlet, Benedick, Angelo and Oberon/Theseus. Henry V, one of the longest parts in Shakespeare, is a much more difficult role than might at first appear.

Working with Alan made me think a lot about what Kenneth Tynan and later Jonathan Kent would call 'high-definition acting'. I once had a conversation with the great director Tyrone Guthrie when he had argued that great acting should be 'convincing, illuminating and compelling'. The bottom line is 'convincing' – does the audience suspend its disbelief and accept that the actor is for the next three hours Willy Loman or Hedda Gabler? I have known many major performances fall at this first hurdle. 'Illuminating' is where the hard work of rehearsal comes in. The actor needs to show how and why the character has reached this crisis and how and why they deal with it in the way they do. What, in short, has the actor got to say about this character? As the pianist Michelangeli provocatively wrote: 'Don't ask whether a musician plays well or accurately, ask them where they stand philosophically in relation to the work.' Often after listening to a Beethoven sonata or watching a leading actor I am left wondering what the performer was telling us, what their imagination was trying to illuminate. 'Compelling' is the hardest to quantify. Is it innate, or can it be acquired? Is it a life force, striking good looks, a suggestion of hidden depths, or just luck? Striving very hard to be noticed is not the answer. It is presumably to do with imagination, truthfulness, focus, self-belief, courage, physicality, but ultimately there's no formula. Compelling is unpredictable. Alan Howard and Alec McCowen had it, and as my career progressed I would be fortunate to work with a number of others.

Montjoy has always been a good part, one of the few wholly sympathetic characters in the play, but Terry seemed determined to make him a mediator between the different ethos of the French and the English. This wasn't imposed upon me; its development was a gradual, continuous process, one of the benefits of a six- to eight-week rehearsal period which gives time to experiment, take stock and if necessary change direction. I began to be called for scenes I didn't speak or even appear in. I was part of the French night scene writing up my journal (an idea of mine which Harold Hobson later picked up on), while the aristocrats boast and bicker. I was also given Grandpre's chilling description of the English cavalry: 'Yon island carrions, desperate of their bones / Ill-favouredly become the morning field'.

Montjoy meets Henry three times, observes him in action and sees the state of his army, which is at its lowest ebb at his first encounter. The second time he bids Henry consider of his ransom because he's clearly going to lose the battle, and we experimented with the idea that Montjoy has come of his own accord to try to stop the slaughter. Terry then had him witness the murder of the boy, which in the text takes place offstage, and he's duly horrified. His third visit is to announce that the battle is over, 'The day is yours', which is often done quite formally. In rehearsal I was doing it half formally, half passionately, and Terry said, "Go on, go on, do it as you feel it," so I let fly with all my revulsion at the needless loss of life, men trapped in their armour and trampled to death in the mud. Once the reading of the dead was over, the English soldiers drifted away, leaving Henry and Montjoy alone onstage. We slowly followed, but then turned to look back at the battlefield, sharing doubt and horror at the scale of the slaughter. It was my first experience of how a supporting part can be given a life and a journey beyond the limitation of words spoken, impossible to achieve in the shorter rehearsal periods of regional rep. The part of Montjoy, of course, was not alone in this process. Terry, who had acquired a reputation for imposing a concept, on this occasion handed over a lot of the creative responsibility to the actors themselves, waiting to see what their instinct and ingenuity would come up with. They responded hungrily and imaginatively. Such an approach can result in a shapeless mess, but in this instance it paid off remarkably.

I understudied the Chorus and together with Henry IV that meant I had 850-odd lines, in addition to my own, milling about in my mind. Every time I walked down a street in Stratford or London I started mumbling an understudy speech – I now almost miss it. Just as in 1954 at school Henry V's arguments in the night scene seemed faulty, now the Chorus appeared to be setting up false hopes. He tells us the French 'shake in their fear' at 'this most dreadful preparation', and then shows us a scene between Bardolph, Pistol and Nym proving they have little stomach for the fight that would have the French shaking in derision. He tells us Henry the night before Agincourt 'visits all his host, bids them good morrow with a modest smile, and calls them brothers, friends and countrymen', and then shows us Henry in disguise as a Welshman having an ill-tempered discussion with soldiers on the justifications for war. At the end of the play he undercuts the euphoria of victory with a reminder that 'They lost France and made his England bleed'. What is Shakespeare up to? Is the Chorus giving us tabloid headlines to create a national myth, and then showing us what was really going on? Shakespeare was taking a big risk in debunking the 'glorious victory' of Agincourt, but then by this stage of his career he was a risk-taker, about to write a four thousand-line experimental *Hamlet*.

The play opened and, to general relief, was an immediate success and later won a clutch of awards. Harold Hobson once again went overboard: 'No words of mine can adequately convey the theatrical, visual, and above all the spiritual splendour of Terry Hands production'. Alan was universally praised, though Eric Shorter in the *Daily Telegraph* wrote perceptively, 'Mr Howard sees the king as woefully miscast... you wonder with his doubts and hesitations whether Hamlet hasn't turned up at Agincourt in error'. Many of the reviews wrote of the 'visual splendours' of the set as if it was highly decorated and expensive, when in fact its triumph lay in its simplicity. Farrah, a great visionary designer (and a lovely man), had stripped the stage to its brick back wall and built a one in twelve rake that ran straight down to the auditorium. When the decision to go to war was taken the music swelled, the actors rushed into their costumes, and a great golden heraldic canopy opened above the bare stage. As the battle approached this canopy descended to the floor, its wires raising the canvas in uneven ridges so that it became a muddy, hillocky field, all grey and brown, a form of alien moonscape. The breach, always a design problem, was solved by a rectangular lift centre-stage, which rose to a forty-five-degree angle. The English army had somehow to clamber up this slope and fall down behind it, while Alan, halfway up and clinging with one hand to a rope, urged them on to 'imitate the action of the tiger'. Three breath-taking effects, and all the set that was needed.

Buzz Goodbody's revelatory chamber production of *Hamlet,* almost conversational in style, also previewed, and expectations were high. On the Friday evening I had a talk with Buzz about the play and her production, centring on the lines 'the funeral baked meats did coldly furnish forth the marriage tables'. That weekend, as she had forewarned many, she took her life. I know that as a communist she could not see the possibility of a more egalitarian society emerging, especially for women – the theatre in general, and the RSC in particular, were such male-dominated institutions. As Ben Kingsley wrote: 'She was aware of the gauntlet she ran, wittily, courageously, sometimes belligerently, and that in my eyes makes her heroic'. It was a staggering loss.

Since no director was keen to take on *The Silent Woman*, the eight people cast had to be incorporated as principals in another play, and John Barton undertook John Ford's *Perkin Warbeck* (1633), a strange, troubling play which T. S. Eliot thought one of the best historical plays outside Shakespeare. Terry Hands had asked me what problems I might have when I joined the company. I replied that I had constantly been playing years above my age, and he assured me that needn't be the case at the RSC. John Barton, however, cast me as a mad old earl in *Perkin Warbeck* (I'd have preferred Sir Amorous Lafoole), and thereafter I played many elderly men for John. It was a great relief when I rejoined the company in 2008 that I had finally got to the right age to play Polonius, Justice Shallow and Pandarus for Greg Doran.

In the *Henry IV*s I was still set to play half a dozen small parts, Wart the ragged recruit being my favourite, and understudy Emrys James as Henry IV. As Emrys was absent for the first weeks of rehearsal, on tour as Mephisophilis in *Dr Faustus*, Terry told me I would be playing the king till his return. Thrown in at the deep end, I knew it was a form of audition, but I had the confidence of knowing I had played many large Shakespeare parts and that I'd had the basics of verse-speaking drummed into me – the drive towards the end of the pentameter, the importance of antithesis, the primacy of breath control. RSC sonnet classes, overseen by Terry and/or John Barton and Cis Berry, were a further revelation. At my first attempt Terry said crushingly: "I didn't get the meaning of that at all."

I persevered over many months till John Barton gave me the final accolade: "I don't think I've ever heard that better done." Once you have understood how to balance sense, structure, variation and rhythm in a sonnet (and it takes time), a Shakespeare speech should hold no terror for you: emotion can then have full play.

Terry later told me he felt embarrassed every time I opened my mouth in the small parts he had given me. So many actors joining the RSC from drama school, fringe theatre, or from a few years in television lack that background experience and find it difficult to cope with Shakespeare in a large space, and that has if anything worsened today.

When Emrys returned I witnessed a fascinating clash of approaches to the part. Terry said he saw Henry IV as worried, downcast, beset by guilt at his usurpation and by problems and rebellions on all sides. Emrys immediately replied, "I don't see him like that at all. He's triumphant at gaining the crown, full of energy, ready and determined to be a strong king and to crush all opposition." He knew that a long part driving two plays is best approached on the front foot. I would say that Emrys got his way, as theatre actors usually do – unless they are replaced.

In June as part of the centenary celebrations the Queen and Prince Philip came to see *Henry V* – an extremely rare visit. We lined up after the performance and the Queen spoke to every third person. She stopped opposite me and remarked that it was a very large stage. I thought that a genuinely interested remark, and I replied that the first time I entered right at the back it felt like the deck of an aircraft carrier and I thought I might take off and fly over the stalls. The Queen eyed me for a moment, perhaps thinking either this man is mad, taking the mickey, or trying to lure her into a surreal exchange, and silently passed on. "You total berk!" chortled Geoff Hutchings on my right, but I remain rather proud of my image.

For the first few months of the season Jenny remained based in London, doing radio work and visiting me at the weekends. At midsummer, now several months pregnant, she moved to join me in Stratford. We were both enthusiastic about the recent encouragement of fathers-to-be at the birth, and we had found a wonderful NCT teacher, Sheri, based nearby. When I approached the company with my plan Terry Hands wrote to say that I could have either of the *Henry IV* performances off if they coincided with the birth, but not *Henry V* as my Montjoy was 'one of the four corner-stones of the production', which was certainly news to me. *Henry V* played opposite Buzz's *Hamlet*, and when the *Hamlet* company heard about Terry's objection to a *Henry V* night they threatened to strike on that particular evening, which would free up their Horatio, the understudy for Montjoy. It was as if Buzz's spirit and beliefs were pitted against a monolithic and very male RSC. As it was I was able to be with Jenny during a long labour, through the whole of one Thursday (a *Henry IV part 1* night) and through the following Friday (*part 2*) when Miranda was born at 5.10pm. Although I had been allowed the *part 2* night off the company manager phoned the hospital begging me to perform as Alan Howard was furious my understudy had appeared as the seven-line Sheriff, so, tired but buzzing, I rashly agreed – was my Sheriff and Wart really so important? David Suchet subsequently had birth attendance written into his contract.

The plays transferred to the Aldwych, and then *Henry V* went on tour. By this time the company had bonded, confident in the production's power and success, and close friendships had developed with no thought of the competitive rivalry I had sometimes experienced elsewhere. In New York we played the huge two thousand-seat Brooklyn Academy, an opera house in all but name. Clive Barnes in *The New York Times* wrote that 'we were given the RSC's definitive staging of *Henry V*, which may well be to history what Peter Brook's *Midsummer Night's Dream* was to romance'. Other notices were equally enthusiastic – 'as glittering a piece of stage craft as you'll ever see' – but following my belief that no production is so good that it doesn't receive one stinker (and vice-versa, a poor production will get one rave) Martin Gottfried in *The New York Post* wrote, 'the readings proved lusciously vacant, modulated voices reading meaningless lines. Alan Howard acted all over the place while standing still – shoulder shrugs and faraway looks – but it was difficult to tell just what he was up to'. As the Governor of Harfleur I had to make my speech from the Upper Circle, which felt about a hundred metres from the stage. To get there I had to go up six floors in a lift, and one night I travelled up with musicians playing a jazz concert in the smaller theatre. The most senior of the musicians remarked that he had liked my speech just now. I thanked him, but as we left the lift I asked one musician who'd hung back, "He didn't really mean my speech?"

"Yes, he did, we were standing in the wings. Do you know who that is?" I didn't. "Dizzy Gillespie." I've always wondered if I might put it in my CV: 'Dizzy Gillespie liked my speech'.

I returned to London, to Jenny and baby Miranda, and to a brown Hyde Park – it was the great 1976 drought. All too soon I had to set off again, this time to a British Council tour of Western Europe, Paris, Amsterdam, Hamburg, Berlin, Cologne, Munich and Vienna. In an effort to save money I agreed with my friends Anthony Naylor and Geoff Hutchings that we would search out rooms for three people. It involved much negotiation and several terrible nights. Berlin was still an occupied city, and I remember the difficulty of passing through Friedrichstrasse station, where you surrendered your passport to an East German official and after half an hour began to fear you would never get it back, in order to see a remarkable production by the Berliner Ensemble of Wedekind's *Spring Awakening*. The reception for *Henry V* took us by surprise with fifteen minutes of curtain calls, ever growing more fervent. At a party given for us by the occupying British army a major told me, "This is the best thing that has happened to us in the year I've been here. I've grown sick of the French and the Germans telling us about their music and culture, and now I can say, well, look at our theatre." I was also very interested in the reaction of two middle-aged Germans to a play that was entirely new to them: "You must understand that we Germans have been brought up at school after the war to regard all war as evil. But I see your play and I realise that war is evil but can also create a band of brothers. I feel a hot flush of embarrassment, but deep down I feel this to be true."

Through a contact in the Berlin Philharmonic our eight-member band had wangled an invitation to an orchestral rehearsal. I managed to tag along with them and we cautiously entered the Philharmonie canteen where many of the Berlin players were having coffee. A hush fell at our arrival: I felt this is going to end ignominiously. Our contact explained that we were the band of the Royal Shakespeare Company when to our relief and amazement the Berlin players broke into applause. Germans hold a respect for culture the British can only wonder at. Our tour continued successfully and in Vienna I was excited to play the Theater an der Vien, where *The Magic Flute* was first performed and where Beethoven actually lived for a time and premiered *Fidelio*, the Eroica symphony and the violin concerto. As usual I had to find my way to the Upper Circle and so great was the crush of people standing I had the utmost difficulty forcing my way through to the front – "Schausspieler," I kept saying hopefully.

On tour we were constantly asked, "What next?", as we were clearly regular members of a world-famous theatre company, and to their disbelief we had to reply, "Probably the labour exchange." I was to learn for the first time that eighteen months or more at the RSC leaves you off the radar of most directors and casting directors, and it is very difficult to find work. It did, however, mean that Jenny could make herself available for work again. She had had to turn down work opportunities in the previous months, including an invitation to meet Mike Leigh about a project. But now all went quiet for us both. I was expecting to start on a two-year contract for the next Stratford season in January '77, but in December it was suddenly and without explanation put back to April. It was my first experience of being out of work for nine months and the havoc it caused to family finances. I duly joined 'Problem Agency', and began to clean houses at 90p an hour – a far cry from the schausspieler of the An der Vien. It has become almost obligatory for actors to say they were the worst waiters/cleaners/ASMs imaginable, but I have always proved a very diligent cleaner. My most unexpected assignation was a run-down house in Mayfair, inhabited by Cicely Courtneidge and Jack Hulbert, both in their eighties and recently retired from the theatre (I had seen Jack star in light comedies in the 1950s). Cicely deputed me to clean Jack's bath (after he had vacated it), and I had it in mind to tell Jack that my father had been taught by his father at King's College London in 1913/14, but he stared at me with such suspicion – with a beard and a red fisherman's smock I looked an unlikely cleaner – that my courage failed me. I could have added that my father had told me the students found it scandalously hilarious that the professor's son was marrying a musical comedy starlet, but I reckoned that was a step too far. I was never asked back.

In January Jenny was offered a part in Granville Barker's *The Madras House* at the National, directed by Bill Gaskill. The contract would run for eight months and overlap my first months in Stratford. We were both committed to sharing childcare and work, equally if possible, and Jenny had my total support to stay in London, take the job, one she very much wanted, and employ childcare. In the end she took the decision to turn the job down, but she has always regretted it. For her it was never a 'choice'. We both had a desire to share Miranda's early years, but couldn't turn down my better-paid two years at the RSC.

The 1977 season finally got underway and comprised six productions, a revival of *Henry V*, the three parts of *Henry VI, As You Like It* and *Coriolanus*. I was in five of these, so I rehearsed almost continuously for seven months, but I understood that it was a mark of the company's faith in me. As Emrys no longer wanted to play the Chorus in *Henry V* I asked Terry if I, as his understudy, could take it over. "No, you can't," he replied. "I can get a very good actor into the company to play the Chorus, but I can't get as good an actor as you to play Montjoy." The RSC has always needed strong supporting actors, the 'engine room of the company', as Terry called them, and promoting the engine room to the bridge was not part of the plan. Terry did tell me that, "We are grooming you to be one of our leading character actors." This was pleasing, but it did throw up the whole question of whether all actors are not 'character actors'. Cary Grant may have given the same performance as romantic leading man but it was always Archie Leach in disguise. Acting is always, as Simon Callow argues, 'a rearrangement of you'. You access thoughts, attitudes, emotions and physicality in yourself that equate to the character on the page. Hamlet is as much a character as Lear.

The *Henry VI*s again showed Terry Hands at his best, with Helen Mirren an unusually sympathetic Queen Margaret. As Somerset, Henry VI's chief general, I was thankfully killed by Anton Lesser at the end of *part 2*, though my severed head did appear in *part 3* and, to my horror, sitting in the stalls on the first night, was used as a football by the triumphant Yorkists, but this indignity did mean I got the occasional night off. At a re-rehearsal in London Helen remarked that she couldn't imagine how she and Alan had ever, in character, fathered a child, and I said, quite without intent, that the contemporary rumour was that it was Somerset's child. "Oh!" said Helen, and onstage began to hug me at every opportunity, which greatly enhanced my part. This continued for some weeks till Helen suddenly stopped. "I got bored with the idea," she said, and my part returned to normal. In *As You Like It*, directed by Trevor Nunn, I was once again Duke Senior, father of Kate Nelligan as Rosalind. Trevor conceived it as an Inigo Jones masque, choreographed by Gillian Lynne, and initially had some of the text sung to Stephen Oliver's music, agony for me and also for Kate and others, and thankfully largely dropped after a few weeks.

Terry Hands' *Coriolanus* reunited many of the *Henry V* company – Charles Dance, Richard Derrington, Philip Dunbar, Julian Glover, Alan Howard, Stephen Jenn, Anthony Naylor, Barrie Rutter, Tim Wylton and Arthur Whybrow. We felt a family once again. Maxine Audley, Tamora Queen of the Goths in the Brook/Olivier *Titus Andronicus*, joined us as Volumnia. Alan was in his element as Coriolanus. On occasions, as his critics said, he could relapse into a kind of rasping rant, but on good nights, which were the majority, he delivered verse impeccably with a speed, clarity and attack that few could match – Gielgud and Olivier of an older generation, Ian Richardson as a contemporary. Today such an approach is out of fashion, actors breaking up the verse in their concentration on sense, not trusting that the sense is contained in the rhythm of the verse. Once again Hobson thought it 'an evening of true theatrical glory', and *The Guardian* wrote, 'I can remember very few Shakespearean productions which have communicated a greater sense of excitement or dramatic energy'. In these late '70s Terry and Trevor had begun to run alternate seasons, Terry's becoming known as the 'butch company', Trevor's as the 'aesthetes'. How I had qualified as 'butch' remained a puzzle to me.

During the Stratford season we rented a flat in The Hill, a large house just outside the town, leased to the RSC. Jenny discovered that a large vacant room on the ground floor had previously been used for an RSC playgroup, set up in the early '60s by Margaret Drabble and others. Jenny sought out Diana Cockerton, the former playgroup leader, who was delighted to be asked to run it again. Company parents would set up and largely fund the playgroup, and Jenny went to the management to ask for some extra funding to help pay Diana. A derisory £5 per week was proffered, a reflection of how little importance was given at that time by organisations to working parents' needs (has it changed?). The playgroup proved a very happy and successful part of the season, provided some childcare, and was also an important social resource. Twenty years later Jenny acted with the company for the '97–98 season and discovered that the RSC playgroup was now a fixture with its own building, and served not only company members but also children from the town. She is very proud to have been part of bringing it back to life.

The productions moved to the Aldwych for the '78 season and by the end of the year, with only occasional performances of *Coriolanus* and *As You Like It*, it became possible for Jenny to accept work and for me to take on the main childcare. That winter Jenny went on tour with Monstrous Regiment and then went to Leeds to play a lead in Richard Woolley's film *Brothers and Sisters*. We employed Di, a teacher who lived nearby, for times when I was performing. I later wrote a radio play *Small Earthquake*, which went out in February '79, based on my experiences of being a rare male at the nursery gates and the One O'Clock Club.

In April '79 we toured *Coriolanus* to Western Europe again, but this time the play was quite well known to German audiences, which I found particularly interesting. The American authorities had banned the play in Germany after 1945 on the grounds that Martius had been represented as a Hitler figure leading the people to a healthier society. De Gaulle, on the other hand, had banned the play in French schools as being too left-wing, and indeed Brecht had rewritten the play to make the people the heroes of the hour (a production I saw with the great Ekkehard Schall as Coriolan). Germans were so used to the play being slanted left or right that Terry Hands' even-handed treatment, whereby each party, Martius and his family, aristocrats, tribunes and citizens, were allowed to present their case as persuasively as possible, was a not always welcome revelation to them. I played Junius Brutus, one of the tribunes of the people, and Terry encouraged both John Burgess and myself to present them not as duplicitous manipulators but as shop stewards certain of their rightful cause. One critic wrote that I came over as an earnest polytechnic lecturer, probably sacked, and I thought 'spot on'. Alan was again much lauded, and was frequently referred to in the German press as 'the greatest European classical actor'. These two tours were of enormous benefit both to the reputation of British theatre and, I think, to Anglo-German understanding. Margaret Thatcher's government and her successors showed no interest in such an enterprise, and by cutting the money to the British Council ensured that large-scale RSC productions would rarely tour Europe again. It is extraordinarily short-sighted, on a par with paring away the money for the BBC World Service.

On my return John Barton kindly incorporated me into the Aldwych company to take over Boyet from Alan Rickman in his beautiful, autumnal *Love's Labour's Lost*, and we then began an eighteen-week rehearsal for *The Greeks*. John Barton had adapted nine Greek plays, mostly by Euripides, into roughly forty-five-minute lengths so that they could play on three evenings, and on Saturdays the complete trilogy. They told the story surrounding the Trojan war, its inception and aftermath, from *Iphigenia in Aulis* through *The Oresteia* to *Iphigenia in Taurus*. As there is no surviving play covering the war itself and the story of the *Iliad*, John himself wrote a tenth play he called *Achilles* – John is never daunted. I played a Barton invention, a generic 'Old Man' observer in four plays (I was by now forty), and anyone beginning with P – Priam, Polymestor and Peleus. The chorus were all women, and in the leads Janet Suzman, Billie Whitelaw, Tony Church and John Shrapnel gave particularly strong performances. The plays were an enormous success, especially trilogy Saturdays, and could have played for much longer than their designated eleven weeks. It is dangerously nostalgic to inflate past successes, but I nevertheless think

1975–80 was a golden period for the RSC with *Henry V, Coriolanus, The Greeks,* Buzz's *Hamlet,* the Dench-McKellen *Macbeth,* the Dench-Sinden *Much Ado* set in the Raj, Peter Nichols' *Privates on Parade,* the glorious *Nicholas Nickleby,* and so much good work at The Other Place and the Warehouse. I was very lucky to be part of it. The '70s had been a grim decade on the whole from the three-day week and the Northern Irish Troubles through galloping inflation to the '78–79 Winter of Discontent and the advent of Margaret Thatcher, but working flat out with the RSC had largely cushioned me against it. I only realised later that a 'golden age' of growth, near full employment and greater equality since 1945 was coming to an end by the mid-'70s, and that financial wealth and inequality would skyrocket and the 1% retake the heights of the global economy.

1980–90: more Rep, more RSC, TV and National Theatre breakthrough

I left the RSC after three solid years and gleefully shaved off my beard (essential to playing old men), to the horror of Miranda, now five, who was appalled at this hairless stranger and refused to eat opposite me. I had learnt a good deal at the RSC, watching a wide range of actors and deciding what worked and, sometimes more importantly, what didn't work. Standing (rarely sitting) on a bare stage in a large theatre speaking as naturalistically as possible a somewhat archaic text with a constant balancing of sense and rhythm is a stern discipline. Very little in film and television would ever prove as challenging. So much film acting proved to be what I term 'behaving', carrying out everyday actions – walking, driving, arguing, eating a meal, making love – close to your own personality. Some movie actors mark most scenes NAR (No Acting Required), saving themselves for the few difficult scenes that will determine their performance. There is little opportunity to just 'behave' in Shakespeare; Acting is definitely Required.

Thanks to the regular RSC income and money saved on tour we had managed to raise a deposit and buy a garden flat in East Twickenham for £13k, a foot on the property ladder at last. But there was no work in London so I went to the Theatre Royal York to play James Tyrone (again much too young) in O'Neill's *Long Day's Journey into Night*, one of my favourite plays, although a nightmare to learn with only three weeks' rehearsal. My friend Brenda Peters, playing Mary, bemoaned that she had so many speeches complaining about 'that old quack Doc Hardy', sometimes she wasn't sure which act she was in. The highlight of Tyrone's career, based so closely on O'Neill's own father, had been when the great American Shakespearean actor Edwin Booth had said, "That young man is playing Othello better than I ever did." Through research with the theatre archivist I found that Booth had played York Theatre Royal in the 1870s, so that every night I stood centre-stage talking about Booth exactly where he himself had stood, perhaps playing Othello.

I followed that with Nigel Gearing's play *Snap* for the touring company Foco Novo, directed by Roland Rees, as Edweard Muybridge, the nineteenth-century photographer (a terrific subject for a film, he shot his wife's lover and was acquitted in California on the grounds of *crime passionelle*). As he took thousands of photographs of naked men and women performing simple actions, still used in art schools today as illustrations of the way the human body moves, I had to strip off with the other three members of the cast (Muybridge took photos of himself performing rifle drill that left nothing to the imagination). One freezing February night in Glasgow I heard a woman in the audience murmur, "They've even made that poor old man take his clothes off." It has proved my first and, to general relief, my last nude appearance. The perils of touring were enhanced when, returning south from Glasgow in the snow, I was driving the van containing props and the other three cast members when I had a burst tyre in the fast lane. The van slewed across the other two lanes, miraculously unoccupied, to the hard shoulder, where I sat rigid in a cold sweat.

Snap, Foco Novo, 1981.
OFD (Muybridge).

In 1982 I played God (my one shot at the part, so far) in Britten's *Noye's Fludde* in Malvern Priory. It was a perfect May day, alive with late blossom, when news came of the sinking of the Belgrano – to the choirboys' elation and my despair, as I imagined the rusty old ship outside the exclusion zone going down packed with young conscripts into the freezing sea. Then it was back to the RSC to play Nestor, an extremely old man, in Terry Hands' production of *Troilus and Cressida*. It is such a difficult, complex play and, among other challenges, requires at least twelve very good actors very well cast, and rarely gets it – as in our production. It was to be the last of my collaborations with Terry. After his initial 'embarrassment', he promoted and trusted me. I learnt many things from him in terms of focus and daring. I owe him a lot and miss him greatly. I stayed with the company on and off for the next six years, though there were often breaks of several months between parsimoniously paid seasons when it was very difficult to find other work. At this period there was no subsistence money at Stratford, accommodation came out of salary, and rehearsal money was less than the playing wage. It took myself and others years of painstaking negotiation, helped by Equity, to put this right. In one such enforced break Miranda reminded us we had promised tomato sandwiches for some school event. We were absolutely broke, waiting for the next dole cheque, so we had to resort to the time-honoured device of raiding her piggy bank and extracting enough pennies to buy half a pound of tomatoes. Signing on at the Labour Exchange had kept actors afloat for decades. All this has now been swept away by the complexities of job seeker's allowance and universal credit and the bureaucratic difficulties of proving that you are looking for work. Actors, young and old, have lost their safety net.

The highlight of the 1983 season was an Adrian Noble production of *Measure for Measure*, with Daniel Massey as a mercurial Duke and Juliet Stevenson as a passionate and, I think, a definitive Isabella. She played the part entirely from a would-be nun's point of view – 'more than our brother is our chastity' – with no thought to make her sympathetic, and she certainly wasn't keen on marrying the Duke. I played the Provost and understudied the Duke, one of the longest parts in Shakespeare, nine-hundred odd lines, and at the very last matinee performance at the Barbican had to go on at three hours' notice, having not rehearsed or run through the part for six months. I had understudied many huge parts for the RSC, and it was the only time I was called on. I dried twice, had to dig myself out of a hole three times, but I got through in some style: it remains the most terrifying three hours of my professional life. To my relief Dan phoned that he could manage the evening performance. I went and lay in the most welcome bath of my life.

In Howard Davies and David Edgar's experimental production of *Henry VIII (All Is True)* I played Bishop Gardiner, side-kick to John Thaw's Cardinal Wolsey (a relationship we were later to repeat in various forms). I had in fact worked with John the previous year in a television series called *Mitch*, when I reminded him how good he'd been in a Marguerite Duras play I'd reviewed at the Traverse in 1965, and urged him to give the stage another go. As we entered each night at Stratford he regularly muttered to me, "This is all your fucking fault." John had had enough of what he called 'institutional Shakespeare' and opted out of coming to the Barbican. I put in to take over Wolsey, but the management decided to bring someone in: I was too good as Gardiner – i.e. 'keep to the engine room'. I was very happy in a Richard Nelson play *Principia Scriptoriae;* in Giordano Bruno's hilarious *Il Candelaio*; in John Barton's production of Granville-Barker's great political play *Waste*, with Dan Massey and Judi Dench, which transferred to Shaftesbury Avenue in 1985; and I particularly enjoyed playing the schoolmaster Hugh Evans in a revival of Bill Alexander's wonderful 1950s production of *The Merry Wives of Windsor*. This was a part I was directed into by Bill's assistant, Roger Michell. Always strike up a good relationship with assistant directors; Roger later put me into two films. His early death has shocked and upset me greatly.

I continued to be useful to the company in strong supporting parts, usually playing anything that needed governing – countries, cities, prisons – not parts bursting with three dimensions or comic possibilities. John Barton told me in his production of John Whiting's *The Devils* that I, town governor, was supreme in my ability to smoke a clay pipe, drink wine, eat grapes and cheese, and talk all at the same time, but it was hardly the height of my ambition. The 1980s had been a difficult time financially, but also politically. Margaret Thatcher's government had rolled back the state and let rip the market, unemployment spiralled, and my efforts at opposition seemed puny. In 1984 we made a company collection for the striking miners' children, and Tilda Swinton and I went out and bought, half price thanks to a sympathetic shopowner, five dustbin liners full of toys, but it seemed a drop in the ocean. I felt trapped at the RSC, so I left in early 1987. It might be family, but I remained a middling offspring. When I started as a professional in 1967 I said I'd give it ten years and perhaps go back into teaching, but in 1977 I was playing good supporting parts at the RSC. I decided to give it another ten years but during that time I seemed to have made little progress. At forty-eight, however, it was probably too late to get back into lecturing; even my mother had stopped saying, "You've given it a good go, why not…" I felt a sense of crisis. Was I ever going to escape being merely 'useful' to managements?

The only thing that would rescue me from smoking a clay pipe was some sort of unforeseen, lucky break. By an odd coincidence Patrick Stewart, a year younger than me, whose career had been more successful but not totally dissimilar to mine, had such a break the same year. The producer of a proposed revival of *Star Trek* saw Patrick at a literary recital at UCLA in California and cast him as Captain Picard in a series that unexpectedly ran for a further seven years. My lucky break was far less spectacular, but over the next three years my fortunes did markedly improve. After twenty years of two-scene television parts as doctors and priests, often telling the hero/heroine they had a terminal disease, or in *Tenko* telling a nun she had to stop talking and re-enter a silent convent, three very good parts were offered me: Chris Mullin's brilliant *A Very British Coup*, adapted by Alan Plater, as Horace Tweed, private secretary to prime minister Ray McAnally (superb), whom I unwittingly betray; a six-part PD James Inspector Dalgleish detective mystery *A Taste for Death* as an unsuccessful vicar shot in the last episode; and a version of Terence Rattigan's *Cause Célèbre* with Helen Mirren, Harry Andrews, David Suchet and David Morrissey, whose character I unsuccessfully represented in court. I was almost fifty, nearing Peter Dews' prediction of 'alright, even better'; perhaps I had come into my own playing unsuccessful civil servants, priests and barristers? At this point David Hare interviewed me for his film *Paris by Night* on the grounds that, "I was very struck by your playing of lack of success in *Cause Célèbre*." He didn't cast me, but fortunately he was about to write a very unsuccessful vicar.

I slept through the 1987 'hurricane', and the next morning noticed the garden looked a little dishevelled but set off without a care to drive to Cheltenham to do a recital of *Venus and Adonis*. After a mile I found my way blocked near Kew Gardens by fallen trees, and realised I had missed something. I eventually linked up with Imelda Staunton and Douglas Hodge, and we arrived in Cheltenham nearly an hour late to find most of the audience had stayed to applaud our efforts to get there. Poetry recitals were very much part of my life. I devised a solo recital of Wordsworth and Hardy, two of my favourite poets, which I also did at the Cheltenham Festival – in 1995 I knew *Tintern Abbey* by heart. I was already a member of the Hardy Society and this led to three recitals at the Dorchester Conference, linking Hardy with Wordsworth; with Larkin (a great admirer of Hardy); and in 2008, partnered by Harriet Walter and Cheryl Campbell, with Edward Thomas and Robert Frost. I find the 'Emma poems' of *1912–13* one of the finest sequences in the language, *At Castle Boterel* my favourite (I have difficulty getting through it without tears). My most bizarre recital was at Glastonbury in 1984. At the RSC I had co-devised a fifty-minute recital *God Keep Lead out of Me: Shakespeare on War and Peace*, which the four of us played to numerous CND groups. Arabella Churchill booked us to play at 6pm in the Glastonbury theatre tent. At 5.30 I noted scores of people leaving the tent to hear Elvis Costello nearby – I rather envied their choice. When we got on stage there were about sixty people prone on the coconut matting, so tired, drunk or stoned (possibly all three) that they were incapable of motion, apart from occasionally rearing up with wild yelps of support for Henry VI. 'Here on this molehill will I sit me down...' "YEAH, MAN!"

The National Theatre had something for me at last. In the summer of 1988 Howard Davies, who had directed me at the RSC, had mounted a much-admired production of Dion Boucicault's *The Shaughraun* (1874) with its wild Fenian hero Conn played by Stephen Rea. The actor who had played Father Dolan was reluctant to return for a revival, so Howard, casting around for someone who could play a priest in two weeks, naturally thought of a vicar expert. I had to master a tricky Sligo accent, which entailed a last-minute session with the dialect coach Joan Washington in a maternity hospital where she was waiting to give birth. The production had a wonderfully detailed and romantic set by Bill Dudley in which the drum revolve caused towers and hillsides to rise and fall as if by magic. Unfortunately every now and then it ground to a halt, causing delays and at least on one occasion cancellation. As Howard ruefully remarked, "I was a guinea pig; no one told me the drum revolve hadn't been used for fourteen years." Despite mishaps, the revival was hugely enjoyable for both cast and audience, and during it Richard Eyre, the National's new artistic director, asked me to play the Player King and to fill out the court in his new production of *Hamlet* with Daniel Day-Lewis.

For this we had the luxury of an eight-week rehearsal period, starting most days with an hour-long dance session under Jane Gibson's direction, learning the extremely difficult and exhausting galliard, which was regularly practised by Queen Elizabeth (not the present one – as far as I know) for half an hour before breakfast. Richard had done a much-lauded chamber production of *Hamlet* at the Royal Court with Jonathan Pryce. At the National he decided to go for the monumental with a vast walled set centring on a huge statue of the old King Hamlet. Dan, who hadn't been on a stage for five years, never felt at home in the set or the huge Olivier Theatre, and never felt he could communicate the soliloquies to an audience he could barely see. Although he felt trapped in the part he had a great desire to improvise, to follow the emotion of the moment. In his exuberance after the success of the Mousetrap play in unnerving Claudius he began to perform a mad galliard, one of the few occasions in the production when our hours of dance practice were actually used. His galliard became more and more frenzied until one night he collapsed to the floor and showed no sign of moving. I was on stage with him, and as he seemed to be asking for help I crossed and, with great difficulty (he's a big man), hauled him to his feet. He offered me no assistance, as a stage actor would normally do for a fellow actor: he evidently wanted it to be for real, as a film actor might, and we repeated this every night. It was never discussed.

Dan was determined to leave as soon as he contractually could, as was Judi Dench, who confessed she never felt she was Dan's mother and, like so many actresses, could not come to terms with the omissions in the part of Gertrude. Fate intervened, literally and figuratively, when in August Dan had a sense of his own dead father, the poet Cecil Day-Lewis, on the battlements, and he left the stage during the fifth scene never to return, and indeed never to appear on stage in a play again. Jeremy Northam, his understudy, took over heroically that night, and played the part very well for some weeks till Ian Charleson, Dan's designated replacement, was ready to perform. Stephen Ashby, the dresser I shared with Dan, later told me that on the night of the crisis in his crowded dressing room he had had to beg: "Dan... Dan... If you really are not going on again... I... I need your boots for the understudy." That's what theatre is about, I thought.

Ian, who had had great recent success at the National in *Guys and Dolls*, *Cat on a Hot Tin Roof* and *Fool for Love*, was already HIV positive and, though intensely committed, longing to have another go at the part, was struggling with his energy levels. I felt very close to him, especially because of our previous relationship in *Hamlet* fifteen years earlier. Ian had developed large pouches under his eyes, and the official line was that this was a virus which would recede. After a couple of weeks rehearsal Ian called a private meeting with the cast and told us that this was ridiculous, and of course he had AIDS but that we all had to stick to the official line to avoid press intrusions. I admired him very much for this; it was typical of his disdain for bullshit. As his performance developed Ian brought a wonderful lightness and immediacy to the part. He had always delighted in the quicksilver throwaway, and to my astonishment regularly got a laugh on 'By and by is easily said', as Polonius left after the play scene, by the derisive flippancy of his throwaway. Because the duel in the final scene took so much out of him he delivered the notoriously difficult line 'I die Horatio' as if the breath were leaving his body, which in his final performances in November it very nearly was. I had tears in my eyes every night. As Richard Eyre later wrote, 'His performance was possessed. He stood at the curtain call like a bruised boxer after sixteen rounds battered by applause'. He died four weeks later on

January 6th 1990 and asked that any announcement should make it clear that he had died of AIDS in order to publicise the condition. In 1991 the annual Ian Charleson Awards were established for the fifteen best classical stage performances in Britain for actors aged under thirty, an informal lunch which I attend every year.

Production Five

RACING DEMON (1990–94)

In April Richard Eyre had asked me if I would take part in a reading of a play David Hare had in preparation for 1990, *Racing Demon*. I liked the script very much and to my surprise the part of Lionel Espy offered me was, if not exactly the lead, the central spine of the play. I knew at once that it was my part but that they were very unlikely to risk casting me. The day before the reading I woke with the most terrible headache I had ever experienced. I couldn't stand, and I had to crawl across the floor to open the door. There was no question of my pulling out; I had somehow to be well enough to make the reading of a part I knew I could play. By the following afternoon I could at least walk, and the reading went well. David Hare seemed pleased, probably relieved that so much of it worked and that he had some nine months to produce a final version. I could see that the part would suit a number of leading actors, Nigel Hawthorne, Paul Eddington or Alec McCowen, for example, and that one of them would probably be offered it (and I later learnt that had indeed been the plan). Two weeks later Richard Eyre phoned me and asked if I would like to play the part, probably the most important phone call of my professional life. In my experience such an offer is extremely rare. The major companies of course have to risk casting a Juliet or a Romeo with a relatively untried young actor, but to promote a middle-aged actor with no track record

Racing Demon, NT, 1990.
OFD (Lionel Espy).

of playing leads in the national companies seldom happens: the RSC had had fourteen years to give me such a break. I felt relieved that the offer had come after over twenty years in the theatre; I had certainly put in my '10,000 hours'. Surely I had the experience not to mess it up?

David Hare had set out to write a play about the church, the first of a trilogy that would also embrace the law and politics. It might seem strange to start with the church, in many eyes the least important of the three subjects and certainly the one that drama had given the least attention to. It was a considerable risk: if the play appeared of little interest to the majority, the trilogy might be in danger. But as David wrote in his book *Asking Around* (1993), 'I never lost my conviction that on £8000 p.a. loving God and trying to clear up society's worst problems, here were some heroes for our age'. David and I shared an Anglican background through our respective schools, Lancing and King's Canterbury. David was, I think, a religious sceptic from the start, but I did not finally leave the church until my first year at university. As I embarked on learning *Racing Demon* I was very disturbed by a major church scandal, which David also refers to in *Asking Around*. The Oxford supervisor of my doctoral thesis had been the chaplain of New College, Gareth Bennett, a noted historian of the early eighteenth century. I found him kind, helpful and very tolerant of my abandoning academia for the stage. In 1989 he was invited to write the preface to Crockford's, the church directory, a point of view that was traditionally anonymous. In it he voiced his scarcely concealed criticism of the liberal Anglican consensus, betraying its Catholic inheritance, and by implication of Archbishop Runcie, his sometime tutor. He wrote nothing that hadn't been aired in the Synod, and that he hadn't said directly to the Archbishop. By malign fate the popular press, who until then probably hadn't heard of Crockford's, latched on to this criticism and made it into a scandalous whodunnit – 'Which cleric had written this attack on the Archbishop?' The *Daily Mail* whittled it down to three possible people and, though Runcie had assured Gary that he had taken no offence, Gary presumably decided that the public notoriety of his unmasking would be unbearable, and in December he took his own life. To the participants in clerical wrangles the stakes can appear very high. I heard the news of Gary's death at of all places the departure lounge of Heathrow airport, waiting for a plane to take the *Hamlet* cast to Hong Kong. I was deeply upset by the whole saga, and have remained so.

We started rehearsing *Racing Demon* on December 11th, two days before Ian's final performance. It was one of the most enjoyable read-throughs I can ever remember. Several of the cast had worked together before: Michael Bryant, David Bamber, Stella Gonet and myself were in *Hamlet*, and I had worked with Richard Pasco in *Timon of Athens* at the RSC. After the turbulent times we had been through there was such a sense of relief that we were working on a beautifully constructed small-scale play bound for the intimacy of the Cottesloe rather than the huge open space of the Olivier. Richard Eyre later wrote: 'Extremely benign atmosphere at rehearsals... It's partly the actors, presided over by Oliver Ford Davies – slightly donnish, ineffably good-willed; he's like a really effective vicar'. I have reluctantly to admit that this is a reasonable summary of the character I present to the world: I was playing close to my public self. David Hare had worked considerably on the text, cutting one character and one scene and also cutting a speech of mine.

"But it's my favourite speech and I've learnt it," I protested.

"I knew you'd say that," replied David, "but it's sentimental and doesn't forward the action, and it's cut." It's the writer's bible: learn to kill your darlings.

The play has been revived a number of times in regional theatres but never on screen or in the West End so its themes and plot require some introduction. Lionel Espy, my character, comes from a distinguished clerical family, and his wife Hester (played by Barbara Leigh-Hunt) probably thought Lionel was destined to rise high in the church, not end up as a South London vicar. I am reminded conversely of wives married to an archbishop who admit that they had assumed they would be organising the village fete rather than having to run Lambeth Palace. Lionel has a new curate Tony Ferris (Adam Kotz), an evangelical fundamentalist who believes that the clergy should fill the churches by telling everyone that Christ has come to heal and preach repentance. The other two members of the team ministry are Donald 'Streaky' Bacon (David Bamber), who can't do theology but believes 'the whole thing's so simple. Infinitely loving. Why do people find it so hard?' Harry Henderson (Michael Bryant) is the most balanced, pragmatic member: 'There is people as they are. And there is people as they could be. The priest's job is to try and yank the two a little bit closer'.

Lionel is summoned to his bishop (Richard Pasco), who complains that his parishioners are not sure that Lionel still believes in 'the rules of the club', the administration of the sacraments. Lionel counters by claiming that trying to serve ordinary working people becomes more important than 'ritual'. The bishop insists a priest has only one duty, that's 'to put on a show'. When Lionel argues that Christ is in our actions – 'Don't you think that some of this other stuff just puts people off?' – the bishop knows that one day he will have to sack him (or as he later puts it, 'You were dead'). The main argument of the play therefore lies between these three interpretations of a priest's duty: to give the faithful what they have traditionally been promised, to help people lead better lives, and to tell all people that Christ has changed the world. Lionel lies in the centre between two fundamentalists, one reactionary, the other evangelical. Lionel thinks 'A priest should be like any other man. Only full of God's love', though he can only bring himself to call the deity 'God, as it were'.

As rehearsals progressed it became clear to me how well it had been cast: it is not enough to fill a play with good actors; they have also to fit the roles they are playing – even the best of actors can't convince in everything. Richard was perfect as a conservative bishop, David as a happy-go-lucky minister, Adam as a doggedly neurotic evangelical, Stella (Tony's girlfriend) as a pragmatic non-believer, Barbara as a long-suffering, neglected wife, Malcolm Sinclair as an ambitious suffragan bishop. Michael, whose Polonius I had so admired, seemed to fit any part he was given – in this case a gay priest desperate not to be exposed to his parishioners. Michael's acting, in large parts and small, always commanded attention. It is true he tended to gravitate centre-stage – there is a place on the Olivier stage known as the 'Michael Bryant spot', centre, a third of the way back (if you come to the front of the stage you can't command the house) – but I think it was his air of contained certainty that really drew the eye. Once he had decided what he was going to do with the character, he was direct, clear and unswerving. I learnt a lot from Michael about clarity. The perfect casting was completed by Joy Richardson, Paul Moriarty and Euan Stuart. As part of our research we went to talk to the head of a theological training college, and he made the point that he had earnest discussions with his students about homosexuality in the priesthood, aware that none of his students was prepared to come out (this was 1989, remember).

David Hare was present at most rehearsals, frowning in concentration at his text. Some actors interpreted this as displeasure at their performance, but I soon came to realise that he was trying to decide if something in the text could be elaborated, cut, or improved rhythmically. David's sense of rhythm was a major help in playing, and learning, the part – 'But people also think, I didn't realise when he said *nothing*, he really did mean absolutely nothing at all'. Rhythm is, of course, central to comedy: it has become another of my obsessions. After a time Richard asked David to leave us alone for a week or so. One of his main reasons for this was to inject more energy, more danger into the action, and my character was one he had principally in mind. David had filled the text with directions that Lionel is at times 'impassive', 'frowns, coming out of a dream', 'is very quiet, as if the others weren't there'. This impassivity, mind elsewhere, I was playing to the hilt. "No," said Richard, "we've got to get Lionel onto the front foot, or we don't have a play." We began to experiment with a more active, spirited Lionel as I didn't want him to appear a victim or to sentimentalise him. A writer gives a character lines and actions, but the way the writer envisaged these being carried out may preclude multiple possibilities of interpretation. We are probably fortunate that we have no idea how Shakespeare envisaged Hamlet or Lear being played. Burbage may have greatly surprised him.

One example of upping the stakes, apparently trivial, will serve. Heather interrupts the four team members stapling pages of roneoed bumf together:

HEATHER: The paper man's here. You haven't paid the bill.
LIONEL: Oh Lord, I haven't had time to go to the bank.

We initially played this exchange very innocuously, mild reproof followed by reasoned explanation. As we came to energise the action Heather showed acute exasperation at her husband's amnesia over money, and Lionel exploded at the hundred and one things expected of him. In one brief exchange the tension in the marriage is revealed. It doesn't need to be described; it's been shown. This was not lost on David when he returned: "The Espys are getting very beady with one another," he remarked with considerable understatement. Richard and David retired for several hours, presumably to hammer out this change of direction, but returned in apparent agreement that it was on the right lines.

In a scene where Lionel and Frances play chess together Frances asks after Lionel's daughter Lucy, whom we later learn has an alcohol problem, and all Lionel says is, 'It's difficult. We don't have an address. It's very hard on Heather'. I said that I longed to say more about Lucy, and David replied, "Yes, I know you do, and so do I, but it's too painful and you don't know Frances well enough to confide in her." I remember this cautionary note whenever I see, particularly on television, a character revealing the most intimate and agonising things to an acquaintance, just in order for the writer to explain the backstory or forward the plot. David also urged me to play each scene for its apparent worth: "The audience don't think, 'He doesn't seem the same person he was ten minutes ago'; they think, consciously or unconsciously, 'This is a new side to his character'." One of the best pieces of advice I've ever had. There is no more destructive sight than an actor ironing out the apparent inconsistencies that the author has painstakingly written in.

The action certainly catches fire in the final confrontation between the bishop and Lionel. But even here Richard urged us to go for broke, and Richard and I took full advantage. Lionel questions the grounds for his dismissal:

'In part you see I think it's just a generalised impatience. I can hardly blame you. The Christian virtue is forbearance. It would be crazy to think it didn't take its toll. Yes? After a day? After a year? After fifty years? What do you have to show for turning the other cheek? What happens while you do it? What's the price? An accumulation of massive bad temper.'

This provokes the bishop into a passionate tirade:

'In any other job you'd have been fired years ago. You're a joke, Lionel. You stand in the centre of the parish like some great fat wobbly girl's blouse. Crying for humanity. And doing absolutely nothing at all. Yes, I chose you. Because you are the reason the whole church is dying. Immobile. Wracked. Turned inward. Caught in a cycle of decline. Your personal integrity your only concern. Incapable of reaching out. A great vacillating pea-green half-set jelly.'

Lionel: 'You told me the issue was theological'. It was to get one of the biggest laughs of the evening. The scene certainly worked as a climax, but did it come too late in the play? Will the audience accept the quiet gathering of the issues in the first half? Should this degree of voltage have been applied much earlier? David Aukin, the NT's executive director, saw a run-through and said he loved the second half but was bored by the first. We shall see.

We moved into the Cottesloe and found Bob Crowley's stage set, a floor in the shape of a cross with the minimum of furniture and the audience on four sides: 'Bravura minimalism' left us nowhere to hide. It increased the feeling that we had no idea whether the audience would come with us or not. Were they really going to be interested in the problems of vicars with congregations of fifty? On February 2nd 1990 we had our first preview, and the full house seemed eager and concentrated. At the end the applause continued even after the house lights went up. We stood offstage, uncertain whether to go on yet again, and Michael Bryant said, "Well, I've never known that before." Judi Dench and her family came to a preview and wrote to David: 'I think it's the BEST play you've ever written – and is probably one of the best plays we've ever seen. Everyone is wonderful in it, and Richard has directed it beautifully. Clever you! I feel so jealous I could SPIT'.

A week later we had the press night and it went well. In the bar the following night Peter Brook came and held my hand: "So truthful, so truthful," he kept saying.

I wanted to beg him, "Could you please write that on the back of my other hand." To my surprise the next day I received a card from Peter Hall, whom I hardly knew. It was one of the most generous and insightful compliments I have ever received:

'Sometimes you see a piece of acting which just is: character, play and actor make a seamless whole. It's rare and it's a wonderful experience – I suppose it's because of it that I work in the theatre. Your performance as Lionel is such a piece of work and I just want to thank you for it. It is marvellous.'

All this was fine, but writer, director and theatre wanted to know what the reviews would be like. As Richard wrote, 'We wait now for the inevitable disappointment when the press fail to match our aspirations'. I read them much later and found them unusually interesting. Many were glowing. Edward Pearce in the *Sunday Express* wrote, 'It is didactic Wilde – and unbeatable. Mr Hare has, quite simply, written a classic'. John Peter in the *Sunday Times* wrote:

'We are in the presence of a real debate, one between expedience and faith; and all the combatants have a case, as well as a case to answer... and the result is, quite simply, serious drama at its athletic and magisterial best.'

But any discussion of religion and the church is always going to encourage doubters. Benedict Nightingale in *The Times* found the play 'enjoyable but fatally flawed... How can Hare satisfactorily analyse the Church of England when he clearly thinks the idea of Someone Up There is a delusion and distraction, a folly and a snare?' This of course would preclude writers from tackling any subject they were not in sympathy with – Howard Brenton and David Edgar, not to mention Shakespeare, would be out of work. Charles Osborne in the *Daily Telegraph* evidently wanted to turn it into the farce *See How They Run* ('Arrest all those vicars!'): 'I thought all the clergymen rather terrible people in one way and another. If their prayers were to be scrapped, a few more jokes inserted, and the play recast as high comedy, it would be more appealing'. The bulk of the reviews were, however, positive enough, along with a sold-out Cottesloe, to ensure that David and Richard could go ahead with their planned trilogy – the law next and then politics.

A few Sundays later I opened *The Observer* to find I'd been nominated for an Olivier Best Actor award, the other nominees being Ian McKellen for his Iago, Nigel Hawthorne for C. S. Lewis in *Shadowlands*, and Michael Pennington for his various kings for The English Shakespeare Company. Much to some people's annoyance John Wood's Master Builder and Richard Harris' Henry IV (Pirandello) hadn't made the cut. It was a very strong year, and the smart money was on Ian or Nigel. I was just surprised and pleased to be nominated; I had no thought of winning. The award ceremony was in the cavernous Dominion Theatre, and I was disappointed to find that Best Actor was the second award of the evening – though I thought perhaps best to get it over with. Susannah York, the presenter, broke protocol by lamenting that John Wood hadn't been nominated, and then said, 'The winner is...' At this point I seemed to hear my name, but I thought obviously the other two thousand people heard

'Ian McKellen'. I didn't move, determined not to appear a fool. Jenny nudged me. "It's you." I staggered up onto the stage. Fortunately I had a speech prepared. I have no truck with 'Goodness, I never thought I'd win, so I haven't thought of anything'. If you have ninety seconds on prime-time television don't waste it. After various thanks I lambasted the Thatcher government and the Arts Council for their cuts to small-scale theatre, the vital nursery of performing arts. This went down well. *Racing Demon* continued to be rewarded: Michael Bryant won Best Supporting Actor and David Hare Best New Play. The rest of the evening and the dinner afterwards passed in a haze. Somehow Jenny, Miranda and I got home. My main thought was I've won a major award, thank heavens I don't have to go through that again (and I haven't, despite several nominations). Years later I told this to an eminent actor, who said, "Oh, my main thought was I really need to go on winning these." I have always been somewhat lacking in worldly ambition.

I was, however, very moved by the number of congratulatory messages I received from fellow actors and the public. A card from Juliet Stevenson best sums up one reaction from the profession:

'For the first time ever I saw the point of awards when I saw you standing there. That somebody whose work had been so committed, sustained, and who has supported so many others with such generosity, imagination and heart for quite a few years, should now receive such general recognition and acclaim seems to make sense of the otherwise rather dubious event.'

Tony Church put it more succinctly: 'It is great when one of the character breed breaks through – gives us all hope. 10000 cheers'. I put down my success not only to my suitability for the part but to the fact that I, for years an identikit bearded Shakespearean actor, was virtually unrecognisable to the London audience and probably the Olivier award panel. Instead of a well-known, familiar actor doing his thing and doing it very well, if predictably, I was a new face, perhaps to some not an actor at all, possibly the thing itself. My sister-in-law told me when she saw the play that she overheard two women discussing my performance, and one concluded: "I'm surprised the Church of England allows him to do matinees as well."

The play was a sell-out in the Cottesloe, and in August we moved to the Olivier, where we stayed in repertoire till the New Year. I assumed there would have to be additions to the set on such a vast stage, but Richard and Bob were determined to stick with the simple cross. So many designers faced with the Olivier either fill it with scenery or truck in small representational rooms, and usually neither approach works. It is hard, as always, to analyse why the play was such a success. I don't think the public had a burning desire to understand the problems of the Church of England. It might have a strong ensemble cast, but that has never guaranteed a play's survival. What I think registered most emphatically was the play's universality. Many insiders argued that it was clearly a study of the BBC. One bank manager said it showed an uncanny understanding of the workings of the Midland Bank. David Hare said the play was obviously about the current state of the Labour Party. What emerged from this was a similarity between all large institutions where three philosophies collide: a conservative wing who want to concentrate solely on what has traditionally been expected of them by their regulars, a fundamentalist wing who want to return to what they see as the core objectives of the original foundation, and a liberal-minded centre who want to understand and serve as best they can customers of any persuasion. It is easy to see why so many audiences related to David's analysis.

This is not to say that the play was not of considerable interest to the church itself, who were generally relieved, even surprised, that the issues were being dealt with sympathetically, rather than being satirised. Many priests told me they could think of fellow clerics who would fit all the characters portrayed. The play, rather like Alan Bennett's sermon in *Beyond the Fringe*, came to be much used in church and in training college discussions. On an impulse, perhaps prompted by my mother's death earlier in the year (she lived long enough to

learn of my award but was alas too ill to see the play), I attended on
my own a packed Christmas Eve communion at Twickenham Church,
and saw to my dismay that there was to be a sermon. The preacher
took as his text: "God. Where are you? I wish you would talk to me.
God. It isn't just me. There's a general feeling..." (the whole of my
opening speech in *Racing Demon*). It was a kind of dream/nightmare,
and I sank lower and lower in my pew. My presence had been clocked
(there had been a church outing to the play), and I was introduced
afterwards to the preacher. All I could manage to say was, "You spoke
it better, but I get more laughs."

We were not to be idle during the run of the play. David Edgar
(*Mary Barnes, Destiny, Nicholas Nickleby*) had been commissioned to
write a play on the upheavals in the Soviet block following the fall of
the Berlin Wall in 1989, *The Shape of the Table*. Richard Eyre's idea
was the play should be largely peopled by the *Racing Demon* cast, and
David tailored his characters accordingly, but in the event I was the only
member to accept my casting. Michael Bryant and David Bamber were
enticed by the offers of Badger and Mole in Alan Bennett's *Wind in the
Willows*, and other *Demon* actors either didn't like their parts or didn't
relate to the play. As Richard said, his attempt to found a permanent
company fell at the first fence. Rather than cancel the production, he
bravely, and expensively, brought in an entirely fresh group of actors,
including Karl Johnson, Stephen Boxer, Katrin Cartlidge, and Stratford
Johns, to be directed by Jenny Killick. I played the prime minister of
a communist puppet regime, akin to Czechoslovakia, collapsing under
a mixture of string-pulling from Moscow, an internal power struggle,
and the influence of television pictures of world-wide demonstrations.
Rather than being an anti-communist diatribe, Edgar asked if the
demonstrators realised 'that they're exchanging the Red Flag for the
pop song. *Pravda* for *Playboy*. The hammer and sickle for the strip-
joint, cola-tin and burger-bar. To have expelled the German and the
Russians to hand the whole thing over to America'. The reviews were
largely positive, though there were complaints that the voice of the
protesters was not sufficiently in evidence. But as a former historian

I have always thought that what goes on in the corridors of power is of importance, even if dramatically unfashionable. I warmed to David Edgar's very nuanced political understanding, and it was to prove the first of five Edgar plays I have appeared in. I had become a Hare and Edgar actor, breaking free at last from Shakespeare and the classics. I probably should have engineered my escape years earlier.

Richard Eyre had warned me that there was no largish part for me in David Hare's next play *Murmuring Judges*, which encompassed lawyers, the police, and the prison service. Fortunately there were many offers elsewhere, and I was unable to go on a short regional tour of *Racing Demon*, with my old friend Ben Whitrow taking over as Lionel. These offers seemed to indicate that I had, in some sense, 'arrived'. It may have taken twenty-three years, but I was now fifty and, as Peter Dews had predicted, I seemed to have come into my own. An Oscar is said to put a million dollars on your fee, but an Olivier alas doesn't work like that. A friend said: "The best you can hope for is that when you go for an interview and give your name the receptionist/p.a. will say, 'Yes, of course'. She probably won't have recognised you, but she will think she ought to know the name." He proved right. While it has never brought us great wealth it did at least free us from the dole, shop work and the cleaning agency, and Miranda has kept her savings.

During the run James Fox and Peggy Ashcroft came to see the play and over a cup of tea in the canteen James said, "What are you doing next, now you're a star?"

"Well, hardly," I objected.

"You've won the Olivier and Peggy and I have just seen you give a star performance, what more do you want?" I don't think it works like that, I thought. And it didn't.

During the runs of *Hamlet* and *Racing Demon* Miranda, now thirteen/fourteen, had started to accompany me on many Saturdays to the National, following the example of Judi Dench and Richard Eyre with their daughters Finty and Lucy. I usually managed to get her into matinees and evenings, if only on an usher's seat, and it proved a crash course in drama. She estimates that she saw *Hamlet* seven times,

The School for Scandal three, Trevor Griffith's Chekhovian *Piano* six, *Accidental Death of an Anarchist* three, and *Racing Demon* twenty-three (she practically knew it by heart). She told me she found 'the variant styles of Hare, Griffiths and Dario Fo fascinating – so many ways to write a modern play'. It must have confirmed her desire to become a writer.

I returned to the National in June 1993 to rehearse for the trilogy of David's plays, due to be presented in September for twelve weeks. Because of cast changes this involved re-rehearsing *Racing Demon* and also *Murmuring Judges*, in which I was now to play the prison officer. In tackling the law David had concluded that it was not enough to examine the old-boy network of the judiciary without considering the role of the police in presenting alleged criminals to the legal system and the role of the prison service in dealing with the aftermath. This had made for an unwieldy structure which, despite all David's ingenious rewritings, never found a cohesive dramatic solution. It was also the occasion of my worst 'dry'. Following a difficult family 'difference' I arrived at the theatre, considerably upset, and five minutes before leaving the dressing room thought 'I have absolutely no idea what I say in my first scene'. I seized the script, managed to read the first two pages of a five-page interview scene, and hoped the rest would come back. I started the scene and after the two pages my mind went blank again, almost as if a switch had been turned off. I knew there was no point as interviewer in trying to busk it so I left the stage and my amazed fellow actor Paul Higgins. In the wings an alarmed Trish Montemuro, the stage manager, gave me the line. "It's no use," I said. "Give me the script." I returned to the stage and openly used the book, which had a certain logic in an interview scene – it is even just possible the audience thought it part of the action. A total memory lapse is what actors and musicians fear most. It's never happened again (so far), but it frightened me for days afterwards. Memo to me: always arrive at the theatre already focused.

In researching *The Absence of War* David had been given considerable access, both public and private, to the Labour Party's

1992 election campaign. It was therefore inevitable that audiences would identify the Labour leader George Jones, played with passion and commitment by John Thaw, with Neil Kinnock, and comparisons were made with other members of his team. I played Oliver Dix, his political adviser, a role loosely based on Charles Clarke, whom in 1993 I had never met or even heard of. Despite this I was later assured by various MPs that I was uncannily like Charles in voice, mannerisms and even the way I sat in a chair. Spectators see what they want to see. The nub of the play, as David wrote in a Fabian Society lecture, was that Kinnock when he became leader 'became convinced for reasons that were entirely honourable that the party could not be re-elected unless he was willing to make a pact with respectability – a quality Neil himself called "a fourth-division virtue". This pact, like all such pacts, was tragically unnecessary... the gamble did not pay off'. It was to pay off in 1997 with Tony Blair's landslide victory. George Jones felt he was shackled by spin doctors, focus groups and advertising agencies so that he must not appear unsound on the economy or soft on defence, and in a passionate outpouring of frustration that he could not say what he really thought about Northern Ireland, nuclear weapons or even taxation. This view was attacked by several Labour Party chiefs, including Roy Hattersley and Gerald Kaufman, and the ensuing turmoil disguised the real merits of the play, which was, as David said, more a work of imaginative fiction than a documentary drama. We later made a BBC television film of the play, well worth revisiting, in which John Thaw excels. Subsequent regional productions have shown it to be a more considerable play and a more prescient analysis than was first allowed.

It was an enormous technical feat to get all three plays ready, particularly when they were to be played in order of their composition on six Saturdays. Many people felt that *Racing Demon* emerged as the best play, and in terms of clarity of theme, structure and handling of tragicomedy I think, though clearly biased, that is true. Also applauded by some were the old-fashioned virtues of 'character acting', as actors appeared in markedly different roles as they had once done in the days of permanent rep companies. Michael Bryant, Richard Pasco, Barbara Leigh-Hunt, Saskia Wickham, Paul Moriarty, Adrian Scarborough and myself enjoyed ourselves hugely. There was also a general recognition that the trilogy was a much-needed justification of the title of National Theatre. These Saturday trilogies remain the most satisfying and exciting experiences of my working life. Richard Eyre felt the same: this is why he wanted to run the National Theatre and now he'd achieved it. The trilogy showed how far the National, and British theatre itself, had moved from the '60s, when there had been little attempt to commission 'state-of-the-nation' plays. The '70s ushered in a developing political theatre, and indeed Olivier's final stage performance was in Trevor Griffith's *The Party* in 1973, a socialist analysis of modern Britain and the reasons for the failure of revolution. Hare, Howard Brenton, John McGrath, David Edgar and others showed that the new energy in theatre lay in political analysis, and in certain ways the trilogy was a beacon of this.

The Absence of War played on after the end of the trilogy, but it turned out we were not finished with *Racing Demon*. In October 1994 we were scheduled to take it to a UK Arts Festival in Los Angeles. Having agreed to this I was then offered Mr Bennett, and Barbara Leigh-Hunt Lady Catherine de Burgh, in Andrew Davies' television adaptation of *Pride and Prejudice* with Jennifer Ehle and Colin Firth. Much as I longed to play Mr Bennett I felt my first duty was to the National. Great efforts were made to fit the filming round the two of us, and they succeeded with Barbara, but Mr Bennett proved to be in too many scenes and the part eventually went to the 'other Lionel Espy', Ben Whitrow, who was, of course, excellent. I was very sad to miss out, although I consoled myself that it was after all just another BBC Jane Austen. How wrong I was. The critical and public response was staggering, the wet-clothed Colin Firth was proclaimed a star, and many years later David Bamber, a definitive Mr Collins, told me the repeats, residuals and royalties had proved eye-watering – "You'd have made a quarter of a million."

In Los Angeles we played the James A. Doolittle Theatre in the centre of Hollywood, which now seemed a ghost town, beleaguered and dangerous, and we were bussed in from arty West Hollywood four miles away. The *L.A. Times*, the only review that really mattered, related the plot, praised the direction and acting, but concluded that for Anglicans these might be weighty questions but for LA the play 'is preaching to the converted' – a criticism that is hard to unpick. Another notice thought it was, like all the best British drama, 'a costumed panel discussion' (which would also be true of all Greek drama). *L.A. Life* dug deeper: 'Pray to get a ticket if you're someone who enjoys issue-oriented theatre that comes packaged in a rich story and vivid characters'. Hollywood, however, is about plot, bodies, emotions and success, not 'issue-oriented' drama. The play did excellent business and many familiar faces were very complimentary; Louis Malle and Candice Bergen reduced me to tongue-tied awe when I met them backstage. *The Hollywood Reporter* told me I had a voice like a symphony orchestra, but vocal skill is not much in demand in LA, though Disney did summon me with a view to voicing animations. Other unsuccessful auditions followed, mostly to play Russian villains. A highlight of our stay was a reception given for us by the 'Last Mogul', the legendary Lew Wasserman of MCA and Universal Studios – Degas and Picasso on the wall, Kirk Douglas telling us about his latest book. As I wrote in an article for *The Guardian*, 'praise for British stage acting is much appreciated but makes us feel remote and rather like the Peking Opera, remarkable but not quite on the same planet'.

Production Six

HEARTBREAK HOUSE (1992)

When *Racing* Demon finished its first National run in April 1991 I was reunited with Brian Cox as his comic side-kick in a television adaptation of Fay Weldon's *The Cloning of Joanna May* with Patricia Hodge, Siri Neal and Sarah Badel. I knew Fay well from her play *The Hole in the Top of the World*, which I did at the Orange Tree in 1987, a prescient climate change saga. I had a speech describing as a scientist my presence at the test dropping of the first atomic bomb in the New Mexico desert. At 10pm the supersonic Concorde would fly over Richmond and the noise was so deafening that in the pub theatre we regularly had to stop speaking for a whole minute. On the nights when this happened in the middle of my atomic speech the effect on the audience was electrifying. Each night I would look at my watch, start the speech and pray for Concorde. After *Joanna May* I played an unpopular teacher in a bizarre television film *The Police*, which proved a strange, upsetting experience. The young boys, most of whom came from an ordinary primary school, captured me, put me on trial in a deserted house, and then left me locked in over the weekend, only to find on Monday that I had hanged myself (hours in make-up). On the last day of the shoot we finished filming an earlier night scene as dawn rose, and I was then driven forty miles across country, had two sleepless hours in a hotel bedroom, and at

7.30am started an episode of *Inspector Morse: Second Time Around*. Was this what it meant to be 'hot', job after job jostling and colliding with one another? I knew you didn't remain in demand for very long, perhaps eighteen months, so best to cram them all in. It was another world from my struggles in the 1980s. I felt both elated and troubled.

The RSC grabbed me to play Gabriel Utterson, the narrator of *Dr Jekyll and Mr Hyde*, a David Edgar adaptation which experimented with two actors, Roger Allam and Simon Russell Beale, playing Jekyll and his alter ego, a device which enabled the two to talk to one another in a way Stevenson never envisaged. David later reverted to the conventional, and rewrote the play for one actor at the Birmingham Rep. My chief memory of this Peter Wood production is of finishing the technical at 6.30 on Friday evening, a day late, and opening an hour later, supperless and without any dress rehearsal. The ingenious set by Carl Toms had three different rooms on a revolve. At one point I made my entrance by crossing a dark room and opening a door, confident of beginning the scene. But the next room was also dark and I began to lose my nerve – where was the audience? I retreated. "That's definitely the back wall of The Barbican," I reasoned. "So the audience must be in the opposite direction." I hurried through the first dark room, opened the door, stumbled through the furniture in the second dark room and cautiously peered through some huge curtains (which should have been drawn back). There was an anxious Roger Allam waiting for me to speak. It is the only time, so far, that I have failed to locate both the scene and the audience. The hoped-for transfer didn't materialise, but this did enable me to join a Trevor Nunn production of Shaw's *Heartbreak House*.

Shaw described the play as being, like himself, an 'inexplicable phenomenon'. He thought it his masterpiece, in which case it should qualify as one of the great plays of the twentieth century. But he also thought at times that it was a 'flawed' masterpiece, and critical consensus would agree. It is an immensely attractive tragicomedy, a 1910s version of a state-of-the-nation play, ambitious, daring, full of good acting parts, but quite what it is saying remains opaque. I first saw the play in 1961 at the Oxford Playhouse. In the twenty years after his death in 1950 Shaw's plays were very out of fashion, swept away by Ionesco and Beckett, Arthur Miller and Tennessee Williams, and the working-class drama of Wesker, Arden and Bond. John Osborne, in full rhetorical excess, called Shaw 'a fraudulent inept writer of Victorian melodrama', his plays 'posturing wind and rubbish'. But Frank Hauser at the Playhouse was one of the few directors in the '50s to believe in Shaw, and there I saw *Misalliance, Candida* and *The Apple Cart. Heartbreak House* had the gravel-voiced Roger Livesey as Shotover, Judy Campbell and Dulcie Gray as the daughters and Michael Denison in his element as Hector. I remember a review that said 'Gales of laughter at the Playhouse, and as usual it's Bernard Shaw'.

I had a background in Shaw having played St John Hotchkiss in *Getting Married*, Colenso Ridgeon in *The Doctor's Dilemma* and Colonel Pickering in *Pygmalion*. When Trevor Nunn offered me the play in 1991 the part was Mazzini Dunn, an idealistic dreamer – back to the 'unsuccessful'. The attraction, apart from the play and Trevor, was Paul Scofield as Shotover. Paul was in many ways the idol of my generation. We of course admired Olivier, Gielgud, Richardson and Redgrave, but they all seemed to belong to a pre-war era. Scofield was the new-wave classical actor of post-war theatre, and his Thomas More in *A Man for All Seasons* the epitome of a new style. I had seen him in the '50s in *Ring Round the Moon, Venice Preserved* and *Hamlet*, a production which toured to Moscow. I relish the story that some Russian actors who had revered his Hamlet came to London in 1958 and were excited to find he was appearing in the West End – in *Expresso Bongo*. On seeing it they concluded that it was a prime example of degraded Western capitalism that a great actor who should be nurtured in the classical theatre was now forced to earn a living by appearing in a third-rate musical. Paul's singing is nearly as poor as mine, and his choice of material has always been eclectic, some would say mysterious and foolhardy. He greatly enjoyed himself in *Expresso Bongo*.

In the same Peter Brook 1956 season as *Hamlet* Paul also played the unnamed 'whisky priest' in an adaptation of Graham Greene's novel *The Power and the Glory*, which some consider his masterpiece. His picture of the very fallible Catholic priest who has fathered a child is thought to have cost him the Nobel prize, constantly blackballed by a die-hard Catholic committee member (despite the fact the Pope had assured Greene that he liked the novel). If I were forced to choose the greatest male performance I have ever seen it would be Scofield's whisky priest. Olivier saw it several times and, thinking it 'the best performance I can remember seeing', played the part himself on American television in 1961, though not apparently with the same distinction. Paul's performance has disappeared without trace, though John Ford made a movie of the book with Henry Fonda called *The Fugitive*. In 1962 at the RSC Paul played Lear aged forty-two, and it is by general acclaim the finest Lear of the last sixty years. Paul's hard despotic descent into frailty was a great achievement, but I felt his iron implacability left him too little room for manoeuvre. It was not a definitive template, but then no performance of Lear ever is. The 1971 film gives some indication of his power, but it is heavily cut and is not an accurate record of his stage performance.

In addition to the lure of Scofield there was the attraction of the play. I was determined to use the experience to try to fathom what Shaw was saying, why he thought it his masterpiece and what was the nature of its flaw. Other actors approached the production with a variety of motives. Felicity Kendal (Ariadne Utterword) said, "I never thought it was something I wanted to do and neither of the sisters was an obvious part for me. In the end I decided to do it for the collaborative element. Working with this group of people was too good to miss." Vanessa Redgrave (Hesione Hushabye) was even more forthright: "I never go to see Shaw's plays, except *Mrs Warren's Profession*. He's not in the same league as O'Neill, Ibsen and Chekhov. He is always putting in laughs where I think they don't belong just for the sake of it. Hesione really is a difficult challenge for me." She admitted, however, "I just wanted to be in the vicinity to hear that voice when

Paul opened his mouth." And why did Paul want to do it when he had turned down so many plays in the last ten years? "I read the play and was drawn to it. That's all I can say. It's the only criterion you can have. It's as though some little light comes on." I asked Paul if he'd always wanted to play Shotover, and he guardedly replied, "Well, let's just say I've had my eye on it." Shaw had said 'Behold my Lear', but Paul felt, "This is an ensemble play, we all share it, so it's not like Lear in that respect, though there are parallels." The parallels are not exact. Shotover does tell Ariadne, his putative Regan, 'You left because you did not want us. Was there no heartbreak in that for your father?' Ellie Dunn, a Cordelia figure, enters into a 'spiritual marriage' with her 'second father', which Lear would have delighted in. But it is hard to make Hesione a Goneril, despite her insistence that her father should make money out of destructive inventions.

The rest of the cast were very imaginatively chosen. Daniel Massey, who much admired Paul, was an inspired choice for Hector; Imogen Stubbs, Trevor Nunn's recent Desdemona and now his partner, had depth and integrity as my daughter Ellie; David Calder, avowed enemy of capitalism, was his own nemesis Boss Mangan; and Joe Melia, who always claimed to me that he was a performer not an actor, did his revue turn as the Burglar. On publicity material all eight of us were placed above the title, with only Peggy Marshall (Nurse Guinness) and Shaun Scott (Randall Utterword) featured below. As Jack Tinker of the *Daily Mail* wrote, in typical Tinkerish style, 'Probably not since Binkie Beaumont [of H.M. Tennent fame] popped his ruby slippers has such a stellar collection been assembled on the West End commercial stage'. Rather improbably I had now found myself part of a commercial 'stellar collection'. Public expectations were alarmingly high, particularly since Paul hadn't been in a major stage success since *Amadeus* in 1979.

The play was being presented at the Theatre Royal Haymarket by Duncan Weldon, who between 1978 and 2003 produced sixty-three plays at the theatre. Duncan had a straightforward formula: 'I have always concentrated on trying to do starry revivals of very good plays with very good directors… Some of the great plays were written for stars'. To this end Rex Harrison had done eight plays for Duncan, though Rex's grasp of the lines became increasingly sketchy. Duncan did, however, present some more enterprising revivals: O'Neill's *Strange Interlude* with Glenda Jackson, Tennessee Williams' *Sweet Bird of Youth* with Lauren Bacall (directed by Harold Pinter) and Osborne's *A Patriot for Me* with Alan Bates. Presenting a play with a cast of a dozen or so for only three or four months was always a financial challenge: the theatre had to be near capacity for Duncan to get his money back, let alone make a profit. When he started out he said he could put a straight play on in the West End for £15,000, *Heartbreak* was to cost him £300,000, and by 2010 a large-cast ambitious production needed half a million (today nearer a million). We were not on huge salaries (I was on £850), though more than the National Theatre or the RSC, but we were undoubtedly a gamble for Duncan. A European tour, a transfer to Broadway, and a possible television version were all mooted and would prove profitable.

The play is subtitled 'A Fantasia in the Russian Manner on English Themes'. Shaw claimed that it was full of 'the same nice people, the same utter futility as *The Cherry Orchard*'. That is a reasonable parallel so far, and when he wrote that it is 'cultured, leisured Europe before the war' you might substitute the 1917 Revolution for the 1914–18 war. It is Shaw's attack on Edwardiana: 'The nice people hated politics. They did not wish to realise Utopia for the common people; they wished to realise their favourite fictions and poems in their own lives'. The problem is that Shaw was not cut out to be so politically analytical. He was far too interested in a certain mystical moral purpose, in the relationship between the sexes, in turning every preconceived notion of character and society upside down and, as Vanessa noted, he couldn't resist a comic diversion. Brecht said of him: 'Shaw is a terrorist. The Shavian terror is an unusual one and he employs an unusual weapon – that of humour'. The first act is country-house comedy, very loosely akin to *The Cherry Orchard* but in reality much closer to Noel Coward's *Hay Fever*, written some four years after *Heartbreak*'s first performance. Characters, relationships and situations are superbly set up, but there seems an uncertainty about the end in sight, though Shaw claimed that he conceived of an ending in June 1916 when, walking on the Sussex Downs with Virginia Woolf, they heard the guns on the Somme.

The character of Mazzini Dunn interested me greatly. We know that Shaw based him on Ebenezer Howard (1850–1928), who is principally known for his foundation of the Garden City Movement, in which Shaw had a financial interest. Letchworth Garden City was begun in 1903 and Welwyn in 1920, and was influential in the setting up of a number of American Gardens. Howard was therefore far from being an unpractical dreamer, and even his seemingly bizarre notion that aeroplanes could drop propaganda pamphlets over enemy territory has been used in every subsequent conflict. I found this a great help. Mazzini clearly isn't Howard, but knowing that Shaw had him in mind enabled me to bring depth and substance to the character. In the play Mazzini is wrong in many of his judgments, but his forthright goodness shines through. Far from condemning the Edwardian middle classes, Mazzini calls them 'rather a favourable specimen of what is best in our English culture… charming people, most advanced, unprejudiced, frank, humane, unconventional, democratic, free-thinking, and everything that is delightful in thoughtful people', a view still held by many a member of the Conservative party. Hesione says of him, 'I thought you the most odious, self-satisfied, boresome elderly prig', but concedes 'you become quite clever when you talk about your daughter… I shall fall in love with you presently'. To which Mazzini imperturbably replies, 'The fact is you don't strike on my box, Mrs Hushabye, and I certainly don't strike on yours' (which provoked a major laugh). Mazzini is a hopeless money-maker, as Howard was – knighted in 1927 and died nearly penniless the next year. As Shaw wrote, Mazzini is 'one of those heroic simpletons who do big things while our prominent worldlings are explaining why they are Utopian and impossible. And of course it is they who will make money out of his work'. I obviously had a niche in heroic simpletons.

Once rehearsals began it was evident that Trevor had cut very little and we were in for a long evening. There had to be an interval before the short third act to allow a major set change, and since the first and second acts were so long they had to be divided by another interval. We could be looking at four hours, but Trevor was determined to give the full text a chance since he argued that it was an urgently relevant play that asks 'what sort of England do we think we have, what values are worth sustaining, and how does it need to change'. To emphasise these he eventually had his cast in the final beat of the play stand in a line at the front of the stage to express their vision of a disintegrating society, Hesione and Ellie hoping that the bombs will come again tomorrow night, 'radiant at the prospect'. Many people feel that Shaw plays itself; the only thing to do is speak it fast and clearly, which may be why directors are not drawn to his plays because they don't feel they can put their imprint on them. Trevor, however, was determined to find the essence of the play, a great strength of his, and he constantly urged us to, "Stay in the moment; don't move on till we've extracted all the juice." This meant that rehearsals proceeded very slowly, but I knew it would be worth it. The more the actor can establish a relationship with each intention, word, sentence and move, the richer will be the moment in performance. Our approaches varied, however. It was not easy to discern Paul's personal method, but he was certainly very concerned with the sound and rhythm of the language. Felicity was intent on precision in language and comedic stress, and also in moves. Vanessa let it all hang out while she tried to establish the truth of the moment, experiments which could vary wildly.

Since my best, and longest, scene was with Vanessa I had a particular interest in how she was approaching the part. I was initially daunted by the fact that, just as I thought Paul's whisky priest was the finest male performance, I also felt Vanessa's Ellida Wangel in Ibsen's *The Lady from the Sea* (directed by Michael Elliott, 1979) the outstanding female performance I had ever seen. I also knew from David Hare, who had directed Vanessa in his film *Wetherby*, that she could be very uncertain about character, accent, costume and props, and could be reckless in changing them. Vanessa had said Hesione would be a challenge and sure enough after a couple of weeks she suggested she might play it half-Jamaican on the grounds that Shotover says 'I have a wife somewhere in Jamaica: a black one. My first wife'. Felicity visibly blenched at this and said she had no intention of playing Ariadne part-black. Vanessa parried by proposing they could be half-sisters, but Trevor pointed out there was no indication of this in the text and managed to persuade Vanessa to drop the idea. A week later I arrived for a rehearsal of our big scene to find Vanessa was playing Hesione Irish. This was a tricky moment: before entering the scene should I enquire why Hesione had suddenly become Irish? I decided to plough on, and it emerged that Vanessa thought that as she was brought up largely by Nurse Guinness she had adopted her accent, her sister refusing to do so. It's interesting how even the best actors often feel the need of something to cling on to, whether an accent, a costume or a piece of business. The next day Vanessa was no longer Irish, Trevor having presumably persuaded her the audience would find it confusing. I was relieved, but it left me feeling predictable and unadventurous. Perhaps I should try playing Mazzini Italian?

My relations with the other cast members was less problematic. I knew Daniel well from the RSC *Measure for Measure*, and I had played Friar Laurence to Felicity's Juliet. I got on very well with my stage daughter Imogen Stubbs, and I had left-wing politics in common with David Calder and Joe Melia. I even had a slight personal connection with Paul, which pleased him, as in 1957 Jeremy Paul and I had shown Paul and his wife Joy Parker round King's Canterbury with a view to their sending their son Martin to the school. Martin duly arrived in 1959 and, I was later delighted to hear, had been responsible for a production of Arden's *Sergeant Musgrave's Dance* – times had changed indeed. Paul would sometimes have lunch with us at nearby restaurants, and though he would chat away he had little desire to talk about acting or past productions. A certain enigmatic quality was a strength of Paul's on- and offstage, though this stood at variance with a wicked and very larky sense of humour that burst out at unexpected moments, particularly unnerving as you were entering a scene. It was as if he was signalling that he didn't want us to think that he was taking himself or his acting too seriously. His sense of comedy had been very evident in plays as different as *Staircase* and *The Government Inspector*. It was to prove very important in *Heartbreak*.

When we reached run-through stage the problem of length became urgent. The first act worked well as country-house comedy, though its excesses could be trimmed. The short last act out in the garden at night time, with the menace of bombs dropping nearby, presentiments of death and destruction and the explosion that kills Mangan and the Burglar had incident enough, even if Shaw's argument was hard to follow. The second and longest act seemed to me the problem. At first the act has a coherent development central to the spine of the play, which marks Ellie's loss of romantic infatuation and apparent determination to marry Mangan for his money. The Hesione-Mazzini scene is essentially an interlude, in which Shaw couldn't resist the temptation to have his siren make a pass at the least likely character in the play. At this point Shaw seems aware that he needs a new injection of plot and so he introduces the Burglar with all the attendant ramifications. There the act could end but Shaw wants to reveal Ellie's new dependence on her adopted father Shotover and in turn his dependence on rum in a long duologue that I feel rambles and overstays its welcome. There follows a largely pointless scene between Randall and Hector, as if Shaw realised that he hadn't given them enough stage time. The plot is not advanced and the act loses pace and focus. Trevor accordingly started to make cuts, but there is always a problem in introducing cuts late in rehearsal or in early performances. Actors lay down pathways in their memory as they navigate from moment to moment, sometimes forced to find a way to make coherent the development of an incoherent argument. Cuts, even if apparently helpful, disturb these pathways and mean that new routes have to be devised. Cuts can also destroy an aspect of the character you rely on. Inevitably there came a moment when Paul said, "No more cuts," just as Felicity had told me in *Amadeus* he had said, "No more rewrites."

Paul had spoken; Shotover's text was fixed. Others, particularly Shaun as Randall, were not so lucky.

We moved to Guildford for a three-week try-out, and discovered Bill Dudley's extraordinary design. The set is usually the stern gallery of a large, wooden galleon, but Bill had developed a huge steel rib-cage, a skeleton of an ancient steamer, windowless and open to the elements, establishing a non-naturalistic world from the outset, an enormous asset. It was a nervous period for both director and cast. The play was too long and needed not just cutting but greater pace: leisurely staying in the moment had to be jettisoned. As Shaw himself wrote: 'My plays must be acted, and acted hard. They need a sort of bustle and crepitation of life which requires extraordinary energy and vitality and gives only glimpses and movements of the poetry beneath'. He might have added that the helter-skelter comedy of the first act needed to be played fast if the more philosophical debates of the final two acts were to be earned. Vanessa seemed particularly unsettled and her experiments continued. Though she was no longer part-Jamaican she still insisted on a black ponytail that reached almost to the floor. Only when it ended up several times in a fire bucket half-full of water was she persuaded to cut it to waist-length, but her lack of inhibitions I still found inspiring. Benedick Nightingale later wrote that she was 'a loose-limbed gypsy queen in an improbable Afro hairdo twirling and laughing with glee as she amiably destroys those unwary enough to venture into her force-field'. Paul, meanwhile, was proceeding in quite a different manner. He was the detached, self-absorbed patriarch with the great snarling, rumbling voice, but he also took care to inhabit the dedicated inventor. His delicate, wicked sense of humour suggested, despite his evasions, that he knew at all times what was going on. But he had plenty in reserve for his 'second childhood': 'I feel nothing but the accursed happiness that comes as life goes, the happiness of yielding and dreaming instead of resisting and doing, the sweetness of the fruit that is going rotten'. I was in awe, I found it so moving.

The opening at the Haymarket went well, the notices were mostly excellent, the cast were much praised. The play, however, remained an enigma. Michael Billington thought it 'the missing link between Wilde and Pirandello', but 'even with so lucid a director as Nunn the play remains tantalisingly mysterious'. Paul Taylor found it 'part allegory, part debate-play, part sub-Wildean comedy of manners, it seems to fastforward at times into the Theatre of the Absurd'. There was a great sense of relief that Paul, the great Lear, the great Salieri, had returned to the classics, but the praise was laced with a certain puzzlement, often expressed in the past, at his unvarnished presentation of the text. Michael Coveney put it most bleakly: 'This is either very fine acting or monotonous phrase-making, and I cannot for the life of me decide which'. At the time it reminded me of the pianist Alfred Brendel's playing – this is what Beethoven wrote; I'm not trying to embellish it. Shotover is undoubtedly Shaw's mouthpiece. He yearns for moral purpose, for enlightenment, for the life of the spirit. Shaw claims that the play 'has more of the miracle, more of the mystic belief in it than any of my others', but at this point in his career he could never resist undercutting anything so serious, so otherworldly, and he reveals that Shotover gets most of his inspiration from rum. Like Shaw, Paul is not a creator to go for the obvious; he is not easy to read; he confounds your expectations. For me, therefore, it was a clash of enigmas, Shaw and Scofield, which some found elucidating, some frustrating.

I have always learnt most about acting not through directors but through working with other actors (keeping good company), and Paul, Vanessa and Felicity presented such different and intriguing models. Because Mazzini's surname is Dunn, Shotover immediately pretends to believe he is Bo'sun Dunn, a pirate in the China seas who stole from him, despite Ellie's indignant protestations. When the Burglar is revealed to be the real Bo'sun Dunn Shotover turns on Mazzini: 'You are not Billy Dunn. This is Billy Dunn. Why have you imposed on me?' One night several weeks into the run Paul suddenly thundered this last sentence at me in the manner of Lear ranting at Goneril. His titanic force left me momentarily speechless.

In the interval I ventured to ask him, "That was extraordinary – where did it come from?"

Paul thought for a moment. "I have no idea." The next night he did it again, but the force had lessened. He never risked it again. Sometimes in rehearsal or performance, or when filming on a certain take, you instinctively do something new and unexpected, that stops everyone in their tracks. You (and the director) then have to decide: is that warranted, helpful, does it fit into the structure of the scene and your way through it, or is it misleading? I think Paul decided it was striking but untruthful, even self-indulgent (he knows all along Mazzini is not Billy), and after one more try he dropped it. An actor such as John Malcovich would probably say, 'It just came to me one Tuesday. Don't censor it. I did something different on Wednesday. Do you have a problem with that?'

I hugely enjoyed my scene with Vanessa and the anarchy she brought to it. This anarchy, however, could extend to throwaway and slight inaudibility. She had a line about Mangan: 'He is not in his first youth, is he?'

I replied, 'After all, no husband is in his first youth for very long'. This could be relied upon for a good laugh, but not when Vanessa started to swallow her key words 'first youth'. After a while I plucked up courage to point this out. Vanessa seemed puzzled, so I tried to explain, "Yours is basically a feed line."

"A feed line," repeated Vanessa slowly, as if this was a totally new concept, and the next two nights she obediently banged out the line at triple volume. With another actor you might have thought she was being ironic, but not with Vanessa; it was just that comic feeds, comedy technique were not part of her repertoire. I had to beg her to pull back. Felicity's approach to comedy was quite different. In performance she had a line she knew merited a laugh but wasn't getting it. She tried in various different ways to no avail, and then enlisted the three other actors surrounding her to come to her help, moving them slightly back and forth, suggesting pauses and different stresses, which were carried out by the other three with varying degrees of enthusiasm. After many evenings the laugh finally came, and Felicity never lost it. It's the mark of a comic technician, as most stand-ups know. Judi Dench once told me that it was only on her hundredth performance as Cleopatra that she finally got a laugh on a moment she knew was earned. "That's why the theatre wins over film and television every single time," she said. "You get more out of it, and the audience teach you so much."

The run came to an end after sixteen weeks. I had learnt and enjoyed myself so much, but to my disappointment there was to be no European tour, no Broadway, no television. The set was too heavy to travel, the play was too long, and Paul may not have wanted to go to New York. What had I learnt about Shaw's 'flawed masterpiece'? He intended it as a tragedy and yet he courted laughter, which has proved confusing to audiences. There is an uncertainty of tone throughout, which is at times liberating, at times exasperating. The whole play has a dream-like atmosphere with sleep and trance to the fore, and yet Shaw attacks the hopeless infatuation with dreams. Happiness is a worthless aim, yet Ellie says she and Shotover are happy when stripped of everything. Anger, despair, wasted passion run like a virus through the play. Shaw's heartbreak is a 'chronic complaint, not a sudden shock', the chronic effects of nature and nurture, heredity and childhood. At the end of the play he intends a collective heartbreak when 'the house breaks out through the windows, and becomes all England with all England's heartbroken', but do we feel that all England is represented here? It is more Shaw's despairing reaction to the war. As Hector says of the drumming of the Somme guns, it is 'Heaven's threatening growl of disgust at us useless futile creatures'. Even the siren Hesione says, 'When I am neither coaxing and kissing nor laughing, I am just wondering how much longer I can stand living in this cruel, damnable world'. It is a bitter, pessimistic play, yet I suspect most audiences come out delighting at the attractive, amusing, cultured characters rather than the 'heartbroken imbeciles'.

1994–97: television and movies

One unexpected outcome of *The Absence of War* was a television series *Kavanagh QC*. John Thaw had finally finished the hugely successful

Kavanagh QC. ITV, 1995.
OFD (Foxcott), John Thaw (Kavanagh), Nicholas Jones (Aldermarten).

Inspector Morse and had agreed to try a legal series. Chris Kelly, the producer of the new series, saw us together in *The Absence of War* and cast me as John's closest colleague and Head of Chambers. John was the Bolton boy made good and I was his establishment counterpart: fortunately he couldn't claim his casting was 'all my fucking fault'. The series was a success, ran for five years, twenty-eight episodes in all, opened to fourteen million viewers and never dropped below ten million – numbers almost unattainable today. Since John had to be the defence counsel in almost every episode it was impossible for me to prosecute very often as that rarely happens to two barristers in the same chambers, unlike many legal series where the same two or three barristers seems to officiate on both sides in every case. This meant that sometimes I was heavily involved, sometimes lightly, which suited me fine. I very much enjoyed the research, sitting in the public gallery of various courts including the Old Bailey, and talking to and observing friends who were now barristers and judges. We took it all very seriously and were often commended for our accuracy. Set in the Middle Temple, it inevitably had an old-fashioned air about it, but it covered a vast range of topics, from cot deaths to court martials. John Thaw, whom I knew quite well by this time, intrigued me as an actor. His take on situations and the text was subtly unpredictable. Whether this was premeditated or instinctive was hard to tell (and he certainly wouldn't have discussed it), but I came to think the latter. I admired his freedom and sense of self, though I couldn't help pondering after a particularly difficult two-hander that John had (reputedly) just earned nearly twenty times as much as me. But that's how television works. Nicholas Jones was a splendid Wodehouse figure, the archetypal posh cad always on the make and always frustrated, Cliff Parisi was the devious Clerk of Chambers with a larger house than any of us. Among our fellow barristers were Anna Chancellor, Geraldine James, Jenny Jules and Rebecca Front; writers were as diverse as Russell Lewis, Charles Wood and Malcolm Bradbury, and directors ranged from Charles Beeson and Jack Gold to David Thacker, Tristram Powell and Paul Greengrass. We delivered our final series in 1998, but made a one-off in 2000. We had the script for a second one-off in 2002, which a far-from-well John told me he was determined to make. He died before filming could start. He was only sixty. It was a great loss, and I miss him.

One benefit of *Kavanagh* was that I came to terms with film acting, all the 'save it for the take', 'adapt to the close-up', etc. In 1973 Robert Lang had advised me that the only way to feel at home with a camera was to get in front of one day in and day out, whatever the script. In the 1990s I finally achieved that, not just in *Kavanagh* but in a number of other films and television series, starting with *Anglo-Saxon Attitudes*, an adaptation of an Angus Wilson novel, which Anthony Burgess considered 'one of the five great novels of the century', in which I played the archaeological professor who misinterprets a pagan wooden object. It had a wonderful cast in Dorothy Tutin, Elizabeth Spriggs (inspired), Richard Johnson, Tara Fitzgerald, Douglas Hodge, Simon Chandler, and as my disaffected son who plants the object in the wrong grave a very early appearance of Daniel Craig. It was exactly the sort of serious family drama, covering two generations, with no violence and little sex, that television has no use for anymore and it has never been repeated, a criminal waste.

A Dance to the Music of Time, adapted by Hugh Whitemore and directed by Christopher Morahan and Alvin Rakoff, suffered a similar fate. Anthony Powell's twelve-book saga has always divided critics, some arguing that it a social and comic masterpiece, a worthy rival to Proust's *A la Recherche du Temps Perdu*. Cramming the twelve books into four two-hour-length episodes was always a risk, not only losing the authorial voice but much of the nuance and philosophy of the original. The first episode was written off by many critics as a portrait of an upper-middle-class 1930s world that had no relevance today. The Second World War sequence and the study of literary bohemia are both superb, and among a multitude of fine performances Miranda Richardson as the terrifying self-destructive Pamela Fitton, Edward Fox as the wayward cantankerous Uncle Giles and Paul Rhys as the disillusioned melancholic Charles Stringham are outstanding. I played Le Bas, the Eton housemaster, who has a stroke when Widmerpool (Simon Russell Beale) hijacks an Old Boys reunion dinner with an interminable speech about the balance of payments, a moment of typically insightful tragicomedy. On the first day of shooting Simon expressed to me his anxieties about playing Widmerpool, and I tried to reassure him by arguing that Widmerpool was like Jeeves. Because everyone has their own take on such an iconic comic character they are never fully persuaded by any portrayal, so the actor might just as well go for his particular concept and let any doubters go hang. I later thought that on day one of a long shoot this was a particularly crass reassurance, but I needn't have worried – Simon was superb. Another immensely rich series that will never be repeated.

I at last got a foot in television comedy. Geoff Posner cast me in a *Coogan's Run, Natural Born Quizzers*, written by and starring Steve Coogan and Patrick Marber. They escaped from prison, took hostage the prison therapist (me) and, for reasons I can't now recall, gagged and tied me to Rebecca Front in the back of a taxi, both of us wearing gym slips. I must have passed the comedy test because Geoff Posner asked me to do another one, but *Kavanagh* filming prevented me. Surprisingly few actors managed in those days to bridge the straight and comic TV drama worlds – Timothy West, Prunella Scales, Jim Carter, Anne Reid and Julie Walters were exceptions. Too often they seemed insulated worlds. Some actors conversely felt themselves trapped in comedy: Duncan Preston, a Victoria Wood stalwart, bemoaned to me that he longed to do Chekhov and Ibsen. It was to be over twenty years before I did another thirty-minute comedy, an episode of Sharon Horgan and Rob Delaney's groundbreaking *Catastrophe*, but things are changing: Anna Maxwell Martin, Roger Allam and Tamsin Greig are as likely to be found in sitcoms as straight drama. In 2000 I met up with Patrick Marber after the Almeida *Coriolanus*. He said, "I sat there watching your Menenius and thought, I can't believe we dressed you in a gymslip." But more of that, please.

I also began to do a lot more radio work, both plays – I particularly remember *The Summer of a Dormouse* by John Mortimer, directed by the great Marilyn Imrie, with Paul Scofield (whose rendition of 'Night and Day' is a collector's item), Alex Jennings, Imelda Staunton and Gemma Jones – and readings for *Book of the Week*, memoirs ranging from John Bayley and Ferdinand Mount to Oliver Sacks. I also fulfilled a dream fantasy by appearing with the London Symphony Orchestra in two John Williams concerts as the elderly narrator of a twenty-minute suite from his score for *The Reivers*, a 1969 film starring Steve McQueen. This involved a tricky Mississippi accent and, since I don't read music, painstakingly working out when to come in, i.e. two beats after the entrance of the oboes. John Williams was very encouraging and after the second concert his agent told me John thought I was the best narrator in his thirty years of performing the piece. I took this as generous American hyperbole, when to my amazement the following year he asked me to do it on an American tour with the Boston Pops. I couldn't as I was filming, but I have remained inordinately proud to be asked.

I began to infiltrate the film world. When Emma Thompson's adaptation of *Sense and Sensibility* was being cast it was first suggested I might play Mr Dashwood, whose death triggers the whole plot. Could I ride a horse? This is the question actors most fear. If you mean could I trot to a mark on horseback, deliver a speech and move gently out of shot, that I can do. But in this instance they required me to gallop amidst a real hunt and fall off my horse. That I can't do, and the part went to Tom Wilkinson, who presumably brazened it out (or may, of course, be a very accomplished rider). When I saw the final edit I enquired what had happened to the hunt. "Oh, we never shot it because it was too expensive." Actors never know what to risk saying about their riding abilities. Instead they found me the part of Dr Harris, who treats and successfully cures Marianne (Kate Winslet) of her pneumonia. In my first scene at Montacute House I was explaining in long shot Marianne's condition to an assembled group when Ang Lee, the director, crossed the huge hall, stared at me fixedly and, after what seemed an agonisingly long pause, said, "Can't you stand up straighter?"

Alan Rickman murmured, "Don't worry, he's asked me 'Can't you act better?'", and Emma concurred, "He's told me not to look so old." Ang was an inspired choice for the film, even if his then-limited command of English caused him to be brusquely direct. His film *The Wedding Banquet* (1993) showed that he loved to mix family drama with social satire – perfect for Jane Austen. He was also a stickler for detail. When he worried what else I could do to appear to be treating Marianne, I suggested bleeding her (a favourite period remedy that probably did little good). This he liked, but he decided it would need the correct bowl to catch the blood. The propmaster said that sending for something so obscure could take hours; Ang insisted, and four hours later we recommenced, blood dutifully dripping into bowl.

I have always found *Sense and Sensibility* a very uneven novel with too many long, lumpy digressions. It has, however, a strong if complicated plot, a plethora of interesting characters, the most social satire in any of Austen's novels, but a faulty structure which makes it difficult to adapt faithfully. I remarked to Lindsay Doran, the producer, that Emma Thompson had written a wonderful television sketch of a newly married nineteenth-century wife spying her husband's enlarging penis and, thinking it must be a mouse, had rung for a maid to remove it. "That's it!" said Lindsay. "When I saw that I knew Emma had the wit and sense of period to adapt Austen." Emma had worked on the script on and off for five years, producing draft after draft, and the reshaping continued during filming and editing. Among the principal changes was the need to build up the character of Edward Ferrars (Hugh Grant), whom Austen had scarcely developed early in the book, leaving the reader uncertain why Elinor was so smitten. As a consequence there is a good fifteen-minute section of the completed film which is entirely Emma's invention. It won Emma an Oscar, and she remains to this day the only person to win an Oscar for both acting (*Howard's End*) and screenwriting.

A year later I did two BBC television films for the director John Madden. In *Truth or Dare* I played the head of an Edinburgh law firm, whose latest recruit Lorna (Helen Baxendale) is hounded by a sadistic university friend Nick (John Hannah). My main memory is filming on interior sets in an enormous deserted tobacco factory in freezing cold Glasgow, trying to stop our breath showing. In the second, *Her Majesty Mrs Brown*, I played the Dean of Windsor, who, judging by the letters between them, acted as a kind of Anglican confessor to Queen Victoria (Judi Dench). Victoria asks him, in a roundabout way, if it was permissible to make new friends some years after Albert's death. The Dean, who knows perfectly well that she's talking about John Brown (Billy Connolly), assents. On her very first close-up Judi caught so miraculously both her relief at his permission and her resentment at having to reveal herself that John Madden said, "Perfect. No need to do another." When John Thaw had heard I was going to work with John Madden he'd told me Madden was the originator of one of Thaw's favourite sardonic complaints about directors: 'That was perfect – just one more'. Perhaps Judi is the only actor so perfect that John Madden decided against 'just one more'. He and the BBC thought *Truth or Dare* could well be turned into a feature film, but when Harvey Weinstein saw *Mrs Brown* (he removed, I think wrongly, *Her Majesty*) Miramax plumped for the period piece. It won Judi an Oscar nomination, which many people think she should have won in preference to her brief appearance in John Madden's subsequent *Shakespeare in Love*.

The third film was *Mrs Dalloway*, a script which Vanessa Redgrave had commissioned from Eileen Atkins since they had worked together before on Virginia Woolf. Because the novel is dominated by Clarissa Dalloway's stream of consciousness it was very difficult to translate this to a predominantly visual medium, but I thought Eileen had considerable success. Clarissa prepares for her grand party where she will meet so many friends from the past, but is assailed by memories of the different choices she might have made when young (Natascha McElhone) if she had gone with the dangerous but exciting Peter Walsh (Alan Cox/ Michael Kitchen) or even the alluring Sally (Lena Headey/Sarah Badel), rather than opting for the security of MP Richard Dalloway (Robert Portal/John Standing). Vanessa was unexpectedly good casting for the part of the apparently conformist upper-middle-class woman since she too understood what it was to have made a life choice, in reverse as it were, by committing for so long to the Workers Revolutionary Party and the overthrow of capitalism rather than becoming a leading film and classical actress. The aftermath of the First World War hangs over the film in the suicide of Septimus (Rupert Graves), plagued by shell-shock and his memory of the trenches: the story perhaps asks whether Clarissa and Septimus have both been living doubt-ridden, meaningless lives. One significant aspect of the film was that both the director and the director of photography were women, Marleen Gorris and Sue Gibson, still today a long way from this becoming an unremarked norm. I played the Dalloways' friend Hugh Whitbread, a portly (more padding) establishment toady with some opportunity for comedy which I relished. When I later went to complete some post-synching on the film Marleen remarked that I had 'turned out very funny' – though I was never sure if this was a compliment or an accusation.

I hadn't entirely deserted the theatre and found that huge leading parts are in many ways easier to play than two-scene support. As Ralph Richardson once said, the target is so enormous you're bound to score some bullseyes (with two scenes you're lucky to hit an inner). In 1993 I did an Alan Bennett play *The Old Country* at Watford Palace, directed by Roger Smith. Hilary and his wife Bron (Ann Firbank) appear to be living in a country retreat in the Home Counties, Elgar playing in the house, when they are visited by Bron's sister and husband (Lucinda Curtis and Edward de Souza). It gradually emerges that we are in Russia, Hilary an exiled spy, and that a trade-off return to England is being mooted, though the play lacks momentum as it meanders through some beautifully written set speeches. Alan Bennett explained to Roger and myself over tea that no management had shown interest in the script until in 1977 Alec Guinness said he wanted to do it. The snag was, according to Alan, that Alec, fresh from his success in the television *Tinker, Tailor, Soldier, Spy*, had wanted to repeat his part of Smiley, while Alan had written a cross between Kim Philby and W. H. Auden. "Auden liked wearing slippers. No, no, said Alec, well-polished black shoes." The part contains many of Alan's concerns – loneliness and isolation, guilt and disappointment, the insecurity and sacrifice of spying, and an ambivalent nostalgia for the best of England. I revelled in all these contradictions and apparently my 'crushed corduroy features proved a marvellous vessel for Bennett's concerns' (*The Guardian*), so at last I knew what I looked like. Alan said he might 'creep in' during the run, and some weeks later he revealed that he had, unknown to box office or cast. He seemed pleased – or not displeased.

Virtuoso about the pianist John Ogdon proved a quite different challenge at the Wolsey Theatre Ipswich in early 1995. In 1962 John, aged twenty-five, had been joint winner with Vladimir Ashkenazi of the International Tchaikovski Competition in Moscow. John had a huge talent, phenomenal sight-reading abilities and a prodigious memory. He married a fellow pianist Brenda Lucas and for ten years he toured and played ceaselessly, often two hundred concerts a year, until in 1973 he had a severe breakdown, possibly schizophrenic, probably bipolar.

In 1981 Brenda and Michael Kerr produced a very frank book about his life and troubles, *Virtuoso*, and in 1989 William Humble adapted this first into a successful television screenplay and then into a stage play, where, not tethered to screen naturalism, he could be more symbolic, even expressionistic. Caroline Smith seized the opportunity to give it a daring production. John was a colossal part, never off the stage, and as I had flu during our three weeks of rehearsals I began to doubt whether I could learn it, let alone accurately chart his breakdown and recovery. It also involved a good deal of piano playing, Liszt, Rachmaninov and particularly Beethoven's Appassionata sonata, all done to John's recordings. There was no question of the audience seeing my finger-work (I am a non-pianist), so the fake piano was built up to disguise my hands, but it was vital that my arms and shoulders were always in the right place for major chords and racing up and down the keys, and I spent many hours with a professional pianist, Timothy Ravenscroft, trying to match some very explosive music. In one scene I was 'playing' a little-known Dutch concerto, chain-smoking, drinking whisky and talking manically, all the while straining to listen to Ogdon's recording – John Barton would have been proud of me

Diane Fletcher, an old friend, played Brenda, and approached the part with trepidation as in the television version a critic had thought Alison Steadman had 'performed a hatchet job' on Brenda for pressurising John into too much work. Brenda had made it a condition of permitting this stage version that she could attend any rehearsals, and was frequently in attendance. Diane gave, not surprisingly, a much more sympathetic reading of the part. Physically I might seem odd casting for John's bear-like frame, but once I had huge padding, wig, glasses and his strange goatee beard Brenda confessed herself shocked by the likeness. The day of the press night it snowed hard in Ipswich, traffic was gridlocked and it took me two hours to drive to the station to pick up Jenny, where Benedict Nightingale and Paul Taylor begged a lift to the theatre as the taxi queue was so enormous. Both gave it an excellent notice (well, they had to), and Paul wrote that the lift was 'a case of the accused driving the jury to court'. We were hoping for a six-week tour and a radio version, but our producer Andrew Welch confessed that regional theatres were not keen. One replied that they couldn't see 'a Poole audience wanting a play about a pianist they'd never heard of having a mental breakdown'. My daughter had made the complicated journey to Ipswich from Oxford, where she had gained a place to read English via Richmond's Sixth-Form College. She insists to this day that it is one of the best performances I have ever given, and all this to a few thousand people for two and a half weeks in snowbound Ipswich. Performers don't necessarily do their best work in the West End and the national companies.

During this period I had been elected to the Equity Council, where I served for eight turbulent but very rewarding years. I had been an Equity deputy for innumerable companies, but the Annual General Meeting had too often descended into belligerent turmoil as different factions on the left attacked the right-wing leadership. I became secretary of a committee to draw up a constitution for Equity branches, at that time 'unofficial', in the hope that the AGM would be based on a branch and delegate structure in the trade union mould, and a form of Representative Conference was finally achieved in 1995. It had been a difficult time for Equity. The ending of the closed shop in 1988 gave employers the chance to cast inexperienced actors on diminished wages, and their written promises to employ only actors of 'proven professional experience' were often flouted, particularly in film and television. It was feared that Equity's influence and membership would diminish, but through sheer tenacity and hard work of staff and members the opposite has happened. Membership now stands at 46,000, though I often find that young actors don't realise how much they owe to Equity in terms of minimum wage, subsistence, sick pay, holiday money, legal aid, insurance, conditions of work, royalties and residuals, and pension contributions. It has been worth all those bum-numbing negotiations with managements, sometimes stretching over several years.

Production Seven

AN ALMEIDA DOUBLE:
IVANOV (1997); NAKED (1998)

fter thirty years in the theatre I had at last been offered a part in a Chekhov, not one of his great four but his first produced full-length play, *Ivanov*. I had seen the play twice before. In 1965 John Gielgud was attracted by its mixture of farce and tragedy, humour and compassion. At sixty-one he was clearly too old for the thirty-five-year-old Ivanov, and the production left me puzzled – what was Chekhov trying to say? I thought Gielgud failed to find enough variety in the part, and this lack of development in the character I also found in John Wood who played it at the Aldwych in 1976, but that is the great problem of the part, and in a sense of the play, as I was to discover.

Chekhov claimed he wrote the play in ten days in September 1887. Having established a reputation for comedy in both sketches and short plays, he was urged by Fiodor Korsh to write a full-length comedy for his private Moscow theatre, and Chekhov duly obliged calling *Ivanov* 'A Comedy'... 'light as a feather without a single longueur – an unprecedented plot... I wanted to do something original. I haven't produced a single scoundrel or a single angel'. But his hopes were dashed when he attended rehearsals. Ten had been promised, but only

Ivanov, Almeida, 1997. Maly Theatre Moscow.
L to R: Ralph Fiennes, Ian McDiarmid, Tony O'Donnell,
Bill Paterson, OFD, Jonathan Kent.

four took place and two of these were wasted. Only Ivanov and Anna knew their lines, and at the first performance, according to Chekhov, Riselevski as Count Shabielski (my part) 'did not utter a single sentence correctly. Literally not one. He just invented his own dialogue as he went along'. There were cheers and boos at the final curtain, and though Chekhov was elated that he had created 'a ferment in the theatre' by his originality he felt tired and disappointed. The Moscow notices were mainly good, although there were those who found it 'essentially immoral', and even 'horrible, disgusting cynical filth'. Chekhov set about rewriting it, particularly the act 4 denouement, as 'a Drama' for a St Petersburg production in 1889, where it was deemed a great success.

Why then this 'ferment in the theatre'? Ivanov is in one sense a stock figure in 1880s Russian novels and plays: the young liberal intelligentsia setting out to change things at a local level, building schools, improving health, rationalising farming, even trying to solve 'the peasant problem', but then losing heart at the government's political repression and the all-pervasive provincial skulduggery, and so descending into inertia and melancholy. It was this 'whining hero', this hackneyed 'superfluous man' that Chekhov was determined first to explain and then put an end to. His Ivanov fights his depression, refuses to become its victim, and stays active and eloquent in his disillusion (all quotations from David Hare's excellent adaptation):

> 'Don't take on the world. Don't tilt at windmills. Don't waste your time bashing your head against brick walls… at all costs stay away from progressive farming. And progressive education. And most of all, God help us! progressive rhetoric. It's a killer. Just pull your little shell over your head, and get on with your life… I did the other thing, and it has destroyed me.'

I was so pleased that Jonathan Kent, who ran the Almeida in tandem with Ian McDiarmid, had cast me as Count Shabielski. Although I had been constantly in work since the Hare trilogy the National and the RSC had had nothing for me, and *Kavanagh QC*, though rewarding in many ways, scarcely stretched me. With *Ivanov* Jonathan had thrown me a theatre life-line, and I was to do four further productions at the Almeida culminating in *Lear*: my stage career was back on track. I was also lucky to be part of a very talented cast. It must be like playing your instrument in a world-class octet: you revel in upping your game. Ralph Fiennes, who had played Hamlet under Jonathan's direction in 1995 and had had a great success in the movie *The English Patient* in 1996, was Ivanov. Harriet Walter was his Jewish wife Anna, dying of tuberculosis; Anthony O'Donnell, whom I knew well from the RSC, was Ivanov's irrepressible steward Borkin; Colin Tierney was the young doctor Lvov, blurting out offensive truths; Justine Waddell was the twenty-year-old Sasha, in love with Ivanov; Bill Paterson played her long-suffering father Lebedev and Rosemary McHale her miserly overbearing mother; and Diane Bull the bourgeois heiress Babakina desperate for social advancement.

The first act is particularly challenging: everyone is in a bad mood and very little happens. It is more like the opening of a Dostoevsky novel. Right from the start Ivanov runs the risk of losing our sympathy when he tells Anna, 'When I am in this state, I begin not to love you. That's why I run. When I do not love you, I have to get out of this house'. Anna feels that 'life has somehow short-changed me', and there is an aura of stalemate which never quite leaves the play. The second act, in complete contrast, is a party scene out of Gogol or Ostrovski, quite the most farcical Chekhov ever wrote. Zinaida's reluctance to provide any food other than gooseberry jam (she has made 'twenty barrels of the stuff') causes the First Guest to exclaim, 'I'd eat the carpet, I'd eat the paintings on the wall... if she came in now, I'd sink my teeth in her thigh... It'd be food! Supper at last! Raw, bloody hunks of your hostess'. This is the tenor of the high farce that Chekhov clearly delighted in. The third act starts in the same mood with the funniest drinking scene I have ever worked on, but this is soon supplanted by a succession of duologues between Ivanov and Lebedev, Lvov, Sasha and Anna, which is the real meat of the play. In the fourth act, the wedding of Sasha and Ivanov, Chekhov's first version had Ivanov suddenly dying, presumably of heart failure, but he soon realised this was 'amazingly bad', and after many rewrites he decided that Ivanov should pull out of the wedding, and persuade Sasha that she doesn't really love him: 'You're in love with an idea. You set yourself the task of saving me'. He feels the 'old Ivanov is stirring again'. 'Where on earth could we go... Time to get out of here, yes. Thank you, Sasha. Time to go... Let me free!' and he shoots himself – curtain. It's a more effective ending but difficult to persuade the audience of its abruptness. It is also the first of the pistol shots that bedevilled Chekhov's dramatic writing until *The Cherry Orchard*, though at least he contrived to have Vanya miss and Konstantin and Tusenbach die offstage.

Jonathan and Ian had a strong belief in 'high-definition acting', and this suited *Ivanov* particularly well, because the danger of the play is a descent into melancholic listlessness. Rehearsals proceeded at a furious pace. Ralph, faced with a character who barely develops until the final moments of the play, tackled the part in meticulous detail. Ivanov is suffering from what we would now call clinical depression, a state Chekhov as a doctor would often have observed. Ralph, shoulders hunched, experimented with a toneless voice, sudden bursts of pettish anger and barely suppressed violence, all the time burning with shame and self-contempt. The variety he managed to find in a state of constant despair I thought a tour de force. It encouraged everyone else to go for broke, Tony O'Donnell to bounce with devious, manipulative optimism, Colin Tierney to push his meddling, holier-than-thou honesty to the limit, and myself to wallow in misanthropy and self-loathing. In contrast Harriet Walter could highlight Anna's pain and understanding love, which she did superbly, and Bill Paterson could find Lebedev's humanity beneath his all-consuming disillusion.

I had seen the Moscow Arts Theatre at a World Theatre Season in a production of Gogol's *Dead Souls* and knew just how far Russian actors were prepared to push farce and melodrama. I was encouraged by this in the third-act drinking scene. Lebedev, Borkin and Shabielski are sitting in Ivanov's study getting plastered, arguing about the vital issues of whether the French or the Germans are the greater cowards and whether herring, caviar or gudgeon are the best accompaniments to vodka. Shabielski drunkenly upholds the gherkin: 'Man struggles up the lonely rockface of evolution, but for all his ingenuity he invents nothing finer than the pickled cucumber'. Kosykh enters and explains in excruciating detail how he came to lose all his money at cards the night before, so that we ended up, to Jonathan's delight, banging our heads against walls and table. Ian McDiarmid, brilliant in the part, carried on regardless. I was especially pleased to be playing such a harshly misanthropic character as Shabielski because I had come to fear that I had been pigeonholed as a saintly, unsuccessful vicar. It was a great release for me to be back in the realm of Falstaff.

In all this flurry of heightened activity David Hare's adaptation was an enormous ally. One critic later said, 'It's as if Hare had chucked away an old Victorian photograph and replaced it with a Howard

Hodgkin'. His adaptation, like the production, set out to make passive characteristics active. Often the words 'boring' and 'boredom' had been cut from the text; 'melancholy' had become 'anguish'. It reminds me of how my heart sinks whenever a Chekhovian character says 'Let's philosophise for a while'. I have a special interest in adaptation, perhaps through playing Shakespeare abroad and wondering when Shakespeare is opaque or chooses a multi-meaning word what decision should be made? David had worked from a literal translation, which he perhaps rashly left in the rehearsal room. Chekhov's dialogue is very plain and unadorned; he seems uninterested in highly crafted eloquence. For example, when Shabielski is imploring Ivanov to take him to the party he says in our literal version, 'It would be such fun to see those ne'erdowells'. Elisaveta Fen in the Penguin faithfully translates it as 'It might be amusing to see all those nitwits and bad eggs'. In David's version I said 'I need people I can despise, I need entertainment'. It's a brilliant line, much picked on by reviewers, but it is hardly what Chekhov wrote, though arguably what he intended. Perhaps the hardest decision concerns Ivanov's attack on his wife as a Jew. Innokenti Smoktunovski, a famous Hamlet, had refused to say the line during the fifteen years he played Ivanov at the Moscow Arts Theatre. In Fen's translation Ivanov says, 'I can hardly stop myself saying something horrible and insulting. Be quiet, Jewess!' Ronald Hingley has him call her 'Jewish bitch!' David went further: 'I cannot stop myself. The words will burst out of me. You dirty Jew!' The choice of this adjective, so often used by extreme antisemites, is horribly shocking – as Chekhov intended.

We approached the press night confident in ourselves, but apprehensive that our bravura would be too 'high-definition' for critical taste. The notices, however, were almost uniformly excellent for the adaptation, the direction and the acting, Ralph and Harriet were particularly praised. The drinking scene was much liked, and Stephen Fry later told me he 'just wanted the scene to go on for ever'. I was particularly pleased that William Fiennes in *Punch* thought my Shabielski 'a marvellous creation, pitched somewhere between Falstaff and Basil Faulty but with a slouchy gait all of its own'. Falstaff and Basil Faulty are two of my role models for the part, but the slouchy gait isn't character acting; it's just me. Most important of all the play came in for major re-evaluation. 'You leave the theatre in no doubt that you've seen a great production of a great, and unfairly neglected, play' (Charles Spencer). Last word to Jane Edwardes in *Time Out*: 'Those who usually find Chekhov too languid will be amazed'.

The production was a sell-out, with long queues for day tickets and returns. We heard of one woman in Calgary, Alberta, who, reading the notices, got on a plane, sat in the pavement queue all night, secured her ticket, went to the British Museum during the day, saw the performance and took the next flight back to Calgary. A transfer to the West End and New York seemed a possibility (Ralph's film commitments permitting), but the one definite booking was the Maly Theatre in Moscow, promoted by the British Council to the tune of £80,000. A Peter Brook *Cherry Orchard* with an American-British cast had been before us, but *Ivanov* would be the first all-British Chekhov to play in Moscow in English. Colossal cheek. The Maly's thousand-seater auditorium is very 1840 – unraked stalls, three circles of boxes set very far back, and Stalin's stage box with bullet-proof curtains. We dress rehearsed in front of 300 invited drama students, who were largely silent (no laughs), and then had a Q&A (rare in Russia). Many found our acting too energised; one even used the word 'hysterical'. Then one young woman said that although she didn't understand the language she was gripped by the human emotions and dilemmas onstage. The audience applauded frantically, and we applauded back in relief. But doubts remained.

The next day we were shown round the Moscow Arts Theatre, and we saw Stanislavski's carefully preserved dressing room. "On the block you will see the wig he wore for Count Shabielski in *Ivanov*." It is a very neat and sober piece of hair, clearly not the way I am playing the part. An American student told us that we have divided the Moscow Arts Theatre School, some relishing our exuberant freedom, where in the place of directorial concept (paramount in Russian theatre) power has been handed back to the actors, while others felt we were not 'inhabiting the roles', the great cry of Stanislavskian naturalism. We then had a press call with a hundred journalists. Most wanted to ask Ralph if he preferred stage to screen, is Ivanov the Russian Hamlet, etc. Towards the end a woman suddenly asked, "Aren't you tired of all this about the Russian soul? If you were doing Ibsen would you worry so much about the Norwegian soul?" Good question. A journalist doubted whether British youth knew much about Russian culture. I piped up: "My daughter's school urged her to read Dickens and Austen but she insisted she preferred Dostoevsky and Solzhenitsyn." The British Council were very grateful to me.

We start the play, determined to be truthful and enjoy ourselves: this is the happiest, most generous, least tortured group of actors I have ever worked with. The first half is sticky. The audience is unsure, despite being forty per cent English-speaking, perhaps because $30 tickets have been changing hands for $300. Laughs begin to come in the party scene, and when eighty-one-year-old Sam Beazley as Gavrila the butler exits we are startled by a storm of applause – the Russians revere old actors. In the great sequence of duologues with Ivanov in Act 3 the extremes of emotion begin to flow in the big theatre. The audience are fixated. This is their Chekhov, a man proclaiming the shame of human existence. Great applause and cheers at the end, many curtain calls, flowers for everyone. A Maly actor comes backstage to congratulate/ criticise us and tells me I am far too sloppily dressed for a Russian count: "Outdoors in Act 1 your tie must be done up." I bet Stanislavski's was. A second Russian says, "You can't cross the barrier, we like our Gogol funny, and our Chekhov sad," but a third argues, "How good to see the great Shakespearean emotions brought to bear on Chekhov." Two Russian directors think we are very radical, largely it seems because we dare to wave our arms about. Lena Krishtoff, our wonderful British Council interpreter, tells me her father hated Chekhov – too depressing. "This is Chekhov for Chekhov haters," she says.

In our remaining two free days we sightsaw and visited Chekhov's grave in the Novdevichi Convent Cemetery. It is very modest, outgunned by the nearby grandeur of Stanislavski's tomb – writers are routinely made to know their place. On our last day some of us were driven out to Melikhovo, fifty-odd miles from Moscow, the dacha where Chekhov lived in the 1890s until his tuberculosis drove him to the warmth of Yalta. Despite the fact that the house and writing hut, where he wrote *The Seagull* and *Uncle Vanya* and many of his greatest short stories, are post-war replicas, I am choked with emotion. Why do these ersatz buildings communicate so much when the homes of some literary figures convey so little? Is it the distance we have come, or that Chekhov loved the house and grounds so dearly and hated abandoning it, or simply that his work means so much to me? Hermione Lee is more prosaic about visits to writers' homes: it is 'a mixture of awe, longing, desire for inwardness, and intrusive curiosity'. We are given lunch, toasts are drunk, speeches are made – by Harriet in tentative Russian, by me in English. The hot cabbage, done two ways, is especially delicious.

Our reception on the last night is stunning, a standing ovation for minutes on end. Some beautiful red carnations are thrust into my hands, there is even a note: 'To Ralph, with love Natasha. Come back soon'. Ah well. The production had no further life, though a little later we did a radio version for the BBC, so it exists – unless the BBC has wiped it. On the plane home I read a Chekhov short story *Ariadne*. A character says, 'A Russian actor will never play the fool. Even in a comedy he wants to express his soul'. Chekhov evidently had numerous problems with the Russian theatre.

Postscripts: Diane Bull, so wonderfully talented and life-affirming as Babakina, knew she was living with a brain tumour, which, though removed, seldom goes away. She died a year later. Medics had advised her not to make the Moscow trip – she was so glad she did, as we all were.

Actors starting out are sometimes warned not to do walk-ons with a few lines, so it makes me doubly happy that Daisy Haggard and Justine Mitchell, our Fifth and Sixth Guests, have had such successful careers in the last twenty years.

Jonathan Kent had a second part for me at the Almeida, oddly enough another play where the central character commits suicide. *Vestire gli ignudi* (To clothe the naked), usually given the title *Naked*, was written by Luigi Pirandello in 1922, the same year as *Henry IV* and a year after *Six Characters in Search of an Author*, which I had performed in 1974. Ersilia Drei, a young woman who is destitute and at her wits' end, is exploited by four men in turn, the novelist Ludovico Nota (my part), the reporter Alfredo Cantavalle (David Sibley), her ex-fiance Franco Laspiga (Ben Daniels) and her ex-employer and lover Consul Grotti (Kevin McNally), though who is exploiting who, and who ends up the more powerful, or the more bereft, is one of the central themes of the play. Jonathan had told me he had hopes that Juliette Binoche might play Ersilia, and though for many weeks I thought this very unlikely, on day one of rehearsal there she was. Juliette was well known to us through her films, principally *The Unbearable Lightness of Being* (1988), *Three Colours Blue* (1993) and the recent *The English Patient* (1996), but although she had started out as a stage actress she had hardly been in a theatre since playing Nina in *The Seagull* at the Paris Theatre de l'Odeon ten years before. A film actor's persona and technique doesn't always translate successfully to the stage, especially if it isn't her first language. It seemed a considerable risk.

I had seen *Naked* before at the Oxford Playhouse in 1960 with Diane Cilento and Sean Connery (they married two years later), and knew that it explored ideas that were also familiar to me through *Six Characters*. The plays chart an ever-shifting reconstruction of the past, where human personality is revealed as endlessly multi-faceted. We all have a series of masks which are stripped away only to reveal a further mask. Ersilia is dismissed by the Grotti family for the death of a child in her care, and the play gradually reveals how the death came about, but the question of who finally bears responsibility is never resolved. She has come to Rome from Smyrna and, penniless, has been driven to prostitution and attempted suicide. She says her life has never had any shape or coherence. She looks for a role which would give her life meaning and dignity, but this is always snatched from her. She has no mask left, no reason for existence. She says at the end of the play (in Nicholas Wright's excellent translation):

> 'I thought I was nothing. And I wanted people to believe me... all we want from life is to be treated with respect. And the more we're covered in filth, the more we long for something beautiful to wear... so I invented a lover who'd left me. You were my beautiful dress... but they wouldn't allow me even that last small scrap of pretence. This time I'll die as I am. I'll die stripped bare'.

Ludovico Nota is a once-successful novelist, now out of fashion, who reads Ersilia's story in the paper and sees 'an entire novel spring to life'. He finds her and brings her to his rented lodgings, but for what purpose? Does he want her as a lover (his early pass is rejected), companion, muse, or simply source material? He presumably is uncertain himself. The first twenty minutes of the play are largely a duologue between Nota and Ersilia, and Juliette was a delight to work with, her English putting my A level French to shame, and she was alive to every nuance and fleeting change of direction. We laughed a great deal, particularly as she kept upstaging herself with her back to the audience and didn't seem to care. The part of Ersilia is an emotional tour de force. In Act 2 Nota and Laspiga 'watch in consternation: it's as though she's been transformed into a different person before their eyes'. In Act 3 she's called on to 'sob, shiver, shake all over, and fall in a faint as her weeping rises to a shrill note that might be mistaken for laughter'. Juliette inhabited all this with faultless instinct.

Nota is a familiar Pirandello figure, the commentator on the subsequent action. As we worked on the play, I felt him increasingly standing apart from the action, occupying as it were a separate time and place, perhaps writing the play himself as it went along. He's the author's mouthpiece: 'Facts are what one takes them to be, so in spirit they are facts no longer, just life that appears to be one way or another' (political leaders should be indebted to Pirandello). Ersilia proved annoyingly hard for Nota to pin down: 'I plucked a tale from life, and peopled it with my imagination. The last thing I needed was a set of heavy-handed interruptions from the source material. It's quite spoiled it for me', and he concludes, 'How odd. I thought she was my creation. Whereas I was hers'. Nota is sardonic, self-absorbed, ironic, forever brooding and grumbling, aware of his own and art's limitations, sometimes engaged, sometimes detached. It proved a wonderful part.

Paul Brown's set had a surreal quality. The stage was raked the 'wrong' way, rising towards the audience, which initially proved very odd to work on. Through the open bedroom door the wallpaper very slowly changed design and colour (it was on a great roll driven by a motor). The audience either didn't notice this or found it mesmerising and/or distracting. Pirandello attached great importance to the street noises outside; 'strada' is a key word in the play. The street is confusion, violence, terror, a reminder, particularly for Ersilia, of the lack of security in her life. In Act 1 there are the sounds of an old man crushed to death by a car and an ambulance arriving. John Leonard, our very experienced sound designer, had such difficulty in finding authentic Italian street and market sounds that one Saturday he flew to Rome, made a wide range of recordings (though surprisingly he didn't capture a car crash) and flew back the same day. When the costumes arrived, Juliette stared at the cheap tawdry dress the text demands and exclaimed, "But it's green! On the French stage green is unlucky." We stayed silent in alarm.

"Are you saying you'd rather not wear it?" Jonathan said cautiously.

"No, pouf... I don't care. I'll wear it."

Juliette's presence ensured that the play sold out, as Ralph Fiennes had for *Ivanov*, but fortunately the notices were uniformly good. All the hacks wanted to know if the film star could do it and, though some found her accent troubling at times, they fell over themselves in confirmation of her talent and her beauty. Benedict Nightingale wrote: 'Her torso writhes and her face seems to gash open as, hacking and wailing, she totters and twists to the floor. It is just one of the many striking, end-of-tether, bottom-of-the-pit moments in the bravest performance I've seen even at the ever-enterprising Almeida'. Jonathan's production was everywhere deemed 'masterly'; the whole cast was much praised.

Charles Spencer found me 'often blissfully funny, getting terrific value out of even unpromising lines'. But of course, like many actors, I paid more attention to the dissenting voice. John Gross wrote: 'I have got so used to Ford Davies giving impeccable performances [good so far] that it took me a while to concede that this time he doesn't. His Nota has some nice growly, humorous moments, but mostly you feel he's only presenting you with the man's external characteristics and he indulges in too much shouting and stomping around'. "Of course he's right," the insecurity in me says. "It's a surface performance and I shout too much." Terry Hands' criticism rises within me – "That wasn't more arrogant, it was just louder." Something to be watched.

It was a hot ticket; visiting celebrities ranged from Sean Connery (the 1960 Laspiga) to Tony Blair (a year into his premiership), who the following week addressed the French Assembly in his very Anglo-accented French and caused great mirth when he said, 'La semaine derniere j'ai vu Juliette Binoche dans *Nue*'. We all had a Monday and Tuesday off so that Juliette could go to Los Angeles to present the Best Supporting Actor Oscar, something she passionately didn't want to do. The night before her flight she somehow contrived to fall off the front of the stage, despite the fact it rose upwards. She damaged her ankle and after the show lay on the battered sofa in the green room, a beatific smile on her face: "I don't have to go to the Oscars." The Academy were not best pleased.

The press had made much of the fact that our company wage was £225 – Juliette told me her two expert massages a week swallowed most of that. As I was currently on the Equity Council I fronted a campaign to get a £275 minimum wage, which got a lot of coverage. Film stars have their uses. We transferred to the Playhouse Theatre for three months, fortunately on more money. John Peter had said that Juliette's stage presence was 'so compelling that it is hard to take your eyes off her'. On one occasion re-rehearsing at the Playhouse, when Kevin McNally and I were on an opposite side of the stage from Juliette, I remarked to Kevin that I never knew how to fill this moment, and he reassured me, "I shouldn't worry, nobody will be looking at us." A realistic, if not a very Method, solution.

1997–99: *Star Wars* and other movies

The *Ivanov* production had yielded something unexpected. Since Ian McDiarmid had played Emperor Palpatine/Darth Sidious in the first *Star Wars* films the casting director of the proposed prequels, Robin Gurland, came to see Ian in the play and asked me to audition for Sio Bibble, the Governor of Naboo. I had seen *The Return of the Jedi* no fewer than three times in 1983 as Miranda (aged seven) had so enjoyed it. George Lucas was I think so amazed at my detailed knowledge of Jabba the Hut that he offered me the part. We gathered to rehearse and discuss the script (a rare occurrence in film), and since George was so approachable I tentatively asked for some expression of protest as Bibble was being captured. To my surprise George obliged after some weeks with a longish speech, amounting to a complete defence of western democracy – though not much of it made the final edit.

Star Wars: The Phantom Menace, 1998.
[Four adult standing] L to R: Ewan McGregor, OFD,
Natalie Portman, Ian McDiarmid.

I soon found myself in Caserta, the baroque marble palace of the Kings of Naples, as governor to Queen Amidala played by the seventeen-year-old Natalie Portman. I shared one scene with one of her decoy queens, the twelve-year-old Keira Knightley, and when we found ourselves waiting for action at the top of a huge marble staircase discussing the relative merits of the Twickenham comprehensives the experience took on a bizarre quality. Since some characters and props were CGI'd in later, I felt at times like an eight-year-old, acting with people and crystal balls that I had to imagine. At one point I was a hologram, which involved my delivering the same speech eight times, each time facing a repositioned camera as I turned a complete circle. At the end George said, "That was amazing, Oliver, you said the same speech identically eight times." I thought, yes, George, that's what trained theatre actors resort to in long runs, unlike American film actors, who try to do something different on every take. The resulting film, *The Phantom Menace*, took over a billion dollars (no royalties for actors) and is, by general agreement, the least appreciated *Star Wars* film ever made. But I did have a dressing room between Samuel Jackson and Frank Oz. I had one scene in *Attack of the Clones* (2002) and a brief appearance at Amidala's funeral in *Revenge of the Sith* (2005). The three films netted me £26,000, a handsome sum but hardly a pension for life. George likes British actors because, theatre-trained, we can handle his dialogue and we are cheap. Fan mail from all over the world continues to pour in: after a wet matinee in Darlington, there will usually be a *Star Wars* autograph hunter or two at the stage door. There is even a small plastic figure of Sio Bibble – the ultimate accolade.

As I have written, it often pays to get to know assistant directors, and later that year Roger Michell found me a part in one of this early films, *Titanic Town*. The script was based on a semi-autobiographical novel by Mary Costello, reworked by Ann Devlin, about a Belfast woman (Julie Walters) who at the height of the Troubles in 1972 devised with a woman friend (Aingeal Grehan) a peace petition, which raised 25,000 signatures, to limit residential neighbourhood fighting. The IRA took this as an attack on them, and indeed the man from MI5 (Nicholas Woodeson) was very supportive of the petition probably because of the names it afforded. I played Whittington, Secretary of State for Northern Ireland, in real life William Whitelaw in Edward Heath's government, who was I think unaware of MI5's motives (how much the secret services keep from government is a much-debated area). Roger proved a watchful, shrewd director. He would say, "It's all there, just do less on the next take," and that came across not as criticism but validation. We filmed one scene on the steps of Stormont, which had been closed to the public since the suspension of devolved government in 1972 and which Mo Mowlam, the current Secretary, had broken precedent to give us access to. "Stormont should be user-friendly," she said. It's a very interesting film, serious with a vein of comedy, with a barn-storming performance by Julie Walters, who later went on to give a magnificent performance as Mo Mowlam herself. *Titanic Town* seems to have sunk without trace.

A television film which continues to gather audiences was Adrian Hodges' adaptation of *David Copperfield* (1999), directed by Simon Curtis. A very television-friendly cast had been deliberately chosen, with Maggie Smith as Betsey Trotwood and Ian McNeice as Mr Dick, Trevor Eve and Zoe Wanamaker as the Murdstones, Bob Hoskins as Micawber, Ian McKellen as Creakle, Nicholas Lyndhurst as Uriah Heep, and a host of other familiar names. I played Mr Wickfield, whom Uriah tries to ruin, and the young David who came to lodge with me was the ten-year-old Daniel Radcliffe. In the completed film David's childhood works well, but the adult David's turns of fortune (the less interesting part of the novel, I always think) are rather truncated. I particularly enjoyed Maggie Smith's company and her very down-to-earth approach to acting. On one occasion filming in Norfolk the watching crowds were so enthralled by the presence of Nicholas Lyndhurst and Dawn French that the two of them had to be driven the few hundred yards from set to base. 'Come on, Oliver," said Maggie. "We'll walk, nobody's interested in us."

Production Eight

LARKIN WITH WOMEN:
1999 & 2006

W hen I asked the director Alan Strachan why he had offered me the part of Philip Larkin he said I was his first and only choice. What my apparent affinity with Larkin says about me I hesitate to analyse. The play, *Larkin with Women*, to be premiered at the Stephen Joseph Theatre in Scarborough, was by a young playwright Ben Brown, who had had a considerable success with his *All Things Considered* in 1996 at Scarborough and Hampstead. I immediately recognised how beautifully the Larkin play was written, obviously well-researched, concise, fast-moving, funny, grittily realistic and finally very moving. Larkin was a great part of enormous variety. Like many of my generation I had bought his two final books of poetry, *The Whitsun Weddings* (1964) and *High Windows* (1974), and I had also seen two remarkable BBC Omnibus documentaries which contained among much else fascinating footage of his visiting a church with John Betjeman. Alan Strachan also sent me tapes of Larkin reading his poetry and, most valuable of all, his *Desert Island Discs* – valuable because an unscripted interview reveals so much more about character and voice. Larkin hated the interview and refused to listen to it when it went out. His favourite record? Not his speciality trad jazz, but Tallis' *Spem in alium*.

I visited Hull University Library, talked to the current librarian and studied the rather grand room that Larkin had designed for himself: he was proud of the fact that apart from the Vice-Chancellor he was the only person in the university with his own private lavatory. I also drove to the two houses that Larkin had lived in, 32 Pearson Park (top flat) and 105 Newland Park, and stared for a long time at the outsides, conscious that Monica Jones, his companion of over thirty years, was still living in the second. I thought of knocking on the door – "Hello, I'm about to play the love of your life" – but courage failed me. It is hard to quantify how useful such research is: I can only play the script, and my Larkin will inevitably be more me than Philip. But things rub off. They may affect the way I say a line, stress a word, light a cigarette, pour a drink, move about the stage, put my arms round a woman – a plethora of decisions that are made instinctively, or rather through immersing yourself in someone else's life.

I was, of course, also aware of Antony Thwaite's *The Selected Letters* (1992) and Andrew Motion's Larkin biography (1993) which had so affected both critical and public opinion. As Motion himself later wrote, 'The nation's favourite poet, lonely but loveable, was condemned [by many readers] as a misogynist, a racist and a porn addict... The teddy bear turned out to be a grizzly'. Larkin certainly relished for a time soft-porn magazines (this was in the play, and the cause of much farcical business), but they were hardly central to his life. His racism was largely confined to showing off letters to Kingsley Amis and other non-pc right-wingers, but he did on rare occasions use expressions like 'wops, frogs, fuzzy-wuzzies'. I discovered what I thought was the measure of his racism in a story his secretary Betty Mackereth told. A student who was exceptionally dilatory at returning library books was sent to Larkin, who duly reprimanded him and later said to Betty, "You didn't tell me he was black." He then stopped himself, according to Betty, and added, "Not that that makes any difference." Larkin was a great lover of traditional jazz and hero-worshipped certain black musicians, particularly Louis Armstrong.

Larkin with Women, Scarborough, 1999.
OFD (Larkin), Carolyn Backhouse (Monica).

Larkin liked the company of women throughout his life and was certainly no misogynist, though he often revealed himself as misanthropic. Small wonder. His father Sidney, sometime Treasurer of Coventry Council, was a great admirer of Germany and what he perceived as the economic and social progress they had made under Hitler. Philip's dislike of 'abroad' may stem from his enforced teenage trips to a Nazi-bannered Germany in 1936 and 1937. He characterised his childhood as 'fear and boredom': 'certainly the marriage left me with two convictions: that human beings should not live together, and that children should be taken from their parents at an early age'. There was something solitary about him throughout his life, despite his affairs and his occasional bursts of gregariousness. In many of his poems he watches other people having affairs and getting married with a mocking, envious, ironic detachment. His fear of sentimental emotion was such that even in his much-admired paean to spring in *The Trees* (1967) that ends 'Begin afresh, afresh, afresh' he would write 'bloody awful tripe' beside it. He had no wish to be a London-orientated celebrity. Malcolm Bradbury wrote in a programme note:

> 'He was the poet of the provinces, the places slightly away from it all. He loved Hull, "isolate city spread along the water", because it was the end of the line. Ordinary people in ordinary places mattered to him, he liked Hull's "cut-price crowd, urban yet simple", the fish-dock, the drab department stores, the war-bombed old town by the harbour.'

I could relate to this: I spent a week on tour in Hull in 1973 (the year before *High Windows* and his ejection from his beloved Pearson Park flat), and I remember Zoe Wanamaker and I catching a battered ferry across the Humber (some years before the bridge) and arriving in a thick sea mist to an ancient wooden jetty that Dickens, or rather Pip, would have recognised.

Many who worked with Larkin described him as 'great fun' in company, with a dry, mocking sense of humour. Ben Brown mined his letters for their elegantly crafted wit. 'When I was a child I thought I hated everybody, but now I realise it's just children I don't like.' 'Virginity is just an undeveloped talent.' 'I have a theory that holidays evolved from the mediaeval pilgrimage, and are essentially a kind of penance for being so happy and comfortable in one's daily life.' Clive James argued that at his best Larkin is as funny as Woody Allen. However, James did bizarrely suggest that the actor to play him should be Jack Nicholson, though he admitted it would entail a few rewrites: 'Your mom and pop, hah, hah. They fuck you over, right?'

Ben's play covered thirty years of Larkin's life, from ages thirty-three to sixty-three (1955–85). The core of the play was his relationship with three women: Monica Jones, Maeve Brennan, an assistant librarian and his most 'romantic' attachment, and Betty Mackereth, his secretary and confidante. Larkin and Monica met in 1947 at Leicester University, when he was an assistant librarian and Monica an English lecturer, and became lovers in 1950. They were the same age, both Oxford firsts, and John Sutherland, a Leicester student at the time, described Monica as 'smarter, wittier, and (not infrequently) better read that many of her colleagues'. She was a very flamboyant dresser, her mini-skirts often shorter than her students. Though brilliant and unorthodox, she held 'it is more distinguished not to publish' and consequently was never promoted (many academics of that period thought it more distinguished not to have a PhD). Maeve Brennan was a junior librarian when Larkin arrived at Hull in 1955, and after tutoring her through her library exams declared his attraction in 1960, though as Maeve was a strict Roman Catholic they took fifteen years to become lovers. She dumped him in 1978 when he asked her to accompany him to a National Theatre visit to Hull with *Larkinland* but not to come with him to the reception afterwards as she wasn't, in her words, his 'official companion – that was Monica'. Larkin had in fact already started a relationship with his secretary of eighteen years Betty Mackereth – 'I'd have asked you sooner, only I didn't want you to think I was T. S. Eliot... he married his secretary'. Betty later said marriage to Larkin would have been a nightmare.

All three women were still alive in 1999 and had read the play and vetted it, though we never discovered what Monica, a very astute critic, really thought of it. Ben's play I came to realise underplays the torture that Monica went through from Larkin's lack of commitment. Maeve had thought that the Motion biography 'doesn't convey his sensitivity or kindness or compassion or the fun of being in his company', and she had concerns that the play might be too unsympathetic or that the actor might do a hatchet job on him. Ben said that he changed some things in the play accordingly, but that they couldn't entirely agree about Larkin's character. Maeve's misgivings were blown up by the media, and gave the production some notoriety, both welcome and unwelcome: it ensured that most of the first-string critics came to the first night, editors sensing a possible scandal, but it increased the pressure on all of us. Monica was too ill to attend the play (or chose not to), but Maeve and Betty came and apparently enjoyed it. Maeve in fact saw it three times and became quite a devotee, forming a friendship with Suzy Aitchison, who played her.

Rehearsals had been largely a delight. Alan Strachan, the best-read man I have ever encountered, is an expert in both the rhythms of comedy and the 'traffic' of the stage, one of Alan Ayckbourn's directors of choice. It was a composite set, one half Larkin's office, the other three different sitting rooms (with much the same furniture). There were seventeen scenes, interspersed with jazz and my pre-recorded readings of various poems, and Alan managed to keep the whole thing flowing with the minimum of apparent changes, though my rapid changes of costumes were a nightmare, especially when loose-knotted ties jammed. He had cast the women perfectly. Carolyn Backhouse had all of Monica's sharp-tongued intellectual forthrightness and, as many critics noted, a 'long-limbed sexiness' to boot. Suzy Aitchison brought great tenderness with a strong comedic edge to Maeve, and Suzy Blake had all of Betty's down-to-earth sparkiness. For an actor starved of 'romantic' parts it was a revelation being allowed to press my attentions on three very different women.

Although I am tall and balding I don't look very much like Larkin. I have a round face, while Larkin's was long and oval, similar, as he himself admitted, to Eric Morcambe. But once I had dyed my hair dark brown (black is too tricky a dye for someone with fair hair) and adopted his heavy black-rimmed glasses the approximation was passable. The voice was a different matter. I listened to the tapes constantly and achieved quite a reasonable imitation, though I am not a gifted mimic. The snag was that Larkin's natural delivery was rather slow and uninflected, monotonous even, not helpful for a fast-paced two-hour show which Larkin dominates. After many trials I finally jettisoned his accent and used my own lugubrious register which contained just a hint of Larkin. Tom Courtenay, in his subsequent one-man show, *Pretending to Be Me* (2002–03), made by his own cheerful admission no attempt to look or sound like Larkin, while Hugh Bonneville, in a television rip-off of the play, adopted a quite accurate accent.

The first half of the play that charts the pornography, chaise-longue sex with Monica and his eventual seduction of Maeve 'would make for an enjoyable if lightweight evening', Charles Spencer wrote, 'what deepens the play is Brown's depiction of the remorseless way in which almost all of Larkin's worst fears came true... You see the passage of time depriving him of almost all consolation except perhaps that of drink'. The second half began with Larkin reading a stanza from *Aubarde*, perhaps the greatest twentieth-century poem on the approach of death. Clive James wrote that 'it unites other writers in a common worship. People agree about its quality who agree about nothing else. Harold Pinter can recite the whole poem from memory while seated at the dinner table' ("That must have made the evening go with a swing," Larkin would have commented). But there was a terrible price to pay. As Ben made Larkin say: 'After my in-a-funk-about-death poem there doesn't seem much more to say... poetry abandoned me'. Margaret Thatcher offered him the poet laureateship, and he felt he had to turn it down, though 'the thought of being the cause of Ted Hughes being buried in Westminster Abbey is hard to live with'. Witty to the last. As he lay dying of cancer in hospital, visited by all three women, Monica meeting Maeve for the first time, Larkin realised that he'd made a bad bargain in putting poetry before personal commitment – 'There's nothing to write which is better than life itself'.

The notices were excellent, particularly for Alan Strachan's 'superb production' (Susannah Clapp). All three women were much praised. Charles Spencer wrote that I was 'an absolute master of baffled, flawed humanity, marvellously capturing the poet's mix of sardonic humour, gauche tenderness, painful honesty and grumbling stoicism. He may indeed be a touch too sympathetic...' This last reservation, that Larkin was a good deal pricklier and meaner than my and Ben's portrayal suggested, was taken up by many with some justification. 'What about the racism?' some grumbled, but neither Ben nor I thought it at all central to his character. Some critics wanted more about the mother, and here I was with them. Eva was undoubtedly the fourth woman in Larkin's life, and it may be that his ambivalence towards her prevented him from committing to Monica through marriage. I begged Ben to include a little more about Eva, if only Larkin's feelings about his dreaded Christmas visits: 'To hell with Christmas. Let us have peace, and not all this blasted cooking and eating (and washing up)'. Yet when Eva finally died in 1977 Larkin was bereft: "What am I going to do for Christmas?" he wailed. Ben, however, was unmoveable. He is what I call a 'watchmaker'; every cog whirs into its neighbour. His writing is so precise, so economical, so considered that it's hard to persuade him to change a word, let alone include a new sentence. The television rip-off did include the mother, wonderfully played by Eileen Atkins, and I felt justified.

The production did not transfer, despite the many optimistic presumptions. Attempts were made to set up a tour – four characters, one composite set, it couldn't be that expensive (and I'm certainly not expensive). In 2002 the West Yorkshire Playhouse presented a mini Larkin festival with Ben's play and Tom Courtenay's one-man show. Because the play centred on Larkin's female relationships Tom deliberately left that aspect out of his script, with the unfortunate result that, viewed on its own, Larkin came across as an asexual hermit. Tom's triumph was to so meld the poems into the narration, the one arising out of the other, so that it was often hard to tell which was which. His show transferred to the West End, was a success, and that ensured that the play would not – Larkin had been sufficiently dealt with. The play has been revived at various regional theatres, and in 2006 the Orange Tree in Richmond presented it with Carolyn Backhouse and myself, Amanda Royle as Maeve and Jacqueline King as Betty. It was once again a sell-out and received four-star notices. Alan Strachan tried to persuade Michael Codron, with whom he had often worked, to put the production into the West End. But the brute truth is that I was not a big enough name to carry the play on my own. We learn where we are in the pecking order in both theatre and movies. A director once told me I had been his first choice for a major movie role, but the American moneybags said they'd never heard of me and certainly couldn't put my name above the title.

Larkin and the two plays at the Almeida had vindicated my belief that I had an instinct for comedy. It is one of the regrets of my early career that I played too many doctors, priests and governors, unsmiling authority parts, when I should have developed my 'rubbery face' as a clown. When I read a script I always see the potential for comedy. Just as I am tone deaf to singing I can usually sense when actors show themselves tone deaf to comedy. It's a kind of mental torture if you're onstage with them and can't point out 'if you'd just stress that word, if you'd just leave a slight pause there, if you turned that into a question...' Laughter is such an ice-breaker. The actor enters, gets their first laugh, and you can feel the audience relax – 'there's a chance that we're going to like this character' – though it's a rapport not perhaps available to you when playing Titus Andronicus. I know actors can be spectacularly wrong about their own strengths and weaknesses, but I trust that Peter Dews was right when he said in 1961, "You have the twinkle, lad." I am a Malvolio not a Hamlet, a Falstaff not a Macbeth.

2000–02: *Poirot* and Almeida Shakespeares

I had twice turned down uninteresting parts in hour-length television *Poirots*, so I was not thrilled when Belinda Wright, my agent, said I'd been offered The Doctor in a two-hour *Poirot*. The script had been sent, however, and I saw to my amazement that it was *The Murder of Roger Ackroyd*. I phoned my agent: "Belinda, when you say 'The Doctor' do you mean Dr James Sheppard?"

A long pause, then, "Yes, Dr Sheppard."

"Belinda, that is one of the most famous parts in the whole of Agatha Christie." Christie claimed that she was challenged by her brother-in-law, and later by Lord Mountbatten, to write a novel entirely narrated by the murderer. She succeeded, though earlier examples of narrator-murderer have since been unearthed. Dr Sheppard tells the story, just leaves out a lot of backstory and the forty-five minutes in which he kills Ackroyd. Poirot, in retirement in the village, works it out through a process of elimination and leaves Sheppard twenty-four hours to take a terminal sleeping draught. As Sheppard writes in the famous conclusion to the book: 'So let it be veronal. But I wish Hercule Poirot had never retired from work and come here to grow vegetable marrows'. Many crime afficionados think it is Christie's masterpiece, and in 2013 the Crime Writers' Association voted it the best crime novel ever. Before turning it down always check that the Doctor/Butler/Cook isn't the best part.

The adaptation was by the immensely experienced Clive Exton and he assured me that he couldn't find a way to indicate that the story was told by Sheppard, so he had written a conventional linear treatment and made major alterations to the plot. The original would have placed Sheppard at the centre of the film, and I couldn't help concluding that the producers had insisted that Poirot remain at the centre. I remember Chris Kelly, the *Kavanagh QC* producer, telling me that ITV didn't like John Thaw being off the screen 'for longer than 3½ minutes' (the precision of that ½!). The same probably with Poirot. Because television crime drama insists on a second murder to keep the audience hooked and provide a good ad break, Exton had Sheppard go on to murder the butler, who seemed to be getting suspicious. Instead of the chilling, downbeat ending he had substituted a wham-bam chase in the huge turbine hall of Sunbury Waterworks where, firing my gun, I (or rather my stunt double) fell to a spectacular death. Before this finale I had been handed the explanatory speech, traditionally reserved for the detective. The speech was punctuated by long flashbacks illustrating the murder, so I had only learnt the passages where I would be on camera. Two days before shooting the scene the director Andrew Grieve told me he wanted to shoot the entire seven-minute speech in one continuous take, as I moved around the room, secretly palmed the gun from Selena Cadell and made my escape, a complicated manoeuvre. Feverishly I learnt the entire speech. On the first take I dried after a minute and felt I was never going to make it. Summoning every relaxation technique, every confidence boost I knew, I started again and this time got to the end, secreted the gun, and ran out. I like to think the crew applauded, but that's probably my fantasy. My admiration for David Suchet for learning all those fearsome unravellings knows no bounds. The episode was a success, Christie aficionados were livid, and a better adaptation of Christie's masterpiece remains to be made.

While we were rehearsing *Naked* in 1998 Jonathan Kent had asked me if I would like to play King Lear in 2002. I thought about it for twenty seconds and said yes. "To get you back into Shakespeare mode why don't you do the Almeida's millennium project, *Richard II* and *Coriolanus* with Ralph Fiennes? You could do Menenius in *Coriolanus* and either Gaunt or York in *Richard*." I agreed, and immediately chose York. Gaunt has the famous speech and can go home early (unless he's required to play Salisbury and the Groom), but York is by far the more interesting part. The setting for the two productions was to be the Gainsborough Studios by the Regents Canal in Shoreditch, where Hitchcock had made his early films *The Lodger*, *The 39 Steps* and *The Lady Vanishes*. The studios were due to be demolished so we could do what we liked with them. Paul Brown set about this with relish, utilising a great crack that ran up the back wall, which symbolised the fractured nations of England and Rome. For *Richard* he devised a grass floor, not a smooth lawn but a real meadow (grown in a field in the Midlands and changed every two weeks), and to ensure its unevenness he placed odd polystyrene lumps under the turf – lethal to act on. For Bolingbroke and Tullus Aufidius Jonathan cast Linus Roache, very similar to Ralph Fiennes in many ways so that they were a mirror image of one another. Volumnia and the Duchess of York, my wife, was the great and formidable Barbara Jefford, fifty years earlier Isabella to Gielgud's Angelo in a Peter Brook *Measure for Measure* at Stratford.

I never felt somehow the *Richard* caught fire (Jonathan later said he wished he'd done it modern), but *Coriolanus* was a different matter. Ralph, who had seemed perfect casting for Richard and questionable for the warrior Coriolanus, turned out to identify far more with the warrior, and in 2011 went on to make a very successful modernised film version of *Coriolanus*, with Brian Cox in my part (an unlikely clash). I had always wanted to play Menenius, having watched Graham Crowden's performance when I played one of the tribunes for the RSC in 1977. Always observe critically a part you've had your eye on. Menenius has to use a lot of voice when addressing the crowds, especially in a large space like the Gainsborough with its poor acoustic. After one matinee I was approached by a man whom I later learnt was a Russian conductor (identity unknown). "You, my friend," he said, "have a voice that can split bricks. You should be singing…" – pause – "…Alberich in *The Ring*." Alas, Bayreuth will never have that pleasure. York, on the other hand, is one of the great underrated parts in Shakespeare. He is a version of the Common Man, or rather Common Duke. Put in charge of the kingdom while Richard is in Ireland, a role he doesn't want and can't fulfil, he is faced by a rampant Bolingbroke, outnumbered and out-manoeuvred. His only solution is to change sides, though with reservations bordering on the comedic:

> It may be that I will go with you; but yet I'll pause,
> For I am loath to break our country's laws.
> Nor friends nor foes to me welcome you are.
> Things past redress are now with me past care. 2.3.168–71

In essence he says to the audience – "Well, what else could I do?" The play ends with a scene of straight farce (often foolishly cut) where his wife pleads with Henry IV for their traitorous son Aumerle's pardon while York insists on his punishment. Barbara Jefford and I enjoyed ourselves hugely. I first realised what a wonderful part York is when Michael Bryant played it at the National to Fiona Shaw's Richard, though Michael had the knack of making any part, however small, seem supreme.

We toured the plays to Tokyo, where we played in a warehouse usually reserved for rock concerts, and with students stuck in their texts I lost all my laughs. In 2000 the Japanese economy was still booming and many Western musicians were in town. Ashkenazi and

Sting came to a matinee, and Sting told me he thought he'd come to *Richard II*, "But when you started on the Belly speech I thought it's got to be *Coriolanus*," so he definitely knows his Shakespeare. Then on to the Brooklyn Academy, where we played not the old opera house as in 1976 but Harvey BAM, a more intimate converted vaudeville theatre which Peter Brook had advised them to leave in its distressed state. The American audience particularly caught on to *Coriolanus*. It was September 2000, two months before the presidential election, and young Americans relished posh Coriolanus having to go down, like rich Bush and Gore, to seek the common vote. Audiences also understood York's change of sides, comparing it to some rich senator who, having opposed a fellow presidential nominee, decides he's better ingratiate himself once his fellow triumphs – plenty of examples there. The Critics Circle, DramaDesk, nominated me for Best Supporting Actor. I did the usual tourist things including visiting the gift shop at the very top of the World Trade Centre – almost exactly a year before 9/11. The thought of that shop on the fatal day has never left me.

The Way We Live Now is one of Trollope's most interesting novels, many think it his masterpiece. Andrew Davies had done his usual excellent adaptation for television, and David Suchet was to play the corrupt financier Melmotte, a kind of Robert Maxwell figure. I was interviewed for the part of a newspaper editor but then offered Mr Longestaffe, a more central part but a very boring man, another piece of casting I'd rather not analyse. Trollope had made a careful study of a major landowner, heavily in debt and hoping, disastrously, that Melmotte investments would bail him out. 'Mr Longestaffe had not any very lively interests in life', Trollope wrote. 'He did not read much; he did not talk much; he was not specially fond of eating and drinking, he did not gamble, and he did not care for the farm. To stand about the door and hall and public rooms of the clubs to which he belonged, and hear other men talk politics or scandal, was what he liked better than anything else in the world'. He had stood for parliament several times without much enthusiasm, never been elected, and thought a barony should come to him by right, not by any worldly achievement. A fascinating study of a petulant, small-minded, upper-class nonentity, a part that can work well in a novel but very difficult to make interesting on film.

He and his wife (Joanna David) had a daughter Georgiana (Anne-Marie Duff), who had rejected various dull suitors but finally, since marriage was a class prerequisite, plumped for a fifty-year-old Jewish banker Mr Brehgert (Jim Carter). Longestaffe was appalled, and to my dismay the scene where he has an antisemitic rant was scheduled for the second day of shooting. It is always galling when your most difficult scene comes at the very start, before you have had a chance to establish and work on your character. Brehgert tells Georgiana that he can't afford a Mayfair house immediately, but she declares that three years in a Fulham house 'would be dreadful'. Brehgert, to her surprise and mortification, breaks off the engagement, leaving her sulking in approaching spinsterhood. *The Way We Live Now* is a beautifully made and cast four-parter, one of David Suchet's best performances, and won various awards.

Production Nine

KING LEAR (2002)

I had had three years to think about Lear, probably too long. "Better do it while you've still got the energy," said Jonathan Kent. There is no right age to play Lear: many have tackled it in their forties – Paul Scofield, Brian Cox, Anthony Hopkins (though he played it again for a television film when eighty). At fifty you still have the energy, at seventy the empathy. I will be sixty-two, ideal compromise or neither one thing or the other? David Hare, who directed Hopkins' first Lear, tried to cheer me in an excess of frankness: "Look, there are eleven scenes, and no one can do them all. You're bound to be able to do some." The part seems to be some sort of ultimate... accolade, test, exploration of the human condition?

"I'm trying not to see it as a test," I tell Fiona Shaw.

"Naturally," she says, "But of course it is."

On tour in 2000 I made a study of what happens in each scene, without coming to any conclusions, i.e. at the start of the play Kent and Gloucester appear to think the kingdom is going to be divided between Albany and Cornwall, yet Lear then reveals he's already decided on a tripartite division and that Cordelia will get the best third – and so on. I then went through the text meticulously noting what other characters say about Lear, while not forgetting that their comments may be 'enemy propaganda' (a favourite Terry Hands phrase). Goneril calls him 'rash even at his best', and 'old fools are babes again'. Regan calls him 'rash, wilful, weak, unconstant', and, very perceptively, "'Tis the infirmity of his age, yet he hath ever but slenderly known himself'. I realise that the three daughters are clear examples of the recent concept of 'Birth Order': Goneril the assertive eldest, Regan the rebel/people-pleasing middle child, and Cordelia the favoured youngest. Psychologically Shakespeare usually got there first.

After my first tour of the text I do a lot of reading – R. A. Foakes, Frank Kermode, Ted Hughes, Harold Bloom, Stanley Wells, Kieran Ryan, Jonathan Bate and many others. I compile a list of outstanding problem areas and write mini-essays on them: I'm intrigued by the changes Shakespeare makes to the accepted story-line after the first two acts; by the use of the Fool; Alan Howard's suggestion to me that in a large theatre you tend to play 'King' (what he does) and in a smaller space 'Old Man' (what is done to him); whether Lear really goes mad; does the play demonstrate 'the very absence of tragic purpose', a meaningless existential universe; or is it a study of suffering that leads in the end to love, of Cordelia to Lear, Edgar to Gloucester. As a historian the hundred knights interest me as they are the outward symbol of Lear's clash with Goneril and Regan. Shakespeare increased the customary sixty knights to a hundred; in Jacobean terms each knight would have had a squire and two or three servants plus female 'camp followers'. Queen Elizabeth's annual progresses were accompanied by six hundred carts carrying equipment. James I, in the audience for early court performances, would have been very alive to the importance of all this. It was about status, Lear's need to retain 'all the additions to a king'. Alas it's only in the Russian Kozinstov film that one gets any impression of this; we'll be making do with three knights behaving as badly as possible.

Does all this research help or hinder? Why not just play the text as you would any other fictional script? Perhaps I'm just covering my tracks, no stone has been left unturned. When I was researching my doctorate I was plagued for months by the fear that I was missing some vital source, some key archive, which everyone else in the field was aware of. With Lear I fear the moment when somebody says, 'Surely you can see it's all about Catholic and Protestant Christianity', or 'Obviously the key is a rare form of Alzheimer's'. But creativity is so much about choice: at this early stage I'm trying to open up as many options as possible. It struck me that all this research, if added to a rehearsal diary, might be publishable, and to my delight Nick Hern agreed. With further additions of a chapter sketching in Lears from Garrick to Ian Holm, a brief manual on acting in Shakespeare and conversations with Jonathan Kent and John Barton *Playing Lear* was published by Nick Hern Books in 2003. It has since sold out but is now available as an e-book.

Jonathan and I meet usually once a fortnight and discuss play, production, cuts, set and casting. It's an important production for Jonathan, his last at the Almeida after twelve years. So many artistic directors have signed off with *Lear*, Glen Byam Shaw at Stratford, Max Stafford-Clark at the Royal Court, Richard Eyre at the National. Not so much a test then, more a culmination of achievement? Jonathan and I agree that Lear abdicates because he fears his mind is going and that uncontrollable anger is his undoing – the words 'anger', 'wrath' and 'mad' (then, as now, a synonym for angry) are threaded throughout the text. I can relate to that. I had a wealthy great uncle who apparently in his last years kept losing his temper with his family in a quite unbalanced way. When I asked Jonathan why he had cast me he talked about power, authority and verse-handling, but then unexpectedly added 'also a child-like quality'. That I found very interesting: will it be borne out?

Jonathan and his designer Paul Brown have given a lot of thought to the set. Jonathan had originally wanted to do it in a panelled room in one of the Inns of Court. We are now performing, because of extensive reconstruction of the Almeida Theatre, in a converted bus garage in King's Cross, but the panelled room motif has been transplanted to a newly constructed auditorium and stage. When the play moves out of rooms into the open air of Act 3, always a design problem, the panels will gradually collapse, revealing a large void behind. It's an exciting concept, but I fear its literalness, signalling too crudely the collapse of Lear's mind. Sets should not tell an audience what is in an actor's mind. There also seems to be a confusion about whether this a chamber production or something more monumental. I voice my misgivings, am reassured, but not totally reconciled. I watch an exemplary production of Brian Friel's *Faith Healer* in King's Cross on a large bare stage receding into darkness and rather wish it was the set, or absence of set, for our *Lear.*

We settle on a cut text, always a problem in *Lear* since there are significant omissions and additions between the second quarto and the folio. We reduce it to 2,700 lines, which optimistically means three hours' playing time. The casting I leave to Jonathan and Fiona Weir, with the great Mary Selway advising. Some castings come easily, some after protracted audition and negotiation. Anthony O'Donnell is the Fool, Paul Jesson Kent, David Ryall Gloucester, all RSC stalwarts. Tom Hollander and James Frain are Edgar and Edmund, Suzanne Burden and Lizzy McInnerny Goneril and Regan, and a talented newcomer Nancy Carroll Cordelia. My Orange Tree friend Paul Shelley is Albany (never undercast Albany) and has played Lear himself, as had David Ryall. No pressure there. Costumes will range from 1930s to contemporary: it pays with *Lear* never to be too specific about place and period. The British Council are keen on a tour, and there is considerable interest in Europe, Australia and the USA (particularly Chicago). We are to do seven shows a week – no midweek matinee, thank heaven. Whether my body and voice will last out twelve weeks and an extensive tour remains to be seen. When I was doing a TV show with Albert Finney I asked him whether we would ever see his Lear. "What, eight Lears a week? Huh... I don't think so." And we never did. I give myself eight weeks to learn it. It was David Suchet, when faced with Iago, who first advised me that knowing a major text (no interpretation imposed) is the equivalent of two weeks' extra rehearsal.

One of Jonathan's strengths as a director is that he had once been an actor – and a good actor at that. It's not imperative that a director knows how to act or that an orchestral conductor was once a former player, but it helps. Just as the conductor will understand why the oboes are having difficulties with a certain passage, so a theatre director will appreciate why an actor seem stuck or dissatisfied with a particular scene. Terry Hands once said to me, "It's not my job to teach people how to act," and I wish I had replied that it should be your job to help actors to unlock their potential. Directors often act simply as a perceptive audience member reporting to an actor the effect of what they are doing and suggesting what they might do to improve this effect, without realising that something other is holding them back. Among much else a director needs to be a psychologist. In a production of *Uncle Vanya* the actress playing Yeliena had clearly lost confidence to the director's puzzlement, and it took Anna Calder-Marshall as Sonya to fathom the reason, that she didn't think she was attractive enough for the part. I prompted Anna to suggest to her that because Vanya and Astrov are starved of new female visitors and find her attractive it doesn't mean she has to be a radiant beauty. To appear to be giving 'notes' to a fellow actor is hazardous, and I usually back off. Wendy Hiller once told me Gielgud had a good formula: he used to say, "I have something I think you'll like." I wish I'd tried that.

On 10 December 2001 we finally get to day one of rehearsal. Scene 1 is always a difficulty. The problem is the lack of backstory: why is Lear abdicating and dividing up his kingdom, when did his wife die, why does he have a daughter as young as Cordelia, how long have Goneril and Regan been married? The old play *King Leir* (author unknown), which Shakespeare presumably knew, answers many of these but takes 700 lines, a third of the play, to do it (Albany and Cornwall have recently been imposed by Lear on his elder daughters, etc.), but Shakespeare treats his version as the start of as folktale – you just have to accept the story starts here. John Barton counselled me not to worry too much about it on the grounds that halfway through the performance the audience will have forgotten about scene 1 – possibly true but not one of John's more helpful pieces of advice. The play and the part of Lear start in a measured way, but from Cordelia's 'Nothing' it turns into a three-hour sprint. Words tumble out, both Lear and Cordelia say things in the heat of the moment which they probably later regret – Lear certainly does. I am immediately faced with the anger problem. He warns Kent 'Come not between the dragon and his wrath' and over a hundred lines later he is still saying to Cordelia 'Better thou / Hadst not been born than not to have pleased me better'. Does he seethe with uncontrollable anger throughout, does the anger come and go, is it mixed with different emotions? Anger is such a difficult and tiring emotion to play, so hard to find variety, and it is not a state the audience, especially a British audience, find sympathetic – 'Temper, temper, Lear'.

Then comes the confrontation with Goneril, and he realises Cordelia's 'Nothing' was a 'small fault', and *striking his head* says 'Beat at this gate that let thy folly in / And thy dear judgement out'. This leads to the terrible curse on Goneril, 'Into her womb convey sterility'. At first this seemed angry yet again, but there is something about its cold implacability that pushed me in an opposite direction and I became quiet and steely. It's partly the need to find variety, but it's also another aspect of patriarchal dominance, or even manic instability. I'm determined in the early stages of the play that Lear should not be likeable – hopefully he will become more sympathetic as his trials mount. In the following scene 1.5 I have this image of Scofield sitting quietly on a bench, scarcely listening to Alec McCowen's Fool. But Jonathan still wants me angry, furiously packing up to leave Goneril, and I submit – don't graft on favourite moments from other productions. The anger turns out to be a helpful contrast to two key moments of revelation: 'I did her wrong' and 'O let me not be mad'. I find these two moments central to Shakespeare's Lear. Hamlet or Macbeth would have enlarged on both for at least fifteen lines, but Lear has no such powers of introspective understanding, though it would make the part so much easier to play. Out of frenzied activity I suddenly stop, stare out front, and say 'I did her wrong', and I would have been happy for a half-minute pause before the Fool says 'Canst tell how an oyster makes his shell?' Sometimes Tony allowed me ten seconds.

Jonathan watches me like a hawk. "Don't get contemplative, don't get measured, don't get benign, don't get ironic. These are all Oliver's attributes, and they are all very English, but they are not Lear's." It's a tough discipline for me. Jonathan is also not interested in the humour in the play, and here we are at odds. I believe in the old maxim: 'In tragedy look for the comedy, and vice-versa'. Lear's meeting with Kent/Caius in the stocks, when they 'yea' and 'nay' one another, is clearly a pantomime front-cloth number, and Lear's admonition 'Stay here' to a tethered man is certainly a gag. Shakespeare (like Shaw?) loved a laugh at inappropriate moments. Michael Hordern, who played it in 1969, wrote that his director Jonathan Miller's view was 'that if you didn't approach it as a funny play about people going gaga you missed a dimension'. Jonathan at his most contrary.

The scene where Lear confronts Regan and later Goneril before exiting into the storm became and remained my bugbear. I understood it, I could play it well enough, but I never felt that I was on top of it. Perhaps I couldn't find enough variety; perhaps I couldn't match the philosophy of 'Reason not the need' to the character I had assumed; perhaps I just feared I was being boring getting angry with my daughters yet again. Talking to other Lears I am always fascinated by the passage they felt they 'couldn't do', and it's never the same scene. In my desperation to keep the love of Regan, my last hope, I seized her from behind, whispering in her ear 'Thou shalt never have my curse', which critics and others pounced on as abusive, incestuous behaviour. I found the final quarrel with Regan and Goneril immensely taxing, and hovering over it is the prospect of the storm to come.

You can argue that the storm is in his mind – it is, like the madness, entirely Shakespeare's invention – and just speak the words, as Charles Laughton and more recently Derek Jacobi did. But the text indicates that Shakespeare saw it as a real storm, probably with much use of thunder sheets. Jonathan has real water pouring down, eighty-seven thunder claps, and metal-framed walls intermittently collapsing which I have to dodge or risk concussion. I have no alternative but to use a lot of voice (Alberich in *The Ring*). Poor Tom is always a conundrum, and Tom Hollander is initially baffled and unwilling to put more than a toe in the water (metaphorically and literally). Eventually he is persuaded to jump in, becomes fast and furious, and the scenes get easier to play. Lear's 'Off, off, you lendings: come, unbutton here' is always a problem. How far should Lear strip? Jonathan is adamant that Lear naked is far too distracting. My experience when Ian Holm stripped is that his genitalia were the sole subject of discussion at the interval: "Didn't look very royal to me," "And they say he's been married three times." I go down to pants and socks, which always looks comic, but Lear's behaviour in the storm is tragicomic. One night as the storm starts I had a terrible feeling that I have forgotten to put on my two pairs of off-white costume pants and that my own pants are red. They are, and Tom Hollander is hysterical with laughter. Fifteen years later an actor hearing I had played Lear remarked, "Oh, the one with red knickers." Has this become in theatrical lore the most famous thing about my performance?

Lear's growing 'madness' remains a disputed area. Jonathan Miller claims it is 'an extreme case of dislocation', John Barton thinks it's a massive breakdown but hardly insanity, the psychiatrist Dorothy Rowe thinks 'madness' is simply a defence people use when they feel under immense threat. Others put forward ingenious theories of dementia and schizophrenia. The folio cuts the mock trial of Goneril-as-foot-stool, possibly for length and narrative line, but possibly because Shakespeare or the 1623 editors didn't want Lear to appear too demented. Most productions keep it in, and I came to think it indicates a return to a state of childhood, which is also present in Lear's first appearance at 'Dover Beach', when he says, 'Look, look, a mouse: peace, peace, this toasted cheese will do't'. They are the words of an imaginative seven-year-old. My 'child-like' character coming into its own? Later in the scene he has all his wits about him when he recognises Gloucester and declares, 'There thou mightst behold the great image of authority: a dog's obeyed in office'. Out tumbles all the hypocrisies, double dealings and injustices he has observed among the elite – 'Through tattered clothes great vices do appear / Robes and furred gowns hide all'. It's political and social dynamite, my favourite scene in all Shakespeare. Under the cloak of a character's 'madness'

King Lear, Almeida, 2002.
OFD (Lear) in the storm.

Shakespeare could at last let his despair at status and authority run riot.

Shakespeare has great difficulty bringing the two unwieldy plots to a close. In the text Goneril, Regan and Gloucester all die offstage, Edgar and Edmund have to fight a duel (give the groundlings a bit of action) preceded by interminable speeches. Lear has three short, beautifully written scenes, which are a joy to play. Diana Rigg (Scofield's Cordelia) had warned me not to lose energy in these scenes, and this is a great help. Some of the best notes I have ever had come from actors in past productions – 'Don't worry about that, this is the real problem'. I'm puzzled by Cordelia's reticence in Lear's presence, until I realise that she cannot 'heave her heart into her mouth', that they have never found a way of communicating verbally.

All the groundwork has now been done; can I now throw it all away? Judi Dench is a great exemplar of this. Late on in run-throughs I've seen her go for the part's jugular, throwing away certain bits of meticulous planning. It's a high-risk strategy which can result in a generalised wash, but it's worth attempting. As Alfred Brendel says, 'If the middle rehearsal period has to be a filtering through the intellect, the end has to be a return to emotion'. Don't concentrate on playing a Liszt sonata note-perfect, just go for it; the work's been done. Iris Murdoch is more daunting about the whole process: 'Any artist knows that the space between the stage where the work is too unformed to have committed itself, and the stage where it is too late to improve it, can be as thin as a needle. Genius perhaps consists in opening out this needle-like area until it covers the whole of the working time.' A genius I have not proved. During rehearsals Scofield and Irene Worth came to the Almeida to do a recital of the Chekhov-Olga Knipper letters. I told Paul I was rehearsing Lear and he said, "Oh, that's interesting. I might come to that." I knew he wouldn't – he was adept at saying 'perhaps' to invitations and then going home – but I was touched that he even entertained the idea.

Although my voice was not in good shape – at the third dress rehearsal I had to insist on using half-voice – the opening went well and by the press night we were up to speed and the production had all the appearance of a success. I didn't read the notices till the production finished, but you always pick up the general drift. Some weeks after the opening someone sent me an article Mark Lawson had written in *The Guardian* shortly after the press night:

'There's a catch in the acclamation of great acting which is that it is generally only seen in those who have previously been declared Great Actors. For example, Oliver Ford Davies, a top-rank character actor, opened this week as King Lear in London. Before the production opened – and without seeing it – I bet a colleague that the critical consensus on him would be almost-but-not-quite... This was because Ford Davies is best-known for playing dons and vicars... rather than the Richard III, Hamlet, Othello and the other favoured base-camps on the way to the blasted heath.'

You can imagine how happy I was to have missed this judgment at the time, but I think Lawson has a point. It applies to creative artists in every genre. A violinist on the regional circuit may play the Beethoven concerto extremely well, but it won't be judged by critical consensus the equal of established stars, despite the fact that many may prefer her interpretation. We may prefer Caillebotte to Renoir, but Caillebotte is never going to enter the pantheon of Great Artists.

Lear's anger proved the major talking point – in addition to the collapsing set. Katherine Duncan-Jones, whose book *Ungentle Shakespeare* I much admire, wrote in the *New Statesman*: 'Davies' Lear is mad almost from the outset, in the Elizabethan or the modern American sense of "mad": he is furiously angry, sometimes comically so. Yet he is always good company... This is an important production. Don't miss the Almeida's last bus'. Several critics had doubted my casting. Benedict Nightingale in *The Times* queried: 'Could this tapering, shaggy actor so memorable as the introverted, self-doubting

King Lear, Almeida, 2002.
OFD and David Ryall (Gloucester).

162

vicar in David Hare's *Racing Demon*, find the size and weight for Lear? I shouldn't have worried. Davies produces stronger and more plentiful emotions than I had assumed to be within his range… Davies makes you believe in the callous egotism of the unreconstructed Lear. Yet when he comes to key lines – "I did her wrong" or the stark "I shall go mad" – you realise that something else is beneath, waiting to be released'. Spot on.

Kate Bassett in the *Independent on Sunday* went even further: 'Ford Davies – the cuddliest old softie in British theatre [the things you learn] – proves a Lear of startling authority and snarling ferocity… his path in and out of madness is superbly charted and the tenderness of his death scene is heart rending. A great performance'. Lear's extreme anger was an unusual, perhaps an original, take on the part, and a few critics wanted the anger toned down. Rhoda Koenig in *The Independent* went the furthest: 'As Lear he lacks a certain variety, Lear arrogant, Lear affronted, Lear compassionate, Lear demented, all speak in the same curmudgeonly rant'. Charles Spencer in the *Daily Telegraph* would have none of Lawson's foreboding: 'This performance triumphantly establishes him as one of our finest actors, offering one of the most moving and intelligent Lears I have ever seen… his transition from snarling tyranny to loving tenderness is played with such truth, and such clarity, that one feels like cheering'.

You can see why I don't read the notices at the time. I somehow survived the vocal anger and the rain for twelve weeks, but I was disappointed, mixed with a certain relief, that the production had no further life. The British Council tour fell through because the set was too heavy to travel round the world, and Jonathan and Paul wouldn't compromise. The Old Vic wanted the production for a further twelve weeks, but again the set was the stumbling block. I was especially sorry to miss the Vic, where I had seen the Lears of Paul Rogers and Eric Porter. An unexpected treat for me was a request from the celebrated artist John Wonnacott to paint my portrait, with shadowy pictures of the production as a backdrop, entitled *Thinking of Lear*. Every few months I would go to his studio in Leigh-on-Sea and only after

AN ACTOR'S LIFE IN 12 PRODUCTIONS

two years did he declare it finished. Playing Lear was a culmination of a character actor's dream of escaping Capulet and Duke Senior into something more testing. If it was a test had I passed? I realised there's no question of 'passing'; you just add one more small building block to the dozens who have gone before.

2002–03: *Johnny English*, *The Mother*, Zeffirelli

As soon as the production finished I developed a bad back. It was as if my body said 'I'll see your Lear out, but then I'll collapse'. The notoriety of the *Lear* brought a number of offers, which I needed to take: working on an Almeida *Lear* for six months had emptied my bank account. I was also 'hot' again, if only for a few months; best to cash in. I went straight into an episode of a new series, *Foyle's War* with Michael Kitchen, playing a corrupt magistrate taking bribes from fathers trying to avoid their son's call-up. I then murdered a young evacuee who knew what I was up to, and was duly shot by my wife, played by Cheryl Campbell. A dozen takes on my bullet-ridden collapse made my back even worse (always demand a mattress when the floor is out of shot). I then left vicars behind to play the Archbishop of Canterbury, real and fake (don't ask), in a big feature film, *Johnny English*. Summoned to a rehearsal at Shepperton Studios, which I assumed involved the whole cast for a read-through, I found to my surprise it was just Rowan Atkinson, John Malkovich and myself, a bizarrely assorted trio, though very good to work with. We spent eight days in St Alban's Cathedral filming this grand finale, where every time I raised the crown to John's head a pain shot through my back, but with five hundred extras filling the nave I could hardly ask for a day off. Rowan swung down on a rope in an attempt to stop me, and, thinking me the fake cleric, spent an entire day trying to pull my face off, with the result that I developed bruises either side of my nose. In an earlier scene my bare bottom was exposed with 'Jesus loves me' tattooed across it. It was not in fact a shot of my bottom (I had asked

Johnny English, 2002.
Rowan Atkinson and OFD (Archbishop).

for bottom approval to no avail), but it soon became the most famous thing about my performance: to this day people cross cafes to hand me notes inscribed 'Jesus loves me'. Dedicated theatre-goers seem to know about my red knickers in *King Lear*, but the whole world seems aware of 'my' tattooed bottom in *Johnny English*.

A welcome contrast was a small-scale film, *The Mother*, written and directed by two old friends, Hanif Kureishi and Roger Michell. My character Bruce was introduced in an attempt to lure Anne Reid, 'The Mother', away from her affair with the much younger Daniel Craig. The Mother and Bruce have a night together in which Bruce dispenses appallingly insensitive sex, also not good for the back: neither Anne nor I enjoyed the shooting of that. At the age of sixty-three I had at last got to play only my third lover, with unedifying results – I added it to my long list of the unsuccessful. After these two films I harboured a secret hope that I might have cracked the movie world, but of course the Powers assume actors have only one or two performances, and archbishops and terrible lovers are not much in demand. Anthony Sher told me after his success as Disraeli in *Mrs Brown* he hoped the same, until a Hollywood insider remarked, "Not much call for Jewish prime ministers."

Once the two films were done I realised I needed a rest. In the fourteen years since 1988 I had been going relentlessly from one job to the next, perhaps afraid to turn anything down. As my first twenty years had been so problematic I had become inured, perhaps programmed, to accept any offer that came my way. Directors don't like to be turned down. Actors are accustomed to rejection, but directors see it as a personal affront. On the very few occasions I had declined an offer I noted the director/producer in question never asked for me again. Actors develop a thick skin; employers are more fragile.

I enjoyed my autumn break in a cottage we had bought in Dorset. My back slowly recovered (much osteopathy), but early in 2003 came an offer that might lead to a series, the holy grail of television. Pauline Collins and I were to be an elderly version of Agatha Christie's Tommy and Tuppence in a modernised version of *Sparkling Cyanide*, directed by my friend Tristram Powell. As there was little filming on offer in cold February it attracted a very strong cast, including Lia Williams, Clare Holman, Susan Hampshire, Ken Cranham, Dominic Cooper and James Wilby. It has been endlessly repeated, but the series never took off. Since ITV had taken over *Miss Marple* from the BBC and had brought *Poirot* in-house, I always doubted there was room for a third Christie, and so it proved. The filming prevented me from going on the huge anti-Iraq war march, but I was delighted when my sometime student Robin Cook resigned from being foreign secretary. I was then summoned to an interview for a Pirandello play to be directed by Franco Zeffirelli. *Cosi e (se vi pare)*, usually translated as *Right You Are (if you think so)*, but in Martin Sherman's new version *Absolutely! (perhaps)*. The interview at first went well, as I knew my Pirandello from my work on *Six Characters* and *Naked*.

Then Franco mentioned Mussolini and I remarked that Pirandello had briefly embraced national socialism. "Never," said Franco.

Unwisely I carried on. "Well, he did once declare himself 'a Fascist because I am Italian'."

"He was never a Fascist," insisted Franco. I saw nervous glances round the room, and I thought that's me finished, stupid Oliver showing off. "So," said Franco, "would you like to play this part?"

"Well, yes."

"And you shall."

Outside I asked Lisa Makin, the casting director, if he meant it. "Oh, yes. He really wanted John Mortimer, and I said you were the nearest equivalent."

Franco had wanted to do a play with Joan Plowright, as they had worked together on several films and stage productions, but not for twenty-five years, and I think both saw this production as a possible West End swan-song (as it proved). Joan warned us: "Don't, for heaven's sake, copy Franco if he demonstrates a line or a gesture. Judi Dench did an exact copy on *Tea with Mussolini*, and when he saw the rushes Franco called what she loyally did 'most embarrassing'." A very strong cast was assembled – who didn't want to work with Zeffirelli? – and included Brid Brennan, Anna Carteret, Liza Tarbuck, Sian Brooke, Darrell D'Silva, Gawn Grainger and Barry Stanton. We all got on very happily, Joan was a delight to work with, though Franco, in true Italian style, was never on time for 11am rehearsals, despite being chauffeured. He was now eighty and had lost a sense of balance through an operation, but once seated he was in total command and directions flowed in a manner he presumably used for film and opera – "Now, darling, move to that chair, cross your legs, say your line, maybe take out a cigarette, have a drink." One day I changed a move. "Oliver, you didn't move when I said."

I decided this was the moment to make a stand. "I'm afraid I couldn't make it work, Franco, can I move later?"

The room froze, Franco paused. "Oliver, you are great actor, move when you like." Franco knew how to keep a cast happy.

We were to be fourteen weeks at Wyndham's, together with the Haymarket my favourite theatre. I moved into a dressing room painted a strange mauve colour at the behest of Madonna, a recent occupant. I relished playing Laudisi, a stand-in for Pirandello, who is a cynical commentator on stage throughout, sometimes a detached observer, sometimes part of the action. The gossiping townspeople are transfixed by the rival claims of madness and illusion by the mother-in-law (Joan) and son-in-law (Darrell), and Laudisi advises them 'to believe them both, or don't believe either of them'. He takes the same stance as Ludovico Nota, whom I played in *Naked*, in his scepticism towards 'facts'. I relished the comedy in the part, and was naturally pleased when Liza Tarbuck said her dad Jimmy kept telling her that I had great comic timing – perhaps a future in variety loomed, straight man to Jimmy Tarbuck in Spanish resorts? To my surprise I was later nominated for an Olivier Best Supporting Actor. Since Joan and I were the two names above the title, in what sense was I 'supporting'? It has always been a strange category. Warren Mitchell won for *The Price*, possibly the right decision.

Production Ten

KING CROMWELL (2003)

In the spring I had had a phone call from Sam Walters at the Orange Tree: "I think I'm going to do your Cromwell play." My writing plays on contemporary subjects had come to a halt in the 1980s when I realised that it might be more productive to combine my two loves, drama and history. I quickly knew my subject would be the English Revolution. Between 1649 and 1660 England had a major revolution followed by a republic. It is a period that has always fascinated me, particularly because the English revolutionaries, unlike their American, French and Russian successors, had no Rousseau or Marx to guide them. They made it up as they went along. A great debate took place, thousands of pamphlets were published, and daring experiments in government were attempted. The period is routinely referred to as 'The Civil Wars' or 'The Commonwealth and Protectorate' rather than 'The English Revolution'. Right-wing commentators to this day write, 'Thank goodness we've never had a revolution'. In 1649 Parliament put the king on an open, if predetermined, trial (a European, possibly world, first), executed him, abolished the House of Lords and the bishops, and declared a republic to be run by parliament. I think that constitutes a revolution in anyone's definition. John Milton wrote that it was 'the most heroic achievement since the beginning of the world'. 'Ah, but it didn't last', conservatives cry, 'in 1660 the monarchy was restored'. Well, the 1789 French Revolution was over by 1804 when Napoleon declared himself Emperor, and in 1815 the Bourbons were restored. The French, however, agree that they had a revolution, and some are even proud of it.

The story of the revolution is full of rich characters – Oliver Cromwell, Charles I, Henry Ireton, John Lilburne, Edward Sexby – and great scenes: Charles' attempt to arrest the five members but 'the birds have flown'; the trial of the king; Cromwell's breaking up of parliament in 1653, 'In the name of God, go!' I knitted all these together and it made a great story, but somehow it remained a pageant, what I call 'school's broadcasting'. What was I saying, beyond recounting familiar history? It is the curse of historical biopics, so I decided to be more radical. I had an idea for a play in which a university drama department in Africa, probably Nigeria, plans a play about Cromwell with funding from a major oil company. Scenes from the Cromwell play in rehearsal are threaded through the narrative. When the oil company discovers more about Cromwell's revolutionary tendencies they withdraw their funding and lean on the university to sack the perpetrators of the play. I did a good deal of research and worked on the play for eighteen months but finally accepted that the play was technically beyond me and perhaps was really a subject for a film.

I thought it safer to go to the opposite extreme – One Day in the Life of. The choice of day came quite suddenly to me. In March 1657 Protector Cromwell was offered the crown by parliament (they knew where they were with a King, but what were the limitations on the power of a 'Protector'?). Cromwell hesitated for six weeks, and at one point it seemed he would accept. He finally refused, though never explained in full his decision. Reduce the six weeks to one day, and it seemed to me you had a play that could examine most of the triumphs and failures of the revolution. The obvious snags were the lack of developing story and its known ending. Most people, however little they know about the period, will be pretty sure that Cromwell didn't become king and that Elizabeth Windsor is not family. He was nicknamed 'King Oliver', but I feared audiences might book to celebrate the great jazz cornet player. However interesting all the arguments in the play, looming shortly ahead is the death of 'King Cromwell' (bad press) and the restoration of the 'Merrie Monarch' (good press). However enthralling Anne Boleyn's determination to get her man we know it's going to end badly – but that hasn't stopped many a novel and play on the subject.

Why my interest in Cromwell, a difficult and unattractive figure? He seems to me to exemplify the search, the experiment and the ultimate failure of the revolution. He also embodies a number of twentieth- and probably twenty-first-century dilemmas. He was in essence a military dictator, a general of genius, who wanted to find a democratic basis for a republic. General Zia, for example, military ruler of Pakistan in the 1980s, claimed many of the same sentiments, as did many a South American dictator, however hypocritically. Cromwell was a firm believer in the House of Commons, his political alma mater, and kept calling elections but then excluded his opponents. He was a religious fundamentalist seeking godly reformation, who also believed in a broad, tolerant, national church: Roman Catholics were less persecuted in his regime, while Jews were welcomed back into England. He was a leader of unassailable authority who, like Mandela or Tito, could find no one comparable to succeed him. Radicalism and conservatism warred within him, a very English condition.

It was to be a 'corridors of power' play, so out of fashion since the 1970s when Caryl Churchill's *Vinegar Tom* and *A Light Shining in Buckinghamshire* explored how the underclass responded to turbulent times. But I have always argued that there is also a place for what went on in Whitehall's 'smoked-filled rooms'. My 'One Day' concept appeared inevitably a studio play, which required a simple set and a limited number of characters if it was to stand any chance of a production. In consequence, scenes and characters came and mostly went. Cromwell and his wife in their house in Ely, the ghost of Charles I, Bridget Cromwell his pious eldest daughter, the parliamentarian Bulstrode Whitelocke (great name) all went. These all involved agonisingly difficult choices, and in my experience many actors are quite unaware of these difficulties. They assume that the script they are handed arrived fully formed in the writer's mind, rather than the result of endless trial and error, of twenty or thirty abandoned treatments. I have always urged actors to try writing and directing, if only to appreciate how and why choices are made, and how they impact on the actor's performance.

In 1996 I finally showed the work in progress to my friend David Edgar, and received a six-page typed critique:

> 'It is as I expected an erudite, informative, elegant and adult read... The problem at the moment is that the agenda is not set up clearly enough... What you must do is decide on the action of the play and ruthlessly ensure that everything serves that action: i.e. towards the end of his leadership Cromwell is faced with a public and private question. In order to answer them he assesses his achievements and failures. As a result he comes up with answers that neither we, his family, his aides nor perhaps he himself expects.'

This reads like a university tutorial, and indeed David was teaching a Birmingham University playwriting MA, which my daughter Miranda did the following year, and was encouraged by him to regard structure as paramount: a good idea is not an end in itself; if you can't write good dialogue don't even bother to start. David's shrewd critique spurred me into a major rewrite, which I then submitted to Richard Eyre at the National. He suggested a workshop and reading at the National Theatre Studio, which took place in December 1997 with a very strong cast headed by David Calder as Cromwell, Samantha Bond as Elizabeth his daughter and Simon Russell Beale as Andrew Marvell. The National literary department attended, said nice things but neatly side-stepped by telling me there was a two-year waiting list at the Cottesloe, and it would be better if I tried to get it on elsewhere. I sent it to various London fringe theatres, and though they found it 'interesting and beautifully written' they also dodged it on the grounds that they only did plays on contemporary subjects (unless of course written by very established authors). The RSC were intrigued but thought that I hadn't 'sufficiently digested my material'. This last was perhaps true, but it is the curse of historical dramas and always the most convenient excuse for rejection. The main reason so many historical plays and films centre on the Tudors and Queen Victoria is that it can be assumed the audience know something of the characters and the period (Henry kept swopping wives, Elizabeth remained unmarried but had the heart of a lion, Victoria as widow fancied John Brown). But how much knowledge do audiences bring to Protector Cromwell, except that he hated stained glass and cancelled Christmas? As a result, as David Hare pointed out to me, you risk scenes 'bulging with two people telling each other what they already know'. We all sneer at 'Hello, Lenin, my name's Trotsky and I'm also a Bolshevik', but in a play this meeting has to be dramatised somehow.

I have gone on at some length about the many treatments my play went through, as an illustration of the difficulties playwrights, beginners and veterans face, and why so many give up. I had my acting to bolster me financially and I could pretend that was my real calling, but most writers don't. My aim had always been to get the play on in 1999, the quatercentenary of Cromwell's birth, when the subject would surely be of maximum interest. In 1899 there had been great celebrations, mainly due to the Nonconformists whom Cromwell had championed (the former liberal prime minister Lord Rosebery needed their votes) and the Jews whom Cromwell had allowed back into Britain (the statue of Cromwell outside the Palace of Westminster we owe to Rothschild munificence; Oliver should be on a horse but the money didn't stretch that far. Its position and very existence have remained contentious ever since). But 1999 passed with hardly a murmur – no plays, films, few documentaries. To my great annoyance more attention was paid to the 350th anniversary of Charles I's execution: we are such a reactionary, royalist country. I had therefore abandoned any hope of a production when, out of the blue, came Sam's phone call. And would that have come if he had not been an old friend? But then, I consoled myself, all playwrights have needed a friendly producer/management to take a chance on them.

Once the Pirandello was finished I was free to concentrate on a last rewrite. The play had been pared down to one set, an anonymous room in Whitehall Palace, and eight characters (still too many for some fringe theatres, but Sam was never daunted). Cromwell's decision on accepting the crown was examined through his relationship with John Lambert, his second in command in the army, who wanted to succeed him as Protector and establish a virtual military dictatorship. There had been much-recorded gossip of a relationship between Cromwell and Lambert's wife Frances, so she added a welcome personal dynamic (and it got another woman into a terribly male world). His successor as king would have to be his eldest surviving son Richard, who only wanted to be left alone to paint, but their relationship enabled me to examine their mutual pain at the deaths of Cromwell's sons Robert and Oliver – 'it was a dagger to my heart', Cromwell wrote. John Thurloe, Cromwell's secretary and spymaster, to whom Oliver could confide his doubts and perplexities, was in favour of monarchy, as was Cromwell's daughter Elizabeth (Bettie) who, conveniently, was known to hate Frances Lambert's apparent hold on her father – they are recorded as screaming at one another at court 'like Billingsgate fishwives'.

A secondary plot, musical, literary and hopefully comic, centred round the poet Andrew Marvell, who was applying to be assistant Latin Secretary to John Milton (all diplomatic letters were written in Latin). He and Bettie championed Cromwell's daughter Fanny's marriage to an aristocrat with 'fifty violins and mixed dancing till dawn', for which Marvell was to write a masque, hoping to cast Cromwell as a non-singing Jove (which he may have later undertaken). They were also keen on William Davenant's experiments in opera. *The Siege of Rhodes*, England's first home-grown opera, was first performed privately in London in 1657, and there was no attempt by Thurloe and the authorities to close it down. Cromwell was very fond of Tudor music (though not in churches), and this was provided by an

King Cromwell, Orange Tree, 2003.

unseen harpsichordist, John Hingston, stationed in a corridor outside and pre-recorded on tape. We had a lot of fun with trills he gave when he agreed with something. Finally, Cromwell had an impassioned interview with the captured Edward Sexby, a former colonel in his army, who now pressed for Cromwell's assassination for his betrayal of the Leveller cause.

The language of an historical play is always a problem, unless you make it clear from the outset that the speech will be modern and will have no truck with historicism – 'no problem, bring it on'. If you want, as I did, to give it a seventeenth-century feel and match actual recorded speech and writings, then fortunately Cromwell tended to speak very directly, following his maxim that new laws should 'be made plain and short', though he did allow himself the odd religious flourish. 'Nothing will satisfy men unless they can press their finger upon their brethren's consciences, to pinch them there. For indeed Religion was not the thing at first contested for, but God brought it to that issue at last'. I also wanted to use Marvell's writings: 'Much better to breathe free and lively as a republican than pine and fret as a royalist, till wit, soul and all be drowned in ale and melancholy'. Sexby too used typical Leveller language: 'Many of us fought for those ends which we since saw were not those which caused us to venture all in the ship with you. It had been good in you to have advertised us of it, and I believe you would have had fewer under your command'. To invent matching language I spent hours checking individual words and expressions in the Shorter Oxford dictionary, working on the principle that if a word or phrase was recorded before 1700 then it could have been in use in 1657. Cromwell's final speech when he rejected the crown illustrates the best I could do in terms of language: 'All things point to my taking the crown... I see that. The name of king is so great, so understood, so reverenced by the people. But why? Both king and commoner are poor creeping ants before your throne. Lord, I must tell you – I have learned something today: that good men do not swallow this title of king. And therefore I cannot believe it has your blessing. Whichever way I turn today, the title has stuck with me. And does yet stick. At best I should accept it doubtingly – and Christ teaches us what is so done is not of faith. I cannot restore that which providence has destroyed. I cannot.'

A scene that gave me particular pleasure was the job interview (David Edgar likes a job interview) between Cromwell and Marvell on the subject of Marvell's *Horatian Ode upon Cromwell's Return from Ireland*, the one that describes Charles I's execution:

'Nothing common did or mean
Upon that memorable scene:
But with his keener eye
The axe's edge did try:
Nor called the gods with vulgar spite
To vindicate his hapless right,
But bowed his comely head
Down, as upon a bed.'

Marvell scholars have often wondered if Cromwell ever read the poem, which had not been printed, merely circulated in manuscript, and if so what he would have made of it. It is the mischievous prerogative of history plays to invent scenes that almost certainly never took place, Schiller's meeting between Elizabeth and Mary Queen of Scots being the most notorious example. Accordingly my Cromwell quizzes a quaking Marvell about his exact position on the king's overthrow and Cromwell's ascendancy. But is it too academic a conceit? Will it have to go?

The first casting problem was to find a Cromwell. Oliver is a 'heavy' and Britain, unlike America, seems to produce very few de Niros and Robert Duvalls. Richard Harris (Irish) had a good shot at it in the 1970 *Cromwell*, though Alec Guinness as Charles I ran away with the film. I think Charles always does, as Rupert Everett did in *To Kill a King* (2003) and Mark Gatiss in Howard Brenton's play *55 Days* (2012). Mike Gambon would be an excellent Cromwell, but I knew he'd balk at learning it. David Calder, my National Theatre studio Cromwell, proved wary; he probably thought, "You wrote it, you do it." So eventually I did. Is it wise to act the leading part in your own play? At least it will be roughly the Cromwell you had in mind, but what you had in mind might have been transformatively reimagined by another actor. It also meant I couldn't sit to the side, Hare-like, scrutinising, cutting and rewriting as scenes failed to deliver what I had intended.

The rest of the casting went well under Sam's direction, showing, I hoped, that I had written seven good parts. I was especially pleased that those idiosyncratic actors Sean Baker and Hugh Simon agreed to play two of the trickiest parts, Marvell and Thurloe, and that Claudia Elmhirst and Miranda Foster were to be Bettie and Frances. John Ashton (Sexby), Paul Goodwin (Lambert) and Damien Matthews (Richard) made up a strong team. Although we only had four weeks' rehearsals I persuaded Sam to have a day's outing to Cromwell's house in Ely and the Huntingdon Cromwell Museum. We also had a morning reading of my abridgement of the Putney Debates. I think that anything that stimulates an actor's imagination and helps their sense of a very different period is worth pursuing. They are also very good for company bonding. In fact the cast responded more eagerly than I had anticipated both to the politics and the family interaction, giving me hope that everyone's motives and intentions were not only clear but had a familiar ring. My main acting worry was my own performance: was I paying too much attention to everyone's handling of my writing and too little to what I was doing with Cromwell? My hope was that I had immersed myself for so many years in the man's contradictory character that his twists and turns were deeply imbedded in me and would play themselves whether I willed it or not. The play proved relatively straightforward to rehearse as over half the scenes are duologues between Cromwell and son, daughter, secretary, Leveller, etc. But is it therefore really a radio play? It's certainly a 'debate play' – a term beloved of hostile critics. But then all Greek plays are debates, as are so many Ibsens, Brechts and even Shakespeares (*Troilus and Cressida, Measure for Measure*). I'm in good company.

The play opened to uniformly good reviews, good but not outstanding. The acting was much praised, and every member of the cast was singled out in one review or another. Cavils centred round what Michael Billington called the 'retrospective irony', particularly Cromwell's belief that the Irish question would be solved 'in a generation or two' (I grant that was cheeky). Some liked the comedy surrounding opera, a few thought it irrelevant, but most were amused by Cromwell's hatred of 'new music' – Monteverdi et al. Some found a lack of story (as I had feared). *Time Out* wrote, 'The story isn't the play's best feature, but for language, history and acting it's worth a coronation'. The words 'erudite' and 'witty' were much used, though most agreed, like the *Financial Times*, that 'it wears its erudition lightly'. Perhaps I had finally digested my research? Billington thought 'it clarifies big issues without over-simplifying them. It is streets ahead of the tushery and tat of TV historical drama'. To my great relief two reviews actually liked the Marvell job interview. My Cromwell was generally praised though some commentators thought he was probably a nastier brute. I was particularly pleased by *Time Out*'s comment: 'What's most impressive is that he does so little "acting". He simply growls, glares and let's his muscular script punch its historical weight'. Perhaps I had released the Oliver in me? Suzi Feay in the *Independent on Sunday* was the most enthusiastic: 'This was the great pleasure of the week, with wonderful unshowy acting. The play is funny, immensely moving and full of still potent ideas'.

We quickly sold out, with people standing at the back of the circle every night. It was very frustrating to turn so many away: years later Michael Frayn told me he and Claire Tomalin were disappointed not to get in (if they'd only asked). Following Orange Tree custom there was a three-hour seminar/discussion on 'Oliver Cromwell and the English Revolution' one Saturday morning, led by Professors Blair Worden and Justin Champion. Blair Worden has been for many years the doyen of Cromwellian period scholarship, and his biography has been eagerly awaited. As I write this twenty years later it still hasn't appeared, and the reason may be that Cromwell's contradictory character baffles even the best of scholars. As a sometime historian nothing gave me greater pleasure than Blair telling me after he read and saw the play that he was largely in agreement with my summation of Cromwell. He later wrote to me: 'I enjoyed and admired *King Cromwell* even more in performance than on reading it (when I missed many things and mis-read others)'. Coming from a non-theatre person I found this very interesting. The ability to judge how well a script will play in performance is one of the greatest challenges in theatre – and particularly in film. The few who have the knack or the prescience to foresee this are worth their weight in gold, and in Hollywood would be billionaires.

As with most successful fringe productions there was a feeling that it will surely transfer or be revived, but as usual nothing happened. Sam Walters, after two difficult West End transfers of his work, had given up trying to exploit even the best of his productions. In 2003 the idea of fringe co-productions had barely got off the ground; ten years later they would become an economic necessity. I too realised when the run ended that I had been so taken up with performing the play that I had never badgered producers, the National or the RSC to come and see it. Their attitude was probably 'Thank heaven he's got it on somewhere and we can forget all about it'. Admittedly any commercial management would find Oliver Cromwell a hard sell. The following year I did persuade Samuel French to publish it, so it exists, and fifteen years later I received £10 in royalties, so a few people must have bought it out of curiosity. It had taken me nine years to write and get it on, and it cured me of any desire to do it again.

2004–08: plays various, *The Linden Tree*, return to the National

To my surprise Nick Hern commissioned me to write a book, a form of manual on playing Shakespeare. It's a crowded field. John Barton's transcripts of his television series on *Playing Shakespeare* (1982), with its starry cast and accompanying DVD is the longest bestseller; Peter Hall's *Shakespeare's Advice to the Players* (2003) is paramount in analysing the language in a series of speeches; and among many others my old friends Adrian Brine and Michael York published *A Shakespearean Actor Prepares* (2000). I decided on something a little different: a mini-encyclopaedia that would include chapters on the Elizabethan Actor, Shakespeare's Language, Actor Interviews ranging from Judi Dench and Ian McKellen to Harriet Walter and Adrian Lester, and forty odd mini-essays ranging from Memorising and Soliloquy to Irony and Sex. It involved a great deal of work and was finally published in 2007. Fortunately it had several very good reviews – 'this terrific book' (*The Observer*), 'it is hard to offer enough praise... definitive guidance' (*British Theatre Guide*) – and has sold nearly five thousand copies. At the University of York, where I often go and lecture, it has become a set book. When praised I ruefully admit, "If only I could follow my own advice."

From the arduous to the ridiculous, I next played a loathsome bully in *Midsomer Murders*. I mention it only because when John Nettles, Inspector Barnaby, left the series after fifteen years and was asked his favourite murder among the hundreds he had investigated he picked mine. I was drugged and tethered to a lawn with croquet hoops while my collection of vintage wines was catapulted at me, my abused wife (Sara Kestelman) directing the aim from her wheelchair. John particularly liked my dying cry as a dusty bottle hurtled towards me: 'Not the Margaux '68!' I next played the doctor in a film of *Heidi*, directed by Paul Marcus (another former RSC assistant) with Diana Rigg and Geraldine Chaplin, and shot largely in Slovenia. The main attraction for me was that the Grandfather was played by Max von Sydow, whom I had so admired ever since *The Seventh Seal* in the 1950s. In the final scene Max and I sit on the porch of his wooden hut, smoking our pipes and discussing mortality. I was very proud.

Darwin in Malibu at the newly built Hampstead Theatre was set in some contemporary parallel universe above Malibu beach where my Darwin, in shorts and Hawaiian shirt, and a recently drowned young woman were visited by Thomas Huxley and Bishop Wilberforce to play out their 140-year-old dispute about evolution. Crispin Whittell's play was ingenious and entertaining, with hints of Shaw and Terry Johnson, but intellectually underpowered. Nigel Planer's gauche muscular Wilberforce and Douglas Henshall's boisterously challenging Huxley gave the play great momentum, but it remained, as many pointed out, a one-joke concept. I had great fun with an extended riff about the validity of Wilberforce shooting partridges in heaven, since to have got to heaven the birds were clearly 'good and virtuous' partridges. Looking like a 'child's idea of God', Susannah Clapp thought I was 'one better: he begins to convince you that he should be running the world'. A little over-the-top, I thought. I particularly enjoyed the research, one of the great perks of play preparation, reading *The Origin of Species* and visiting Downe House and the recreation of Darwin's study. The hoped-for transfer never materialised. Acting in plays at Hampstead and the Orange Tree, with several months in between, is not good for the bank balance, and suddenly I had to borrow money to pay my tax bill. Casually employed actors, doing 'art theatre', live so precariously.

I returned to the National in 2005 after over ten years for my fourth David Edgar play, *Playing with Fire*, directed by Mike Attenborough. It was a response to the 2001 race riots in Bradford, Burnley and Oldham, the sort of play a 'national theatre' should be programming. In David's view it boiled down to one question: 'Is Roy Jenkins' vision of a society of mutual tolerance and respect now fracturing into isolated communities, glowering at each other across self-imposed ethnic and cultural divides?' Segregated enclaves exist in cities throughout Britain, but the mill towns of Lancashire and Yorkshire, reliant on a single, now-dead, industry, are the most extreme expression of a social exclusion that results from globalisation. Poor white communities vie with poor, non-white, often Asian, communities for recognition and support.

David's play wanted to dig deep into the legacy of past discriminatory policies and the ever-present clash of Whitehall versus Town Hall. A New Labour fixer (Emma Fielding) is sent to the mythical East Yorkshire town of Wyverdale to sort out its social and financial problems with a defiantly Old Labour council (headed by David Troughton). All her strategic plans and performance indicators ensure that faith festivals, translation services and 'anti-social public-space behaviour' (closing down prostitution) are enhanced at the expense of hospitals, libraries and poor white housing. In the second half of the play there is a public inquiry, much like a documentary reconstruction pioneered by the Tricycle Theatre, in which everyone's case is laid out. My part, Frank Wilkins, was a Labour councillor, sidelined by the leadership, who resigned in order to appeal to a white population antagonised by these New Labour changes. At a Holocaust Commemoration he seizes the microphone and makes a rabble-rousing speech: 'Hands up how many people here need, genuine need, their council-tax-collection leaflet translated into Pushtu? Enough to warrant... the closure of two swimming baths?' As a result of this blatant populism he is elected mayor in place of the usual 'donkey in a red rosette'. I seized upon the part, so alien to my own political convictions, with gleeful relish. The unsuccessful heroic simpleton seemed temporarily laid to rest.

Back to the Orange Tree for another state-of-the-nation play, this time written in 1947, but with many resonances for a society sixty years later. J. B. Priestley wrote *The Linden Tree* directly after *An Inspector Calls*, and it had the longest West End run of any of his plays. The Oxbridge Professor Linden is sixty-five at a small Midlands university and is reluctant to retire, though the young vice-chancellor, who believes in 'conveyor-belt educationalising', wants him out. Linden's wife (Anna Carteret) and their four children have gathered for his birthday and nearly all want him to retire to the affluent south. Linden, however, yearns for a 'peaceful social revolution... without the Terror, without looting mobs and secret police'. Should he fight on in the name of progress, making the sacrifice that the taking responsibility for society entails, or put individual happiness first and quit? He is distressed by a new generation of students (we observe them being taught) that has 'a kind of grey, chilly hollowness inside, when there ought to be gaiety, colour, warmth and vision'. The play was a revelation to many, despite the *Times'* misgiving that 'it seldom shakes off its musty debating-society air' (back to 'debate' finger-wagging).

One of the notices wrote that the part of Linden could have been written for me, and indeed I was exactly the right age (at last) and it chimed with so much of my life and thought. Linden's teaching methods are liberal, free-ranging and imaginative, not tied to exams and vocation. The study of history is not, in Linden's words, 'a lot of dim stuff in a book to be mugged up'. When I was teaching at Edinburgh I talked for a while in a seminar about the architecture of Versailles until a student asked, "Is this anything to do with history?" and I knew he meant, "Will it help me to pass the exam?" Today, of course, with the huge sums invested by students, getting a good degree is the be all and end all and teaching for the exam is forced to reflect this. Versailles is out. Linden was in fact the first time, after forty years, that I had ever been cast as a university teacher. I once went for a one-scene television part as a left-wing history lecturer, and I congratulated the casting director on finding the one member of Equity who exactly fitted the bill. I didn't get it. Television casting can be like the army: "What were you in civvy street?"

"A cook."

"Right, I'll put you down as motor mechanic." And vice-versa.

Celebrity actors of course can play anything, however improbable. The imperative with supporting parts is the immediate appearance: do you look like a plumber, a lecturer, a hair-dresser? We all know that such professionals come in all shapes and sizes, but television thinks it has to abide by the accepted stereotype. My friend Patricia Garwood was told, "Sorry, you're too young to have a teenage daughter."

"But I have a teenage daughter."

"You don't look it."

It was a very successful production, well cast, beautifully directed by Christopher Morahan, five stars in two papers, 'If there were any justice it would transfer instantly in to the West End' (Michael Billington). It didn't. But I was so pleased that Mary Casson, the ninety-three-year-old daughter of Sybil Thorndyke and Lewis Casson, the original Linden couple, came and enthused about the production. I had perhaps the best notices of my career. The words 'humane', 'sardonic', 'wise' and 'rueful' were much used, but some risked 'a wonderful creation' and 'simply superb'. The next Orange Tree production was a revival of *Larkin with Women*, again with Carolyn Backhouse as Monica. Both sold out immediately. It was probably the most satisfying three months of my career.

The Life of Galileo is often regarded as the most approachable of Brecht's plays, which belies both its complexity and its ambivalence. At the National Simon Russell Beale was to play the part and Howard Davies cast me as the Cardinal Inquisitor. Howard's modern, naturalistic production in a direct, stripped-down adaptation by David Hare had, as always, clarity and urgency. He was a director I loved working with. He didn't say a great deal in rehearsal, but what he did say always drove to the heart of the matter. I miss him greatly. The play is a battle between both expediency and idealism, secular truth and religious faith. Galileo shifts from believing science must serve only the truth to admitting science must serve society. As the Little Monk says, 'Unrestricted research is a danger to humanity', reflecting a very modern anxiety if we are now on the way to cloning, or even engineering, a human being. The pace of socio-political change, so evident in the seventeenth century, is now galloping beyond our apparent ability to control or even understand it. For Brecht in 1947 it might have been nuclear power; today it might be the future of AI. I thought it was one of Simon's best performances, an authentic scientist, not afraid at the start to appear selfish and devious as Brecht demanded but very moving when compromised at the end. I decided my Inquisitor was initially very friendly, 'almost twinkly and chortling before clenching his jaw' (Kate Bassett), as I questioned Galileo's daughter Virginia (Elisabeth Dermot Walsh) at a party, checking her answers in a large file I leafed through – I am addicted to files, the best prop ever for certain parts.

Sir Davy Dunce is a great Restoration farce part – the very name serves as a character clue – once played at the Royal Court by Arthur Lowe. I was delighted when David Lan, exemplary artistic director, offered it to me at the newly rebuilt Young Vic. I saw it as a celebration of my forty years in the theatre, and dared to hope it might place me in the tradition of Michael Hordern and Alistair Sim. Unfortunately David saw Thomas Otway's comedy-farce *The Soldiers' Fortune* (1681) as a 'dark' social document, influenced perhaps by Otway's own tormented life, and directed it accordingly. He assembled a great cast, including Anne-Marie Duff, David Bamber and Ray Fearon, but it was a laughter-free experience presented on the most tortuous set I have ever worked on. It received poor notices and played to small houses. I was bitterly disappointed. The actor is so often at the mercy of the production. It may be your one shot at Medea/Vanya/Cleopatra/Lear, but if the production is misconceived you will probably sink with it, however interesting your performance.

Anne-Marie and I then escaped down to the National to appear in Shaw's *St Joan*, directed by Marianne Elliott. Anne-Marie was an inspired choice for Joan for, although in her thirties, she came across as an intransigent teenager, 'a slip of a girl' that the text demands. She had the assurance and vulnerability of a permanent outsider, helped by an Irish accent, together with a blazing stage presence. Shaw's play is essentially about Protestantism (the individual conscience), democracy and nationalism, and Marianne and her designer Rae Smith were justified in setting it in the early twentieth century. Their most radical step was to work with the choreographer Hofesh Shechter. The play started with a towering pyramid of chairs (later Joan's funeral pyre), which the cast dismantled and then hovered in the shadows at the side of the central platform, which revolved and lifted at different angles. In battles, not illustrated in the text, the chairs thrashed across the stage as other frenzied actors beat on corrugated iron sheets. It suggests that Shaw productions can be radically reimagined: don't feel hobbled by his very specific stage directions. I once again played the Inquisitor (a new piece of type-casting) and presented the case that the heresy of reckless individualism – believing her voices rather than Church dictates – was a threat to the social order. Marianne and I decided that I should address my mammoth speech directly to the audience as rationally and persuasively as I could, 'hands wringing, brow furrowed like a weary headmaster... beatifically troubled' (the *New Statesman*). After the terror of delivering the speech to the huge width of the Olivier at the first two performances I began to enjoy it hugely.

In *Much Ado About Nothing* I find Beatrice and Benedick work best when played middle-aged: to the humour is added long-delayed self-awareness, and greater vulnerability and emotional depth. Judi Dench and Donald Sinden made it work at Stratford in 1976, and I thought Zoe Wanamaker and Simon Russell Beale even more anguished and truthful, and just as funny, at the National in 2007. In recent years *Much Ado* has been set in Havana, Middle America and India, but Nick Hytner returned it to sixteenth-century Messina

Much Ado About Nothing, NT, 2007.
L to R: Gary Pillar (Friar Francis), Hero (Susannah Fielding),
Zoe Wanamaker (Beatrice), OFD (Leonato).

and there are many gains in this, principally the Sicilian outrage at
Hero's apparent sexual licence. Nick's expert direction gave the play
a great sense of community and social depth, Mark Addy and Trevor
Peacock in their element as Dogberry and Verges. The *coup de theatre*
came when Benedick, to escape detection in the gulling scene, hurled
himself into a pool with a mighty splash that sprayed the front rows of
the Olivier. Robert Lindsay, master comic technician, later described
it as 'the best gag he had ever seen'. The unexpected depth of the
pool (four feet?) enabled Simon to vanish for a time and finally emerge
dripping to preen and posture at his discovery that Beatrice loved him.
Zoe, not to be outdone, later engineered herself into the pool during
her gulling scene.

When preparing Leonato, father to Hero (Susannah Fielding), I
was surprised to be told that it was the second longest part in the play.
Why had Shakespeare done that? The part is usually heavily cut and

often played as an unimaginative bureaucrat out of his depth. I found the text suggested quite a different character, 'Lear-like' (a phrase much used in reviews) in his initial rage at his daughter's apparent infidelity, and then the motor of the second half of the play as he sets out, in the most difficult and complex verse, to restore her reputation. Hero's story is the play's main plot (Beatrice and Benedick the comic sub-plot) and Nick and I tried to honour that. I much enjoyed my attempts at this reclamation, thought it wasn't to everyone's taste – you depart from the norm at your peril. *Much Ado* remains one of the happiest productions I have ever been in.

Production Eleven

HAMLET (2008–09)

While in rehearsal for *Much Ado* the RSC, after a long gap, showed new interest. Greg Doran, then chief associate director of the RSC, offered me the part of Polonius. David Tennant was to play Hamlet and Patrick Stewart Claudius. In one way this was daunting as the production would clearly be An Event, since David was at the peak of his *Doctor Who* fame and Patrick had the international renown of *Star Trek* and *X-Men*. The entire run sold out in minutes, ensuring no one in the audience would be there because they had heard how good it was – always a millstone. At the same time I felt I was ready to play Polonius (I had been offered the part before), as I saw it a mixture of Leonato and Davy Dunce, a patriarch and a buffoon. My two great influences were Michael Bryant (National Theatre, 1989) and Tony Church (RSC 1965 and 1980), and I had discussed the part with both of them. Michael played Polonius entirely seriously as a secretary of state of bureaucratic, almost military, precision, a prurient, even unpleasant father. Such comedy as emerged was the result of his blind earnestness. In 1965 Tony, under Peter Hall's direction, played him as an establishment manipulator and an oppressive paterfamilias with a great sexual curiosity. Again it was short on humour. In 1980 John Barton emphasised the personal over the political. He saw the play as a breakdown of an essentially

AN ACTOR'S LIFE IN 12 PRODUCTIONS

happy family, in which Polonius' eccentricities and pedantries could be endearing rather than oppressive – comedy was back in play. John argued that as his death causes his daughter to go mad and his son to start a rebellion there is clearly love in the family. The text will bear out all three interpretations. Some difficult choices lay ahead.

Like Leonato, Polonius is at first sight a surprisingly long part, some 350 lines, the third longest in the play. Why had Shakespeare written him at such length when Gertrude, a seemingly more important part, has only 157? Perhaps he just enjoyed writing a patriarch he could make fun of. Perhaps it was a way of getting back at Lord Burleigh, who had recently died but had sent a servant to spy on his son in Paris. Never underestimate a writer becoming intrigued by a character not central to the plot; Dickens and Dostoevsky did it constantly. Wives and mothers seem seldom to have interested Shakespeare; young women were different, hence the space given to Ophelia. The many early versions of the story are no help. All they tell us is that 'a friend' of the king offered to hide in Gertrude's bedchamber to spy on Hamlet, is discovered, killed, and in some versions chopped into pieces, fed down a sewer and eaten by waiting pigs. A young woman, known to Hamlet since childhood, is used by the king as a sexual decoy to try to establish whether Hamlet is really mad. It was probably Shakespeare who saw the advantage in making them father and daughter, though it could have been the author (probably Thomas Kyd) of the lost play, the so-called *Ur-Hamlet*.

Unusually for Shakespeare, Polonius' first two long scenes concern his relations with his daughter and son, a rare instance of a family interacting with one another, and establish him as a domineering paternalist with an attentive, though hardly loving, attitude towards his children. Shakespeare is setting up a framework which will later work so well in *King Lear*, two families which mirror one another and end in their destruction. Polonius' advice to his son, so often taken to be comically tedious, is concise and well directed. Two unusual admonitions stand out and tell us a good deal about Polonius: 'Give every man thy ear, but few thy voice, / Take each man's censure, but

Hamlet, RSC, 2008.
OFD (Polonius), Mariah Gale (Ophelia).

reserve thy judgement'. This is the unmistakeable credo of a politician
and a spymaster. The final directive is more riddling: 'To thine own
self be true' could mean either practise noble integrity or pursue
ignoble self-interest – in any event be constant in furthering your own
interest. Polonius is not without self-knowledge. In a later scene he
gives Ophelia a prayer book to read 'to cover your loneliness', and
then admits, 'We are oft to blame in this, / 'Tis too much prov'd, that
with devotion's visage / And pious action we do sugar o'er / The devil
himself' (3.1).

What had always struck me about Polonius were his pedantic
efforts to define and pin down exactly what he was trying to say.
Research suggested that the choice of the name Polonius (in earlier
versions Corambis) may be based on the Polish statesman Grimaldus
Goslicius, whose book *The Counsellor* was published in translation in
1598, in which he comes across as verbose and sententious, imagining
that his 'art is rather to be termed the science of prating', a word

Hamlet is later to apply to the dead Polonius. This prolixity is not confined to Polonius. In his opening speech Claudius qualifies his declaration of 'taking to wife our Queen' with:

> Have we, as 'twere with a defeated joy,
> With an auspicious and a dropping eye,
> With mirth in funeral and with dirge in marriage,
> In equal scale weighing delight and dole...

Hamlet is likewise much given to elaborate lists. He instructs Horatio and Marcellus that seeing him they never shall reveal that they know aught of the Ghost:

> With arms encumbered thus, or this headshake,
> Or by pronouncing of some doubtful phrase
> As 'Well, well we know', or 'We could an' if we would',
> Or 'If we list to speak', or 'There be an' if they might',
> Or such ambiguous giving out to note...

The play is so much about word-play and Polonius outdoes them both in verbosity. This is implicit in his confusing instructions to Reynaldo, where he attempts to act out the conversational openings his servant might adopt in Paris – 'Good sir' (or so), or 'friend' or 'gentleman' – and is so buried in his own musings that he completely loses his drift: 'What was I about to say? By the mass, I was about to say something!' (senile aphasia?). It is a moment of such apparent reality that some in the audience always feel the actor has dried, and Shakespeare must have intended that – a sneaky/brilliant trick. When he tries to explain to the King and Queen his theory of Hamlet's madness he embarks on what I can only call sixty-five lines of stand-up comedy (Shakespeare first establishes the patriarch, then replaces him with the buffoon):

> My liege and madam, to expostulate
> What majesty should be, what duty is,

Why day is day, night night, and time is time;
Were nothing but to waste night, day and time.

Gertrude curtly orders him, 'More matter with less art'.

Madam, I swear I use no art at all.
That he's mad, 'tis true, 'tis true 'tis pity,
And pity 'tis 'tis true; a foolish figure!
But farewell it, for I will use no art.

The acme of his pedantic listings comes with his later attempt to define the Players' range, culminating in 'tragical-comical-historical-pastoral'. Critics interpreted my prolixity in various ways: 'drifting off into a donnishly absent-minded world of his own' (Paul Taylor); 'adrift on senility's stream of subconsciousness' (Nicholas de Jongh); 'very funny, very tragic, his is the noble mind o'erthrown by incipient Alzheimer's' (Martin Hoyle). The other aspect of Polonius I relished was that he is shown so authoritative and so wrong in almost all his judgements: Love ('I suffered much extremity'), Insanity ('a happiness that often madness hits on'), Espionage ('we of wisdom and of reach'), Literature ('"beautified" is a vile phrase'), Drama ('this is too long'), and general judgement ('hath there been such a time… that I have positively said 'tis so / when it proved otherwise'). He is a great comic creation, yet shares with Falstaff a side that is dangerous, manipulative and amoral. But like Falstaff he remains oddly endearing. One night after I was killed and fell out of my hiding place I heard a woman exclaim, "Oh, not him!"

The setting was modern, a black mirrored box designed by Robert Jones for the Courtyard Theatre, an experimental thrust stage which would later be adopted with modifications in the redesigned main theatre. The emphasis was on a camera-obsessed surveillance state, a milieu adopted by many contemporary productions. David Tennant proved to be something of a chameleon. Unfailingly courteous and friendly, he comes assertively alive when he acts. As rehearsals progressed it became clear that he was going to push Hamlet to

Hamlet, RSC, 2008.
OFD (Polonius), David Tennant (Hamlet).

extremes of anger, bitterness and wild humour. It may be that his three series as Doctor Who had encouraged him thus to go for broke. He observed and parodied everyone he came into contact with, from Guildenstern to Claudius to Osric. He was a prankish provocateur, restless and mocking, but also a depressive, reflective and suicidal. It developed into a very intelligent, exciting, unpredictable performance. At the dress rehearsal he appeared after the battlements in a Superman T-shirt but was persuaded the irony might be lost on some and he reverted to a skeleton design. He particularly enjoyed baiting Polonius, 'the foolish prating knave', and this was a great help to me as our clashes became sharper and funnier. Somehow my Polonius kept his temper until finally, having agreed the cloud was like a camel and a weasel, my anger burst forth on 'very like a whale'.

Three things I especially admired about David's performance: firstly, without disturbing the rhythm of the verse he achieved fresh, truthful, even unusual readings of certain key lines. Secondly, he recognised the importance of the pause, the time for consideration, followed by a rapid, quicksilver delivery of the next lines (if you take a pause, don't then think your way haltingly through the next sentence: you can't do both, it sends the audience to sleep). Thirdly, he didn't give us a lecture, as some Hamlets have done. He didn't hold up the text for inspection, as if to say 'This is very interesting; I'll think my way through it slowly and explain it to you'. We don't want the text explained; we want the actor to inhabit it. I know some people found David lacked philosophical weight, but you can't play a welter of opposing facets. You risk ending up with what Kenneth Tynan said of Michael Redgrave's final Hamlet: it was 'a variorum performance... at times he seems to be giving us three different interpretations of the same line *simultaneously*'.

Patrick Stewart is a formidable actor and so was his Claudius. His opening speech was masterly, geniality laced with humility but very much in charge, a supreme operator and politician. Hamlet's 'madness' seemed merely to disconcert him, but it was just possible to detect real fear and vulnerability. His composure in the play scene was remarkable. Instead of the customary cry of alarm on 'Give me some light, away!', Patrick called for a lantern, crossed to Hamlet and shone it in his face with a shake of his head which seemed to say 'Whatever it is you know, don't think you've got me'. A brilliant choice. He decided, as many Claudiuses do, to cut 'How smart a lash that speech doth give my conscience' (Act 3.1), the first admission to the audience of his guilt. Then when he finally faced up to his guilt in the prayer scene, his last line, 'Words without thoughts never to heaven go', was said not with customary bitter acceptance but wryly, as if to say 'I knew that all along'. His Claudius triumphantly demonstrated the maxim, so vital to playing villains, 'keep thinking you're winning till the last possible moment'.

Penny Downie charted Gertrude's disintegration with great precision. In the opening court scenes she looked every inch an aristocratic beauty in love, then came her growing anxiety at her son's behaviour, culminating in her raw despair at David's very visceral assault in the closet scene. Her alienation from Claudius, Ophelia's madness and death, brought her to a state where you felt she was indifferent to her own survival. And all this with 150 lines. Why so few; why not a soliloquy about her dead husband, perhaps? Claudius speaks of his love for her – 'She is so conjunct to my life and soul' – but Gertrude says nothing of her feelings for him. We only have Hamlet's fevered imagination for evidence, and we know how unreliable sons are about their mothers' sex life. She sees 'such black and grieved spots' in her soul but gives us no further enlightenment. She repeats 'As kill a king' but enquires no further. It's as if Shakespeare wanted their relationship opaque, leaving it to the actors to interpret as they choose. As Ophelia Mariah Gale was no out-of-her-depth ingenue, but a mature, intelligent young woman with a sullen, resentful acceptance of her place in society. She stood up to her father and Hamlet as strongly as she could, and I thought her mad scenes, near impossible to bring off, had reckless emotional power as her grief over her father vied with her desired sexual release. She was wonderful to act with, ready to try any range of possibilities. With Ed Bennett as Laertes, John Woodvine as Player King, Peter de Jersey as Horatio and Mark Hadfield as Gravedigger, the cast was particularly strong. I was not surprised that the literary critic Robert McCrum wrote that it was 'one of the best RSC ensembles in living memory'. It was the strongest all-round Shakespeare cast I ever worked with.

An early preview was unexpectedly attended by Gordon Brown, then prime minister and an avid collector of *Hamlets*. He and I talked afterwards of our experiences of the Edinburgh University history department (he arrived the year after I left), but it turned out to be a bad night for Gordon. We learnt later that Labour had lost the Glasgow East by-election to the SNP, a presage of Labour's defeat in 2010. At the press night critics were generally enthusiastic about the production, David's performance and the cast in general. I was pleased that *Time Out* thought I was 'a powerful nasty piece of work as well as a comically long-winded one' and Billington 'brilliant as both a sycophantic politician and a comic pedant': a vindication of playing each scene for what it was worth. I felt Polonius was the apex of my explorations into character acting, and I was hugely lucky to do it in such good company. I loved playing him. Two critics thought at the interval that it was so far the best *Hamlet* they had ever seen. Robert McCrum wrote: 'The first half was almost flawless and utterly spell-binding… the attention to detail impeccable'. But he felt the second half 'peters out when it should be a vertiginous descent into murder, mayhem and revenge'. Would that it were so vertiginous, but it has always seemed to me the second half is a problem. I had never fully realised, despite having been twice in the play, that the murder of Polonius is the major turning point. From that point on nothing will go right for Gertrude, Ophelia and Laertes, and ultimately for Hamlet and Claudius – not to mention Rosencrantz and Guildenstern. Hamlet's absence drains the play of momentum, despite Ophelia's madness and death. Claudius' plotting with Laertes (entirely Shakespeare's invention) is a major weakness: too melodramatic, too complicated, too banal. I remember Peter Wood, recognising this in an RSC 1961 production with Ian Bannen, placed it after Ophelia's burial when Laertes is at his most vulnerable – a fascinating idea, but which caused problems elsewhere. I also find the insertion of not one but two comic episodes (The Gravedigger and Osric) before the denouement a mistake – it slows down the 'vertiginous descent'. The bloodbath at the end is efficiently, if routinely, devised, apart from the difficulty of interpreting Gertrude's insistence on a drink (is it suicidal or merely defiance of Claudius?), but the arrival of Fortinbras is ill-prepared and, after much discussion between Greg and the cast, cut in our production.

As soon as *Hamlet* was on we started to rehearse *Love's Labour's Lost*. The cast was much the same, except that we were joined by Nina Sosanya as Rosaline and Joe Dixon as Don Armado. David Tennant played Berowne in his native Scottish accent. I felt that, released from both the burden of Hamlet and RP English, he gave a wonderfully free and relaxed performance. I played Holofernes the schoolmaster, with my friend Jim Hooper as Sir Nathaniel the curate. They are strange parts, entering after an hour with no introduction. When we exited on the first preview we fell into one another's arms, near-hysterical. "They had absolutely no idea who we were," said Jim, "and half of what we said they found completely unintelligible." The audience gradually got used to us and my relapses into Latin: indeed I found that the more I addressed them as if they understood my Latin quips, and were free to answer me back in Latin if they chose, the more they laughed. It was a joyous production, a great antidote to the pressure of *Hamlet*, but sadly only allowed twenty-five performances.

In December we moved to the Novello Theatre at the Aldwych for six weeks. The proscenium arch meant that our black mirrored set boxed us in and made the production more claustrophobic than on the Courtyard's open stage, a gain in many ways. Once again we were sold out: the two thousand calls a second to the box office had forced BT to suspend the line for a time so that local 999 calls could get through. As we assembled for the technical it was clear that David was in great pain with his back. He managed the first four performances, the last two often in a semi-crouching position, but it was decided at the weekend that he would have to have surgery with a six-week recovery period. Ed Bennett, his understudy, took over on Monday and the following night faced the press and came out triumphantly. His was a younger, more awkward, more emotionally restrained Hamlet. Casts adapt very rapidly to a new leading actor; it gives the production a fresh lease of life: twenty years before at the National we had to adapt to not one but two new Hamlets. David was determined to return for the last week, and then decided he could manage the preceding Saturday night. Our producer, Denise Wood, thought it advisable to go on stage to announce that David would indeed be performing. She could have been announcing the Beatles were reuniting; I have never heard an incredulous cheer like it in the theatre before or since. On the following Monday I went to the box office and the manager said wearily, "I've been telling angry people for a month that David is off. Today I give the good news to a man, and he says, 'But I don't want to see David Tennant, I want to see Edward Bennett.'"

It had been decided that instead of transmitting the production live to cinemas, a technique that had just been mastered, we should make a film for the BBC. The location was an abandoned college for training missionaries at Mill Hill in North London. The cloisters were the battlements, the cloister garden the cemetery, and the hall and chapel the interiors. Greg was able to enhance the spy theme by having occasional shots as if from surveillance cameras high on the walls. Asides and soliloquies to the audience became talking to camera, a more interesting solution in many ways. So tight was the schedule we had to shoot about ten minutes of script a day (feature films shoot two, television four to six). "Good thing you really know the words," said Chris Seager, our hugely experienced Director of Photography. "How do you remember them all?"

A postscript: Patrick and I were both nominated for an Olivier supporting actor award (David alas wasn't eligible for best actor as he hadn't done twenty performances in London, the minimum required). Patrick won, possibly the right decision.

2009–11: *All's Well,*
The Crucible, Goodnight Mister Tom

Back to the National, which made me realise that I was one of the few actors who moved seamlessly between the two companies. In the 1960s the newly formed RSC and National were separate tribes and remained so for many years. I now seemed to occupy the niche of elderly, myopic patriarch in demand from both sides. It wasn't a niche I had sought. What had happened to my rubbery clown's face? Perhaps it had become Polonius.

There is a strong fairy-tale element in *All's Well That Ends Well* that recent productions have often neglected in favour of autumnal tristesse. Marianne Elliott and Rae Smith decided to go the whole hog with Victorian storybook illustrations. There were Gothic turrets,

All's Well That Ends Well, NT, 2009.
Michelle Terry (Helena), OFD (King of France).

Sleeping Beauty briars and Transylvanian silhouettes, with a backdrop of projections of stars, bats, spiders, winking owls and howling wolves. It was bravura staging. Michelle Terry was a superb Helena, wonderful to act with and dressed initially like Little Red Riding Hood, while my King of France looked like a child's idea of royalty with a huge Father Christmas beard and an oversized (and very heavy) crown – another clown, perhaps. I had even been filmed high in a castle turret counting out my money. Clare Higgins was an unusually spirited Countess, and Conleth Hill ideally seedy and devious as Parolles. It didn't all work, but then neither does the play, and the 'happy ending' is profoundly unsettling as Helena and Bertram face the most problematic marriage in all Shakespeare's comedies.

Back to the Orange Tree for another Ben Brown play directed by Alan Strachan, *The Promise*, concerning the Balfour Declaration of 1917 which led to the setting up of the British mandate of Palestine in 1922. Researching the idealistic, if abstracted, Arthur Balfour I realised how inadequate was his advocacy for a Jewish 'homeland' when no guidance, let alone material support, was offered on how they were peacefully to co-exist with the indigenous population. 'An independent Jewish state is a matter for gradual development in accordance with the ordinary laws of political evolution', Balfour argued. No such 'ordinary laws' exist, as has become tragically evident. The complex arguments, for and against, of Balfour, Curzon and Edwin Montagu were laid out with great clarity, and the final scene set in 1925 Jerusalem brought out the tensions between the emerging Jewish 'state' and the Palestinians. Ben also cleverly interwove the story of prime minister Asquith's fixation on Venetia Stanley and her later relationship with Lord Beaverbrook. Another ambitious, beautifully written play.

Many people questioned how the Regent's Park Open Air Theatre could stage Arthur Miller's *The Crucible* when it inhabited a world of small timbered interiors. The director Timothy Sheader argued that an 'epic' play can exist on an open stage without walls, and he enhanced this with characters entering and exiting through woods and shrubs and the 'possessed' girls perching on encircling tree stumps observing, and sometimes reacting to, the ebb and flow of the action. I had long wanted to play Judge Danforth (had been unavailable for an RSC offer) and found Miller's sense of rhythm in the formal language of the part an inspiration – as Scofield had in the 1996 film. Outdoors, however, does have its drawbacks, drizzling rain some evenings making the raked wooden boards treacherous underfoot, and brilliant sunshine some matinees 'unhelpful' for the ominous breaking dawn. I then managed to fit in an obligatory appearance in *Game of Thrones* as Maester Cressen. As the priest of the old religion I tried to kill both myself and Melisandre, the new priestess, through a poisoned loving cup. I died but she didn't and, between takes, I asked Carice why she survived. "I'm four hundred years old," she explained. I thought – should have checked that first.

I was very intrigued when David Wood sent me his stage adaptation of Michelle Magorian's novel *Goodnight Mister Tom* (1981). I had seen the 1998 television version with John Thaw and discussed it with him when we were doing *Kavanagh*. The lonely, grumpy old man and the needy evacuee slowly coming together as father and son is heart-warming, even sentimental stuff, but it is leavened by a scene where William's abusive and mentally ill mother (Aoife McMahon) locks him in a cupboard and abandons him. William and his fellow evacuee Max were to be played by eleven-year-olds, so we had to have three teams of boys and this made rehearsals long drawn-out but very interesting as each of the six boys developed in their own particular way. David Wood, the laureate of theatre adaptations for children, has a great belief in 'suddenlies'. To keep an audience, especially a young audience, interested and entertained a dramatist needs to keep changing tack, producing surprises. It's basic to drama: *King Lear* and *Hedda Gabler* are full of suddenlies. Robert Innes Hopkins devised a very ingenious touring set, and Angus Jackson gave it a sparky and disciplined production.

We opened at Chichester and embarked on a tiring fourteen-week tour that stretched from Plymouth to Glasgow, from Cardiff to Norwich. Everywhere we played to near capacity, partly since the book and the television DVD were so well known but also through the lack of large-scale theatre for eight- to thirteen-year-olds. A particular hit was the puppet dog Sammy operated by Laura Cubitt under the expert tuition of Toby Olié: one small girl asked why that person kept following the dog around. I did get bored with being asked at Q&As if I had based my performance on John Thaw's, and one man actually pronounced, "I didn't think you'd be as good as John Thaw, but you were – just about." Eighteen months later Fiery Angel mounted a second production with much the same cast, though with a new set of boys (voices break so quickly). We played ten weeks at the Phoenix Theatre and toured for another ten wintry weeks. The production won the Olivier Award for Best Family Entertainment. I am very proud of it – and it's absolutely fine to act with children and animals.

Production Twelve

WRITTEN ON THE HEART
(2011–12)

2 011 was the quatercentenary of the publication of the King James Bible (the KJB), the 'Authorised Version'. Since Shakespeare was still active in 1610/11, and indeed various writers, including Kipling, have fantasised that he helped brush up the language of the Psalms or the Song of Solomon, it seemed appropriate that the RSC should tackle the subject. Eccentric Bardolaters even claim that in 1610 Shakespeare would have been forty-six, and the forty-sixth word from the beginning of the forty-sixth psalm is 'Shake', and the forty-sixth word from the end is 'Spear' (I've checked). In 2008 a conference was held at Stratford, and David Edgar was commissioned to write a play, which he titled *Written on the Heart* ('Only love and mercy truly comprehend the law, and he who has not that written on his heart shall never truly come to Christ, though all the angels taught him'). This was then workshopped by the RSC at the University of Michigan in 2010, and opened at the Swan Theatre in Stratford in October 2011.

The problems of writing a play about six years of Hebrew and Greek translators were obvious. As David wrote in *The Stage* (26/4/2012): 'the full, 80-year-plus history of the English Bible is the story of the English Reformation; it is spattered with blood and scorched with fire'. David was alive to the many modern parallels. As he wrote to me (29/5/2020): 'the fundamentalist Protestantism of the 16th and 17th centuries were so eerily resonant of other religious fundamentalism today with their veneration of the book, their hostility to the image, suspicion of music, their sexual puritanism, their desire to unify church and state, and their obsession with martyrdom. Even the beards'. David's first inclination had been to write a play about William Tyndale, the translator in the 1520s and '30s of the New Testament and the first fourteen books of the Old, who was burnt in Flanders in 1536 for his heresy. His story is the obvious dramatic subject and Howard Brenton had already put it at the centre of his Globe play *Anne Boleyn* (2010), and to David's dismay had a section on King James and Bishop Andrewes. David decided to be even more ambitious, not only to link Tyndale and 1610, but to illustrate the terrible upheavals of the interim period.

From working on his play *The Shape of the Table* in 1990 I knew that David was fascinated by middle-aged leaders balancing principle with expediency. As he wrote in *The Stage*: 'I'm interested by the way in which people with political beliefs come to make compromises… There are individuals, radicals in their youth, who decide that a certain amount of what they fought for has been achieved. We didn't get everything we wanted, they say, but we're satisfied with how far we have come. It's this far – but no further. Yet there's a younger, more radical generation who refuse to agree to this. Don't think the battle has been won, just because you say so'. The action of the play therefore was 'men compromising to make a radical idea workable in the world; but at what point does that compromise reverse the radical idea?' He later developed this theme in his one-man show *Trying it on* (2018). The person he alighted upon to personify principle versus expediency was Bishop Lancelot Andrewes, leader of the First Westminster Company, translators of Genesis to Kings, and thought to be, without conclusive evidence, the general editor of the KJB. The central conflict was between Andrewes the establishment Anglican and Tyndale the militant Lutheran. Both David and Greg Doran, the director, were keen that I should represent the establishment. I set out on my research, happy to be back in my obsession with seventeenth-century history. I also recognised that in this, my thirtieth RSC production, I had at last been offered the leading part. It had taken thirty-six years, but better late...

Andrewes was born in 1555 in Barking to a merchant mariner family. He excelled academically, went to Cambridge and later became master of his college, Pembroke. It is said he visited his parents for a month every year and took the opportunity to learn a new language, and finally knew fifteen modern languages and six ancient. As a devoted Anglican and monarchist he became a chaplain to Queen Elizabeth and a known forensic interrogator of puritan separatists, sometimes leading to their execution. He quickly endeared himself to James I by declaring in his sermon on the thwarted Gunpowder Plot that it was an act of God to preserve nation and church, and was therefore quite close to endorsing the divine right of kings. James pressed bishoprics on him, Chichester, Ely and finally Winchester, and it was assumed that he would succeed Bancroft as Archbishop of Canterbury. Many claimed him as the best preacher of his day. His sermons are oddly staccato compared to the rhetorical flow of John Donne, but spoken out loud you can appreciate how well they communicate. In his 1620 sermon on John 21.xv, Mary Magdalen at the sepulchre, he wrote: 'Christ she saw, but knew him not. Not only not know him, but mis-knew him, took him for the gardener'. You are hooked immediately. His most famous opening to a sermon is the one T. S. Eliot lifted for his *Journey of the Magi*: 'A cold coming they had of it, at this time of the year, just the worst time of the year to take a journey, and specially a long journey. The ways deep, the weather sharp, the days short, the sun farthest off, *in solstitio brumali*, the very dead of winter'.

All this seemed straightforward, but he gradually emerged as a more complex figure. There are indications that he was impressed by Calvinism in his early years but turned against it as he began to ascend the church hierarchy. He persecuted Roman Catholics as ardently as Puritans but was drawn to High Church trimmings, vestments, chalices, altar rails, kneeling stools, etc. He sat on various government committees but made a point of asking that ecclesiastical matters be taken first, and he then withdrew before political discussion could begin. He was noted for praying five hours a day, an unusual amount by the standards of the day, and thought himself a great sinner. What was this excessive guilt about? Was he plagued by memories of his Elizabethan persecutions: in a later scene we see the young Andrewes having the gall to tell the imprisoned Clerk (based on Henry Barrow), near to execution, that he is lucky to have this 'solitary and contemplative life. Yours is the life I would choose'? There are coded references in contemporary writings that he may have been gay, and perhaps this was a constant source of guilt. He had refused offers of bishoprics from Elizabeth through his opposition to the alienation of ecclesiastical revenues. Does this suggest that money had a great attraction, perhaps to fund both rebuildings and costly additions? Was he a dogged conformist, devoted to high office and its income, while avoiding political responsibilities? Anyone who survived the sixteenth century in office knew that 'trimming' was the way to stay alive.

The KJB was a translation made at a particular time for a particular purpose, not, as some fundamentalists would have it, laid down and approved by God himself. James I on his succession wanted religious peace in Europe and to bring the warring factions of Christianity together. His Hampton Court Conference in 1604 rejected the puritan faction on all important matters, and the new translation project was a sop to sweeten their defeat. John Wyclif had overseen a translation from the Latin vulgate in 1380 and under Henry IV this was declared a heresy and a burning offence. To allow all classes to read the bible in English and draw their own conclusions was far too great a threat to church control. Five of the seven major English bibles of the sixteenth century were produced in exile and two of their makers were burnt at the stake. Archbishop Bancroft ordered the new translators to defer to the 'ancient fathers' and 'the old ecclesiastical words'. James basically wanted a traditional version, observing the episcopal structure of the English church, deliberately archaic in tone with much use of 'thou', 'hast', and 'doeth', even though such usages were going out of fashion.

Significantly, he banned the word 'tyrant'. The fifty-four translators, who personified different shades of religious belief, knew that they had to steer a course between the Scylla of Catholicism, equated with tyranny, and the Charybdis of Puritanism, equated with anarchy. It was to be a struggle.

David pitches us straight into the struggle. The first scene set in 1610 in Ely House, Andrewes' London home, has seven of the leading translators, frustrated at the failure to finalise a version acceptable to king and archbishop, arguing in terms that an audience initially find hard to follow. David was unrepentant, likening it to estate agents in David Mamet's *Glengarry Glen Ross*, who have a private language the 'laity' can't possibly understand. But we are at least introduced to the key words on the issue of Catholicism v. Puritanism: 'priest' or 'elder'; 'church' or 'congregation'; 'charity' or 'love'; 'confess' or 'acknowledge'. It proved to be a gallimaufry of RSC character acting – James Hayes, Bruce Alexander, Jim Hooper, Paul Chahidi, Joseph Kloska, Simon Thorp and myself. The more we grasped what we were talking about the more heated, and therefore the more believable, we became. Michael Billington in his review couldn't stop himself quoting Groucho Marx that he wasn't sure whether he was watching one man with six beards or six men with one beard. Some enlightenment was offered at the end of the scene when Richard Thomson (Paul Chahidi) explained to Andrewes' maid Mary Currer (Jodie McNee) some of the basic background. Mary, a devout reader of Foxe's *Book of Martyrs*, preferred the 'common speech' of Tyndale's translation to the more high-flown language of the current scholars. Tyndale, by translating the Hebrew word for word, came up with simple phrases that have passed into common use: 'let my people go', 'a man after his own heart', 'the fat of the land', and dozens more.

This proved a useful bridge into Tyndale's last night before execution in a Flanders prison cell. Tyndale had exiled himself in 1525, and published his translation of the New Testament and the first five books of the Old, in Germany in 1526. This was smuggled into England and duly burnt at Cardinal Wolsey's orders. Henry VIII's mind changed however, and he gave permission for Miles Coverdale's translation from the Latin to be published in 1535. Tyndale was lured from his safe house in Antwerp, tried by the Spanish authorities for heresy and condemned to death. At some point he had translated nine further books of the Old Testament and these somehow found their way to England. David Edgar thought it reasonable to suppose that someone had managed to smuggle these out from his prison cell, and chose as the intermediary a young Roman Catholic priest sent at the last hour to seek Tyndale's repentance and save his soul. It proved a fertile dramatic choice. Tyndale, played with ferocious, reckless intensity by Stephen Boxer, runs rings round the young priest (Mark Quartley) of little learning and no great vocation – 'Find me bishops. Find me the Pope. Find me holy relics or the seven sacraments. Oh. Find me purgatory.' But it is the priest who offers to smuggle the nine books out, on the grounds that both he and 'the ploughboy' may read Joshua and Chronicles – an unexpected twist. 'To England. And the word is out', Tyndale concludes. It reminds us of course of the climax of Brecht's *Galileo*.

The third scene is in many ways the most complicated as it has to cover so much ground. It is set in a small Yorkshire church fifty years later in 1586. A deputation arrives to check whether the old Catholic ways have been ditched. These visitors are headed by the Archdeacon (James Hayes), later revealed as the young priest from the Tyndale scene, the young Lancelot Andrewes (Jamie Ballard), and the puritanical Clerk (Daniel Stewart). The local Churchwarden (Ian Midlane) miserably outlines all the successive changes their church has been forced to make under Henry VIII, Edward, Mary and Elizabeth, taking images and painted windows down, putting them back, and then taking them down again. The Clerk tries to recruit Andrewes to his 'true communion of fellowship holding all things in common' but is firmly rebuffed. It is a rich scene, with a vast, if bewildering, amount of information, argument and comedy.

The second half of the play returns to Ely House in 1610, where Andrewes discusses with the young Ward (Joseph Kloska) the final sticking points in their translation, Ward seeing Andrewes as a father figure and Andrewes showing a clear attraction to him. Left alone Andrewes flings himself before the altar: 'O base and loathsome sinner that I am. I have returned like a dog to its vomit. I know, O Lord, the plague of my heart'. In his despair Tyndale is conjured up, whom he recognises to be 'an effusion of my mind'. Tyndale is naturally appalled at the High Church trimmings of altar rails and cloths, and Andrewes counters that 'men still yearn for ceremony in the church'. Tyndale discovers the terrible irony that Coverdale was freely available in England in 1535, the year before Tyndale was executed: the English establishment clearly hadn't tried to save him, preferring him out of the way. There follows much wrangling on the key words, but Tyndale is also critical of KJB's archaic language:

> TYNDALE: So our Lord speaks as no man ever spoke… For 'the old things are gone' 'the former things are passed away'. To sacrifice the clear to the majestic.

Written on the Heart, RSC, 2011.
Stephen Boxer (Tyndale), OFD (Andrewes).

ANDREWES: No, to make the majestic clear.

TYNDALE: To smooth out the rough and rugged places. To sacrifice the meaning to the music.

Andrewes persuades Tyndale that so much of his work has endured, and to prove it they run through the Beatitudes, almost entirely Tyndale's very simple and direct translation. A chastened Andrewes allows Tyndale to dictate the changes he wants: 'love' not 'charity', 'repentance' not 'penance'. It is a wonderful twenty-minute duologue (not easy to learn), but the audience laughter on the slight groan I gave when Tyndale insisted on 'congregation' not 'church' was one of my most satisfying moments of the evening – they'd got it. It is a scene, and a play, about the primacy of language and its many ambiguities, a theme I had struggled with on stage for over fifty years.

The final beat of the play brought the inevitable compromises and a hint of what lay in the future. The translators arrive and argue over Andrewes' new list; an unexpected visit of the Princes Henry and Charles show Henry, heir to the throne, to be a confirmed Protestant (had he not died of typhoid the following year there might have been no civil war); William Laud proclaims himself to a largely sympathetic Andrewes as a zealot for 'tradition, sacraments, good works, and majesty' (which, when archbishop, will lead to his execution by parliament in 1645); Andrewes writes to Archbishop Bancroft, 'It is possible that some amendments were made in undue haste... you might wish to revise them', knowing that 'priest' and 'church' will be reinstated. He declines any thought of the archbishopric, prophesying to Mary, 'I will stay here, in this place... I would not see the fate of kings and prince. Nor my fate, nor yours. Fearing that one day you will strip and smash and burn such places as this'. Tyndale reappears and confirms that his purpose is 'still here... the ploughboy reads the book and sees God face to face'. Such a brief summary, omitting much detail, confirms I think that David had succeeded in giving shape 'to the chaos of life' in outlining the history of the English Reformation.

Rehearsals for the play were hugely enjoyable. We were a disparate lot religiously. David Edgar had been to a very Protestant boarding school, Greg Doran to a very Jesuit, and I to a very Anglican. Stephen Boxer had been at New College Oxford choir school, and others had a similarly diverse background, so we brought a wealth of knowledge and prejudice to discussions. Everyone was sent away to prepare short talks on relevant subjects, and I extended my research on Andrewes. Jodie McNee had steeped herself in Foxe's *Book of Martyrs* and held forth on Mary's burning of three hundred Protestants, which spurred on others to retaliate with the execution of Roman Catholics under Henry VIII and Edward – a Cranmer for a Thomas More. There was much disagreement about the validity of smashing windows and beheading statues. We were fortunate that Diarmaid McCulloch, professor of the history of the church at Oxford, came and talked to us about the KJB. He pointed out the many pitfalls, that fundamentalists who took the Bible literally might feel that if polygamy was good enough for Hebrew patriarchs it was good enough for them, and there was no justification in the Bible not only for purgatory and bishops but even for infant baptism. The Bible (ta biblia, 'The Books') is a library full of questions rather than clear answers. I found that a great help when considering Andrewes' uncertainties.

We had rehearsed in London and arrived in Stratford to find a beautiful ornate set by Francis O'Connor and to hear Paul Englishby's modern take on plainsong (two sopranos, two tenors and a bass). The company had been learning for weeks the motet 'Rejoice in the glorious mother of God', and this was rehearsed nightly and sung live at every performance. This attention to period detail, a great strength of Greg Doran's, is an incalculable help to the actor, both a cushion and an inspiration. The play opened in good shape, and the reviews were almost entirely four-star positive. 'The RSC at its best: fine actors swimming in great words and ideas' (*The Times*). 'Bracing and radical... In Greg Doran's powerfully involving production the piece brings the Reformation and its ideological conflicts stingingly alive' (*The Independent*). Stephen and I were much liked. Most notices agreed it required a lot of concentration from the audience, and some went further – 'The production is weighed down by numerous blokes in cloaks spouting fact-stuffed sentences at each other' (*Evening Standard*).

The play seemed unlikely to have a further life when to our surprise Thelma Holt, in her immense enthusiasm for the production, persuaded Bill Kenwright that they should together transfer it to London. It was shoe-horned into the Duchess Theatre and as we had found with *Hamlet* in 2009 the move from a thrust stage to a proscenium is not difficult: I think the opposite direction would present greater problems. Advance bookings were scanty and it was clear we would have to rely on a second wave of reviews. But critics and papers were reluctant to come to it again. Indeed *The Observer*, one of serious theatre's mainstays, failed to review it in either Stratford or London. Audiences never built, the hoped-for coachloads of Christians and theology students didn't arrive, the notice went up and we were off in five weeks, Thelma and Bill taking a big financial loss. West End transfers are always unpredictable, as many a well-reviewed regional and Edinburgh fringe production have found. The RSC has cachet, but it was a new play on a difficult subject with no stars in its cast. Perhaps it had simply missed the boat: the KJB had been thoroughly dissected in the first half of 2011 (everybody wanted to get their centenary contribution in as early as possible), and it was now April 2012. We were too late. But perhaps it goes deeper. The Anglican Settlement caused such anguish and cost to so many lives, but in our secular age the majority are no longer interested in, or even aware of, the strange compromise that was finally reached, mildly Protestant in doctrine, semi-Catholic in ceremony. The play remains one of the most rewarding experiences of my time at the RSC, the Andrewes-Tyndale duologue with Stephen Boxer one of the most engrossing scenes I have ever played.

2013–21: *Fathers and Daughters*, RSC histories, Peter Gynt

Ever since I discovered in 2007 that Leonato was the second longest part in *Much Ado* the idea of writing about the fathers in Shakespeare had been marinating in my mind. It was unthinkable, however, not to link them to their daughters. From Titus and Lavinia through to Prospero and Miranda, the father and the single daughter obsessed Shakespeare. In long gaps when *Written* was out of the repertoire I set to in earnest at both the Stratford Shakespeare Centre and Institute. The many books on the subject, mostly by American academics, tended to marshal them into categories: fathers reactionary, mercenary and jealous; daughters dominated, defiant, and androgynous. Since I found Shakespeare's characters defy such reductive categorisation, I decided on a chronological approach, play by play. My historical training insisted on putting all this in context, with chapters on Shakespeare's own daughters, fathers and daughters in contemporary society, and in drama 1585–1620 (I had to withstand many attempts from academics to cut these as too well-known). It was clearly to be an academic book and I went through the agony of referencing and checking everything I cited. After some years I sent a draft to the Bloomsbury Arden Shakespeare and to my delight/amazement/dread they agreed to take it on. Margaret Bartley, my wise and supportive editor, persuaded me that it would attract more interest if I were to personalise my accounts of at least Capulet, Leonato, Polonius and Lear, giving them 'an actor's perspective'. She was right, since when my book *Shakespeare's Fathers and Daughters* came out in 2017 it was this aspect that several good reviews picked on. In recent years academics thankfully have attached growing importance to what actors have to say about plays in performance. I was pleased that nearly a decade of work had come to fruition, but knew this would be my final word on Shakespeare. I was Barded-out.

In the same year, 2017, our daughter Miranda Emmerson published her first novel *Miss Treadway and the Field of Stars* (4th Estate) set in

1965 London – 'A fabulous period piece, expertly evoked, that looks at race, identity, isolation and acceptance, and everyone's need to find love' (*Daily Mail*). For a decade she had worked for various charities and freelanced for Radio 4 abridging and dramatising books, while publishing a travel diary, with vegetarian recipes, on China and the Far East, *Fragrant Heart* (Summersdale, 2014). She now lives in South Wales with her husband Chris, a public health consultant, and their two bilingual daughters, Alice and Rosalind. Her second novel *A Little London Scandal* (4th Estate) came out in 2020, at the same time as her PhD on radio adaptation was accepted. Jenny and I are so happy that writing has become her way of life.

In early 2012 Greg Doran told me he was going to do *Henry IV* and V and how did I feel about playing... my heart missed a beat; he's going to offer me Falstaff... Justice Shallow? I swallowed my disappointment; Shallow is a wonderful part: his first duologue with Silence is many people's favourite scene in Shakespeare. The rest of the package was York in *Richard II* and the Chorus in *Henry V*. Various knights and film stars had turned down Falstaff until Ian McKellen suggested Tony Sher, not an obvious Falstaff but such an intelligent and resourceful actor that he can turn his hand to anything, and he proved excellent, one of the best explorers of a text I have ever worked with. Now much missed, taken before his time. Greg's production of *Richard II* was I thought his most successful, David Tennant at home with the many aspects of Richard, Michael Pennington magisterial as Gaunt, and the device of making Aumerle rather than Exton Richard's murderer an added, if debatable, bonus. I went further down the comedic line with York, a welcome, if rare, instance of revisiting a part. As Shallow in *Henry IV part 2* I was reunited with Jim Hooper as Silence and our 'Is old Double dead?' scene was a joy to play. If only Shakespeare had written more about the Warwickshire middle class and less about the Italian aristocracy. And yet when he wrote a small-town comedy set in Windsor it proved an uninspired potboiler. The Shallow-Silence scene must have been a one-off morning of exceptional inspiration. Jasper Britton and Alex Hassell made a fine king and son. I greatly enjoyed

Henry IV part 2, RSC, 2014.
Jim Hooper (Silence), Anthony Sher (Falstaff), OFD (Shallow).

relating to the audience with the Chorus, forty years after I had first understudied it. It is difficult to assess objectively a new production when you have been in such a successful and rigorously examined past production, but I never felt our cast got the measure of *Henry V*.

We took the three *Henry* plays to China in early 2016. A week each in Beijing and Shanghai and two weeks in Hong Kong, though we were never certain how far we were political and business ambassadors. We had been warned the audiences might talk, eat and film, but they proved very attentive – presumably we had been sold as high culture. The one drawback were the Chinese surtitles which often delivered the joke before we had got to it. I found Shanghai the most rewarding city, Beijing fascinating but cold and grey under a pall of pollution, and Hong Kong one vast building site, Versace and Gucci on every major street corner, a depressing advance on my first visit in 1989. Among letters of appreciation was one from a drama student who envied the freedom which she sensed in our acting. China, like Japan, believes in conformity, in not sticking out from the crowd ('if the nail rears up, bang it home'), while westerners believe this an essential part of any art form (Hong Kong was soon to find out that its nonconformity was to be further curtailed). Then on to New York and Harvey BAM for six weeks, when we were joined by *Richard II*. We were a sell-out and audiences were as always very warm and immediate. I am not a great NY lover, apart from the art galleries, theatres and music (Nina Stemme as Strauss' Electra at the Met was breath-taking). My other highlights were the Brooklyn and New York botanical gardens, and my accustomed train journey up the Hudson River, P'keepsie, Cold Springs and Hyde Park. As I travelled I knew that this was my final tilt at the Shakespeare histories, first explored over sixty years ago as Pistol when I was fourteen.

A word about twenty-first-century salaries. Playing Cleopatra or Prospero for the RSC you would earn a little over £1k per week, £55 to 60k if you worked a full year. This is approximately the same as a primary-school headteacher or an experienced train driver (both worth every penny for the responsibilities they carry). The National Theatre has a basic salary plus performance fee, so that in a week of eight performances (rare) a leading actor might earn £1,700, a week with no performances £950. It has been calculated that to live in the more desirable parts of London you need to be earning at least £50k a year, so it is small wonder most actors struggle to survive.

In 2018 I played the Judge in a revival of Enid Bagnold's *The Chalk Garden* at Chichester, directed by Alan Strachan. It's an odd play, part drawing-room comedy, part mystery thriller, part psychological study of grandmother, mother, and daughter. I had seen the original in 1956 with Edith Evans, Peggy Ashcroft and Felix Aylmer. Amanda Root and Penelope Keith were excellent, and I much admired Penny's technique of 'You can laugh at that if you must, but I'd rather you didn't'. I keep learning. Greg Doran then asked me if I would reprise my Nestor from 1981 in *Troilus and Cressida*. I wasn't over-keen, but it is such an interesting and difficult play, which we hadn't cracked thirty-seven years ago, that I agreed. Greg also planned to have fifty-

fifty gender casting, all the rage at the time but a very masculine play to experiment on. Agamemnon, Ulysses, Aeneas, Thersites and Calchas were to be played by women. The great Evelyn Glennie was to devise the entirely percussive music.

On the Wednesday of the fourth week of rehearsals Greg took me aside and told me a far-from-well Desmond Barritt had been advised by his doctors not to continue with Pandarus, and would I take it over? I accepted with foreboding, as I knew what a difficult part it is to learn, at times a wandering stream of consciousness. Eight days later we had a run-through, books down, and not only was I not there yet but I began to have doubts that I would make it on time (I was nearly eighty after all). Pandarus is clearly meant to be a good singer, but my only way to cope was to turn the song into a comic disappointment (that I can do). There is no putting off the first performance because an actor isn't ready: out there will be hundreds of people, many of whom at a first preview will know the play well. The final week of rehearsal and the technical were at times excruciating – nerves before entering are a good thing, but terror is not advisable – but I was more or less there on the first preview. On the third preview I started scene one with my second speech and the rest of my interchange with a perplexed Troilus (Gavin Fowler) was out-of-sync carnage, a nightmarish five minutes, terror rampant. The press night went reasonably well, and by the last two weeks of a five-week run I began to enjoy it enormously, particularly working with Amber James (Cressida). I could feel my feminine side released, and I realised for the umpteenth time Shakespeare's unblinkered, unsentimental view of humanity. Pandarus, the 'loveable, camp softie', learns that his niece is forced to leave for the Greek camp, and in his obsession with Troilus brutally turns on her: 'Would thou hadst ne'er been born! I knew thou wouldst be his death'. It's a strong contender for the cruellest line in the folio. I was elated when a man stopped me in a Stratford street to say I had surpassed Max Adrian, since the 1960 season his favourite Pandarus – actors are so greedy for informed praise. The production proved divisive. The spectacular 'Mad Max' setting, motor bikes and all, seemed to me at odds with a very Homeric/Jacobean play, as did the fifty-fifty gender casting. The hugely versatile Adjoa Andoh (Ulysses) argued she was playing a character, gender irrelevant, and this must be the way forward.

Fifty-two years after I had last been in *Peer Gynt*, 1967 to 2019, I was offered it again, advancing from Madhouse Keeper to Button Moulder. It was a happy occasion as it reunited me at the National with Jonathan Kent and David Hare – David still scowling at his text in the hope of improvement, as he did thirty years ago. Sticking to its basic structure and scene content, he had totally rewritten it for the twenty-first century, where it sat, renamed *Peter Gynt*, probingly and questioningly. David had set his version in Dunoon, on the shore of the Firth of Clyde (Scotland and Norway are a good fit), and the cast were largely Glaswegian, headed by the immensely talented James McArdle. He was sharp, funny, and at times very moving. Guy Henry (Weird Passenger), Jonathan Coy (Troll King) and myself were the English interlopers. Jonathan's carefully orchestrated production divided the critics, achieving the rare distinction of very few three stars. The two stars demanded why the National was wasting time and money on this dreary old play; the four stars proclaimed it, in Michael Billington's words, as 'a sharp satire on contemporary mores', and even the *Daily* Mail called it 'an exuberant reinvention. Swashbuckling theatre'. It was a co-production with the Edinburgh Festival, and we took it there for ten days, where I had my eightieth birthday. I was very happy to be back in Edinburgh seeing old friends, though my main festival memory is ploughing my way through impossibly crowded pavements in incessant rain. As the Button Moulder (the harbinger of death) I came on after three hours. This was not without stresses, but it did enable me to read something I thought I would never achieve, Proust's *A la Recherche, vols 3 & 4*.

In 2020 the Covid pandemic struck but I did manage to go to Sweden and Greece to film a ninety-year-old arms manufacturer blown up by one of his own hand grenades. Ruben Ostlund's *Triangle of Sadness* won the Cannes Palme d'Or. 2021 was dominated by my third Ben Brown play, *A Splinter of Ice*, playing Graham Greene on

A *Splinter of Ice*, Original Theatre, 2021.
OFD (Graham Greene), Stephen Boxer (Philby).

a visit to his old friend Kim Philby in Moscow in 1987. We filmed it
on the Cheltenham stage, streamed it, later toured it for seven weeks,
Bath to Edinburgh, and finally played it at the Jermyn Street theatre.
It was thirty years since Stephen Boxer (Philby) and I had first played
together, ten years since Tyndale and Andrewes had argued the Bible's
wording. It is such a joy to play with an actor whom you know and
understand so well. Greene was eighty-two in 1987, exactly my age
in 2021 – at long last I was the right age for the part. One review
said: 'Watching him listen to the other characters is an object lesson in
stagecraft and mastery of subtext'. Perhaps after half a century I had
grasped how to listen.

AFTERWORD

I am very aware of my privilege. I belong to that group of privately educated, Oxbridge graduates, with no formal drama training, who started in theatre through Oxbridge connections. With that background many got an early break, but then some flourished, many foundered and dropped out. I was white, male, six-foot-tall with a strong voice. Provided I had some talent and a good deal of luck (luck sometimes more important than talent) I might find work in Shakespeare and the classics, and to play authority figures in film and television. I was probably going to make a living, for many the definition of a successful actor. But I wasn't conventionally good-looking, had no powerful agent, few contacts, no inflated idea of my abilities, and was not adept at self-promotion. I was, however, as Chekhov advised, determined to keep going.

Much has changed in theatre in the last sixty years. Let's start with buildings, because without stages actors have nowhere to work. Growing up in Ealing I saw Donald Wolfit's King Lear at the King's Theatre Hammersmith and my first *Carmen* by the Carl Rosa Opera at the Chiswick Empire – all companies and venues long gone. Ian McKellen remembers that in the 1940s and '50s Bolton had three large theatres that had survived, mostly as cinemas, and were demolished in the early 1960s. In their place the Bolton Octagon opened in 1967, a flexible theatre seating 3/400. The Theatre Royal Exeter (1889) closed in 1962, and was replaced by the Northcott Theatre in 1967, seating 464, in the university far from the centre of the city. Other university campus theatres on the edge of town opened at Warwick, Stirling, Aberystwyth and Brighton, but because they were not on the high street, often requiring a car to get to, they tended to make the theatre more elitist. The first civic theatre to be built in Britain since the 1939–45 war was the Belgrade Coventry in 1958. Its elderly partner the Coventry Theatre, seating two thousand and host to Ken Dodd and the Royal Ballet (different weeks), staggered on. In 1983 I remember marching in opposition to its closure, when a Stratford technician argued to me that its lighting board and flying system were a nightmare and it should be pulled down. It closed two years late. With the near-demise of variety many of these huge old theatres had become obsolete and far too expensive to maintain.

The 1970s saw a burst of theatre building in the regions thanks to Jennie Lee and Harold Wilson's Arts Council beneficence and local authority funding: Sheffield Crucible, Royal Exchange Manchester, Theatr Clwyd, Mercury Colchester, Birmingham Rep and others, many with studio theatres attached. In affluent periods some large town councils have been attracted to a theatre project, but unfortunately civic pride often demanded thousand-plus seaters, 'super-venues' ("You can make your money on the panto," as councillors were apt to say), suitable only for large-scale tours, particularly musicals, and no friend to plays and in-house productions: Salford Lowry, Aylesbury Riverside, New Victoria Woking. There is a dearth of attractive middle-scale touring in the manner of the Cambridge Theatre Company, and the national companies have been slow to fill the gap. Theatres have become very dependent on subsidy. New Labour under Tony Blair greatly increased Arts Council funding following the Boyden Report (2000) and this enabled regional theatres to commission and programme new work, but since the 2008 crash, followed by Tory austerity, arts support per head of population has fallen by 35%, with local government investment decreasing by 43% and business sponsorship by much the same amount. Some theatres have become 80/90% dependent on box office. Closures under the pandemic have brought it to crisis proportion, and attempts to reopen in 2021 have been often stymied by Covid outbreaks.

London is a separate state. When I started haunting theatres in the 1950s there was very little off-West End theatre, apart from the Old Vic and Royal Court, though there were a number of theatres in the outer boroughs – Hackney, Stratford, Palmers Green and Croydon. Hampstead Theatre Club opened in a school hall in 1959, but it was not until the late 1960s that the Open Space, the King's Head, The Young Vic and the Soho Theatre opened, followed by the Bush in 1972, Donmar Warehouse in 1977, and the Almeida in 1980. The forty-odd West End theatres have survived more or less intact, mainly hosting musicals, and the National Theatre had finally opened its three auditoria by 1977. Since then small theatres have mushroomed in the inner boroughs, from the Arcola to the Park, the Print Room to the Southwark Playhouse. This huge concentration of venues has had a profound effect on theatre ecology, not all beneficial. It has provided work for actors, writers, directors, designers and stage management, often poorly paid, but tied them to London to the detriment of the regions. London accounts for roughly half of all theatre performances and attendances, and together with museums, galleries and their like has gobbled up a disproportionate amount of funding. It has nearly ten times per capita in arts grants as the East Midlands or East Anglia.

Playwriting has exploded. In the 1950s we were heavily under the influence of France, America and Germany, but in contrast to art and music very little experimentation was taking place in Britain. For my generation our British icon was John Whiting's *Saints Day*, which won an Arts Theatre Festival of Britain prize in 1951 and was dismissed by *The Times* as 'of a badness that must be called indescribable'. Its atmosphere of mystery, violence and military brutality seemed to us startlingly original and my friend Sam Walters directed a production at university, which Whiting came to see and talked to us at length. The Royal Court might become our spiritual home but it had an uncertain beginning. The director/actor George Devine wanted it to be a 'writer's theatre' that was 'original, contemporary and challenging', and his first great success was Osborne's *Look Back in Anger*, though the play has an orthodox plot that even Rattigan or Coward might have used. More influential in the long run were Pinter's *The Birthday Party*, John Arden's *Live Like Pigs* and *Sergeant Musgrave's Dance*, Wesker's *Roots*, Joan Littlewood's work at Stratford East, and Behan's *The Hostage*. The British have always written plays, the 1951 Arts Theatre competition had over a thousand entries, but the plays of the late '50s galvanised writers to think in a different way, to realise that nothing was out of bounds. In 1965 I remember Jim Haynes put on a C. P. Taylor play at the Traverse Theatre in Edinburgh, and told me he asked Taylor if he had any other plays. The next day ten scripts arrived on his desk, and Jim said, with a gleam in his eye, "And they're all different."

The fifteen years after 1956 were a time of growing experiment partly because the new writers came from all backgrounds and had no templates to work from or react against. Anne Jellicoe, whose *The Knack* was an early Royal Court success, had no idea of an end product – 'I created it as a blind man creates sculpture'. But most writers, whether Pinter or Osborne, Arden or Edward Bond, were linked in attacking the Conservative establishment and the imperial inheritance. They showed a Britain divided along lines of class, wealth and generations. Violence lurked or was overt, as in Bond's *Saved* or Arden's *Sergeant Musgrave's Dance*. But in my '60s theatre-going I was excitedly aware of huge contrasts between Joe Orton's high-stylised farce *Loot*, Bond's *Early Morning* (the fantasy Queen Victoria's lesbian relationship with Florence Nightingale was so shocking to the Lord Chamberlain that the Royal Court had to become a club theatre) and David Storey's gently naturalistic *The Contractor* and *Home*, where Storey claimed he wrote a first line with no idea what would follow. There was also the significant development of a writer linked to an artistic director: Wesker with John Dexter, Storey with Lindsay Anderson, Bond with Bill Gaskill.

In 1971 I was overwhelmed by Trevor Griffiths' *Occupations* presented by the RSC at The Place with Patrick Stewart, Ben Kingsley and Heather Canning, and dealing with the 1920 Turin factory sit-in by Antonio Gramsci ('pessimism of the spirit, optimism of the will' – one of my favourite motifs). It exemplified a re-emergence of political writing, helped by the end of censorship in 1968, which was far from one-sided agitprop with Howard Brenton's *Weapons of Happiness*, David Edgar's *Destiny*, John McGrath's *The Cheviot, the Stag and the Black Black Oil*, and David Hare's *Knuckle* and *Plenty*. Hare wrote that 'I can't write unless I know what the politics are', and television's *Play for Today* joined in the debate, with Jeremy Sandford and Ken Loach's *Cathy Come Home* leading the way. Lindsay Anderson at the Royal Court was opposed to political subjects, but as Hare and others argued that was where the energy was coming from. In 1973 Hare, Max Stafford-Clark and later Bill Gaskill set up *Joint Stock* with, at any rate in theory, collective decision-making. Their record is astonishing, most of which I managed to see: *Fanshen*, *Light Shining in Buckinghamshire*, *The Ragged-Trousered Philanthropists* and *Cloud Nine*. Small theatres, often based in pubs at lunch-time, began to flourish, among them the Orange Tree in Richmond, my adopted home. The alternative also made headway with The Women's Theatre Group, Monstrous Regiment, Gay Sweatshop and Tara Arts. Theatrical energy might have returned, but with diminished optimism. It was a fractured decade, uncertain where it was heading after the exaggerated hopes of the '60s.

The '80s seemed at first dominated by the blockbuster musical. *Cats* led the way, followed by *Starlight Express*, *Les Miserables* and *The Phantom of the Opera*. Some writers seemed established, Pinter, Ayckbourn, Stoppard, Hare, Churchill, Frayn and Bennett, but fewer new writers were emerging. As Arts Council funding dropped under Thatcher the market and commercialism came to rule. Dennis Potter claimed the real national theatre was BBC 1. There were still stage plays that attacked the prevailing worship of money: Churchill's *Serious Money* and *Top Girls*, Hare and Brenton's *Pravda*, and Ayckbourn's

A Small Family Business, but as Stafford-Clark later wrote to Richard Eyre, 'The Eighties have been like trench warfare fighting endlessly on the same miserable yards of territory and, of course, being pushed slowly backwards... "marketing" and "security" have been the only growth areas'.

Analysing where Thatcher's shattering of society had left us brought very different responses. I was in the Hare Trilogy at the National (1993) which saw the Church, Law and Politics on the back foot. I was also in Edgar's *The Shape of the Table* (1990), which tackled the crumbling of the Soviet Union, but most dramatists' interests lay elsewhere. Stephen Daldry at the Royal Court argued that 'thesis plays' were outdated and energy now lay in 'a personalised internal search without necessarily a clear answer'. Under his aegis Jez Butterworth's riotous *Mojo* was set in 1950s Soho gangland; Sarah Kane shockingly exposed the link between personal and public brutality; Mark Ravenhill set out to mirror society for whose evils there was no clear solution; and Joe Penhall explored issues that had hardly been touched on, such as a schizophrenic discharged into 'Care in the Community'. Mike Leigh has continued to develop off-beat subjects in his inimitable way. For me Simon Stephens, whose *On the Shore of the Wide World* I had so admired at the Manchester Royal Exchange, best sums up a prevailing attitude towards the public and the personal: 'What does this story say about the world, and what does it say about me?'

I had worked with debbie tucker green when she was a stage manager at the Almeida, and I was very impressed by her monologue *random* at the Royal Court in 2008, and again at Chichester in 2018. There had of course been black and Asian writers in earlier decades, Winsome Pinnock, Roy Williams, Mustapha Matura, and Hanif Kureishi, but now they were being more frequently commissioned, though their work rarely appeared on main stages. It is a serious indictment that Natasha Gordon's *Nine Night* was in 2018 the first black woman's play to appear in the West End. There has also been an explosion of women's writing. Once again there were earlier exemplars, Caryl Churchill and Pam Gens had been writing since the '70s, Timberlake Wertenbaker and April de Angelis since the '80s, but so many talented women writers had found it difficult to escape from the subsidised fringe. The National's Olivier stage had opened in 1976 and it took until 2008 for a woman dramatist, Rebecca Lenkiewicz's *Her Naked Skin*, to be produced there. Since then Lucy Kirkwood, Laura Wade, Lucy Prebble, Nina Raine, Alice Birch and others have enjoyed success in various venues, their widely diverging subjects ranging from the public to the private, from the financial scandal of Prebble's *Enron* to Wade's domestic fantasy *Home I'm Darling*. In television a number of women writers have established themselves, Kay Mellor, Abi Morgan, Heidi Thomas, Sally Wainwright, Victoria Wood, Sharon Horgan, Julia Davis and others, though a recent report showed that only 23% of TV scripts are written by women. Artistic directors like Jude Kelly, Josie Rourke, and Vicky Featherstone have helped the shift, and many theatres like Liverpool, Stratford East, Theatr Clwyd, Lyric Hammersmith and Oxford Playhouse are now, or have been, run by women, though there is a long way to go before there is fifty-fifty representation, particularly in the largest venues. I have concentrated on women and writers of colour since 2000 because I think this is the most significant development of the present century, but of course writers like Butterworth, Churchill, Penhall, Stephens, Martin Crimp, Conor McPherson and Martin McDonagh continued to produce major work. Political theatre re-emerged at the Tricycle/Kiln, the Royal Court and elsewhere. David Hare's *Stuff Happens, The Power of Yes* and *I'm Not Running* were all at the National, and James Graham pioneered a new form of docudrama with *This House, The Vote, Ink* and *Labour of Love*. Few writers can make a living writing for the stage, but Joe Penhall has a good take on the special challenge and reward of theatre: 'I think that the process from the page to the stage is like a chemical change of state. It's like liquid turning to gas, or gas returning to fire. There's an enormous release of latent energy of which nobody is aware till it happens'.

Lastly, what changes have taken place in acting in the last sixty years? This is the hardest to pin down; every generalisation is suspect. The number of actors has undoubtedly increased, though it is hard to put a figure on this. In 2022 Equity numbers stood at 46,000, though non-Equity performers would greatly swell this number. It is also evident from Equity records that the number of BAME performers has multiplied. The reasons for this general increase are much debated. There is certainly more work available in television and film. There is the lure of big money, much of it anecdotal and illusory: in my experience rates of pay for supporting actors in television have actually gone down in the last twenty-five years. There is also the lure of celebrity; appearing regularly on television in even a minor role can bring you a kind of fame, however short-lived. I have a personal theory that attitudes to the viability of becoming an actor have changed. Sixty years ago parents would urge their children to get a secure job in manufacturing, business or banking, and not risk the gamble of acting. Today secure jobs are a fantasy: banks and manufacturers regularly lay off thousands. Acting seems no greater a risk than anything else, so why not go for it?

There are, however, downsides to becoming an actor. Training, either at drama schools or at university and college drama departments, has become far more expensive. We celebrated the influx of working-class actors in 1960, but Tom Courtenay not only got a RADA scholarship but a grant from Hull Education Committee and John Thaw got a grant from Manchester Council. Since the 1990s many drama schools realised that to survive they had to affiliate with universities, and so it now costs £9,250 a year to train at RADA, Central, Guildhall and others. This amount, plus living costs, is a great deterrent to poorer families, and casting directors are already finding it hard to cast young working-class parts: acting is in danger of becoming a preserve of the better-off. Although there may be more work in television, competition has greatly increased, while stage work outside London has diminished. The days when I could spend eighteen months learning my craft at the Birmingham Rep have long gone. Tours of major musicals have become more frequent, but the big touring play companies like Prospect, Compass and the English Shakespeare Company foundered long ago for lack of Arts Council support. In their place are a host of local touring and community companies, from Eastern Angles in Suffolk to Kneehigh in Cornwall and Hull Truck in Yorkshire.

There has been a general decline in skill in speaking, my particular obsession. Peter Gill wrote in 2007 that when he set up the National Theatre Studio in 1984 many felt that young actors were 'a very talented generation, and were on the whole more edgy and real than their seniors, capable of playing a wide range of parts, adept at dialect, and with unusual access to feeling, but they lacked the skill which the speaking required, particularly of difficult texts and more particularly with speaking Shakespeare'. There are many reasons for this. Drama schools have placed less emphasis on speech, on the breath required for handling complicated text; and the whole notion of cultivating an RP accent, which once dominated training, has become old-fashioned and decidedly uncool. Most of their students' work will be in television, very few will do Sheridan, Wilde or Shakespeare, and in film 'naturalism' will be favoured above speech with directors obsessed with the visual. As a result actors in their search for realism have taken to throwing away or mumbling text, hoping the sound department can sort that out. "They call it realism; we call it inaudibility," sound engineers have moaned to me, as they make a quiet mumble become a loud mumble. Inaudibility has also taken hold in the theatre. I have even heard an actor say, "I'm only interested in reaching the front ten rows." When the RSC productions transfer to the Barbican I always ask visiting friends if they heard everything. "Well, not everything," they routinely reply, as if you no longer go to the theatre expecting to hear all the words.

Elsewhere there is good news. Diversity has slowly improved. Cleo Sylvestre appeared in the West End in 1967 and at the National in 1970, but when she applied for further stage work the standard reply was that they would keep her in mind if they did *The Crucible*, which has a black slave Tituba. Other black actors in the '60s, Don Warrington, Carmen Munroe, Norman Beaton, Thomas Baptiste, found it very hard to get parts in plays perceived as 'all-white'. There was no recognition that there are a wealth of parts – Cleopatra, Jacques, Dr Astrov, Solveig – that could be played by actors of colour without even the need to invoke 'colour-blindness'. In 1982 Hugh Quarshie was the first black actor at the RSC to play a leading white role, Hotspur in *Henry IV part 1*. Since then I have worked with so many talented black actors in Shakespeare, Shaw and Otway – Paterson Joseph, Jenny Jules, Cyril Nri, Nina Sosanya, Ray Fearon, and most recently Adjoa Andoh and Amber James. My current worries are firstly that there are far fewer actors from Asian and other ethnicities, twelve per cent of the UK population; and secondly, that there are so few BAME people backstage, in administration and behind the camera. As Sandra Oh observed when filming, "Sometimes it would be me and seventy-five white people."

In the past there were of course many actors we would now regard as truthful and naturalistic – we might be amazed how modern Forbes-Robertson or Eleonora Duse would appear. In *Saturday Night and Sunday Morning* (1960) the performances of Albert Finney, Rachel Roberts, and Bryan Pringle are as fresh and modern as you would wish. Judi Dench in *Talking to a Stranger* (1964) is as truthful, and inspired as she would be now. But if you compare the formulaic, stereotypical acting in British B-movies of the 1950s and '60s with any modern TV series you can immediately see the difference. This improvement is partly to do with drama training. Sheila Hancock said RADA in the 1950s was 'a finishing school for the rich'. Michael Blakemore remembers being told by a teacher, "YOU STUPID BOY! Professional actors don't stand on both legs! They stand first on one leg, then on another. SURELY you see that!" Today RADA can choose from thousands of applicants and has a totally different approach. Drama Centre London, founded in 1967, went further, bringing a mixture of the 'Method', Jungian psychology, Laban movement and Joan Littlewood to upend traditional training.

Some actors think it sufficient to 'learn the lines and say them reasonably naturalistically', as Norman Rodway once disparagingly put it to me. This is common in television where, with little or no time for rehearsal, directors prefer you not to do anything bold or unexpected for fear it might look like Acting. 'Saying the words' I suspect served actors well for centuries, but since the 1930s a more rigorous approach has been attempted, partly under the influence of Stanislavski. Lee Strasberg's so-called Method was never fully embraced in Britain, feeling that it promoted self-indulgence and a disregard for the text. But Max Stafford-Clark, for instance, at the Royal Court and Joint Stock, has always promoted objectives and super-objectives for each scene, and many directors have adopted a modified version of this. Declan Donnellan has emphasised 'the Target': 'You can never know what you are doing until you first know what you are doing it to'. Stanford Meisner has probably the greatest influence today in America and elsewhere. He wanted the actor to 'get out of their head' and behave instinctively to the surrounding environment. The focus is on relating to the other actor to achieve the 'spontaneity of improvisation'. This has become the gold star of modern acting. The best acting has of course always embraced this principle of apparent spontaneity. Spencer Tracy's dictum was: 'I listen, I think, and I speak, and if you think that's easy, try it'. These are versions of Alec McCowen's counsel to me in 1967: 'I clear my mind, listen to what's being said to me, and find myself replying with the words the author has given me'. It's the kind of spontaneity that in their very different ways Ken Loach and Mike Leigh hope to achieve, and it has made a vital difference to British acting.

Harold Guskin, renowned New York acting coach, wrote in his book *How to Stop Acting*: 'the actor's job is to make each moment of the character in the play believable, interesting and thrilling'. He echoed the three words Tyrone Guthrie gave me in 1962, 'the best acting is convincing, illuminating and compelling'. Perhaps less has changed in the last sixty years than we think.

LIST OF PHOTOGRAPHERS

1.   *Romeo and Juliet*, unknown
2.   *Hadrian VII*, unknown
3.   *French Without Tears*, unknown
4.   *Henry V*, Donald Cooper
5.   *Snap*, Donald Cooper
6.   *Racing Demon*, John Haynes
7.   *Kavanagh QC*, unknown
8.   *Ivanov*, own private photo
9.   *Star Wars: The Phantom Menace*, Archives du 7e Art / Lucasfilm
10. *Larkin with Women*, Tony Bartholomew
11. *King Lear*, Ivan Kyncl
12. *King Lear*, Ivan Kyncl
13. *Johnny English*, David Appleby
14. *King Cromwell*, Robert Day
15. *Much Ado About Nothing*, Catherine Ashmore
16. *Hamlet*, Ellie Kurttz
17. *Hamlet*, Ellie Kurttz
18. *All's Well That Ends Well*, Simon Annand
19. *Written on the Heart*, Ellie Kurttz
20. *Henry IV part 2*, Kwame Lestrade
21. *A Splinter of Ice*, Steve Gregson

ACKNOWLEDGEMENTS

I can't claim that anyone encouraged me to write this book; in fact I kept it secret for some time. I am very grateful to the people who have read it in its many stages and made such insightful and encouraging suggestions: Jenifer Armitage, Stephen Boxer, Ben Brown, Miranda Emmerson, David Hare, Anthony Naylor, Alan Strachan and David Wood.

I spent a year trying to find a publisher, such a difficult time in the publishing world due to the pandemic. So I am doubly grateful to Jeremy Thompson and the Book Guild for taking it on and for the help and care given me by Joe Shillito, Fern Bushnell and the team of Philippa Iliffe, Megan Lockwood-Jones, Hayley Russell, Meera Vithlani and Jack Wedgbury.

I want to thank my agents at CDA and in particular my friend Belinda Wright who has looked after me with such care and good sense for at least thirty years. If I were to thank all the actors, writers and directors who have helped and inspired me over fifty-five years the list would be as long as this book. My text and index will have to deputise.

My greatest thanks go to Jenifer Armitage, my partner of fifty years, and to our daughter Miranda, who have helped, encouraged and put up with so much over many difficult years.

INDEX

For writing and publishing news, or
recommendations of new titles to read,
sign up to the Book Guild newsletter: